A Year of Cut Flowers

BLOOMSBURY PUBLISHING
Bloomsbury Publishing Plc
50 Bedford Square, London, WC1B 3DP, UK
29 Earlsfort Terrace, Dublin 2, D02 AY28, Ireland

BLOOMSBURY, BLOOMSBURY PUBLISHING and the Diana logo
are trademarks of Bloomsbury Publishing Plc

First published in Great Britain 2026

Text © Sarah Raven, 2026
Photographs © Jonathan Buckley, 2026
Illustrations © Esther Palmer, 2026

Sarah Raven, Jonathan Buckley and Esther Palmer have asserted their
right under the Copyright, Designs and Patents Act, 1988, to be identified
as author, photographer and illustrator, respectively, of this work.

For legal purposes the Acknowledgements on p. 447 constitute an
extension of this copyright page.

All rights reserved. No part of this publication may be: i) reproduced
or transmitted in any form, electronic or mechanical, including
photocopying, recording or by means of any information storage or
retrieval system without prior permission in writing from the publishers;
or ii) used or reproduced in any way for the training, development or
operation of artificial intelligence (AI) technologies, including generative
AI technologies. The rights holders expressly reserve this publication
from the text and data mining exception as per Article 4(3) of the Digital
Single Market Directive (EU) 2019/790.

The author and publisher specifically disclaim, as far as the law allows,
any responsibility from any liability, loss or risk (personal or otherwise)
which is incurred as a consequence, directly or indirectly, of the use
and applications of any of the contents of this book.

A catalogue record for this book is available from the British Library
Library of Congress Cataloguing-in-Publication data has been
applied for.

ISBN: HB: 978-1-5266-8342-7; eBook: 978-1-5266-8341-0

10 9 8 7 6 5 4 3 2 1

Project Editor: Zena Alkayat
Designer: Glenn Howard
Photographer: Jonathan Buckley
Illustrator: Esther Palmer
Proofreader: Claudia Connal
Indexer: Hilary Bird

Printed in China by C&C Offset Printing Co., Ltd.

To find out more about our authors and books visit www.bloomsbury.com
and sign up for our newsletters. For product safety related questions
contact productsafety@bloomsbury.com

Dedication

To Jonathan Buckley

*My dear friend and
collaborator who has
been taking photographs
for this book for 30 years*

Front cover Two of my favourite
dahlias, 'Labyrinth' and 'Waltzing
Mathilda', with 'White Onesta'
slotted in between.
Back cover An arm-filling bunch of
May cut flowers, including *Digitalis
purpurea* f. *albiflora*, *Anthriscus
sylvestris* 'Ravenswing' and
Hesperis matronalis var. *albiflora*.

A Year of Cut Flowers

A life of growing and arranging for all seasons

Sarah Raven

Photographs by Jonathan Buckley

BLOOMSBURY PUBLISHING
LONDON · OXFORD · NEW YORK · NEW DELHI · SYDNEY

From left to right A handful of Icelandic poppies (*Oreomecon nudicaulis*); *Phlox drummondii* 'Cherry Caramel', *Panicum capillare* 'Sparkling Fountain' and *Zinnia elegans* 'Queen Lime Red'; picking dahlias for our weekend Feast event at Perch Hill.

6 Introduction
The very beginnings of my love for cut flowers

16 My First Cutting Patch
The garden that inspired a lifetime of growing and arranging cut flowers

26 Plant Succession
Flower productivity and seasonal harvests

46 Form
Creating height, movement and interest

56 Colour Palettes
Simple rules for outstanding combinations

78 Vase Life
Extending the longevity of cut flowers

94 January & February
Early colour and the very first cut flowers

104 Hellebores, flower grids and celebratory wreaths
114 Practical: Planning a cut flower patch

122 March
Jewel-like treasures inside and out

134 Miniature vases and floating flowers
140 Practical: Sowing seeds and making frames

152 April
A riot of life and colour

176 Tulips and spring party flowers
190 Practical: Planting out hardy annuals; taking dahlia cuttings; mulching

202 May
Filling the flower-harvest gap

218 Alliums, foxgloves, a mass of one plant and large arrangements
228 Practical: Weeding, watering and feeding

238 June
An early summer show for garden and vase

252 *Roses and sweet peas*
264 *Practical: Creating plant supports*

272 July
Peak flower production in the cutting garden

286 *Hand-tied bunches and edible arrangements*
294 *Practical: Harvesting seed*

300 August
Floral fireworks and bold colours

312 *Nero vase arrangements, summer hand-tied bunches and everlasting flowers*
328 *Practical: Taking tender perennial cuttings*

332 September
It's time for a dahlia show

350 *Floating flowers and table arrangements*
356 *Practical: Autumn sowing*

362 October
Hips, haws, turning leaves and the last of the cut flowers

382 *A galaxy of mini bottles*
386 *Practical: Planting bulbs*

392 November & December
Reliable late colour and festive favourites

412 *Amaryllis, wreaths and Christmas swags*
424 *Practical: Pruning roses and planting tulips*

434 Sowing and Planting Charts
438 Index
446 Acknowledgements

Introduction

I am passionate about growing cut flowers – it's been my main gardening obsession for more than 30 years. It all started when, together with my husband Adam and our ten-month-old baby, we swapped our semi-detached house in west London for a 90-acre farm in the Sussex Weald. On May 4th 1994, we moved into Perch Hill.

Everything was blue: the clear sky, the woods swathed in bluebells and the barely-there garden carpeted in forget-me-nots. Forget-me-nots have pretty much been banned from here ever since (they're prolific self-sowers), but they looked very welcoming that day. There was almost no garden then, just a goldfish pond, an apple tree and a lawn on the south side of the house. Within a couple of weeks I had set to, clearing an area of scrubby blackthorn and brambles to make a six-metre-square cut flower patch.

I had no particular design or plan, but being busy with family and work life (I was then a junior doctor), I wanted a patch that was manageable in size and large enough to give us a vase or two of flowers and the odd handful of herbs every week through the summer and autumn. I knew nothing about growing then, but I was dead keen – and I really wanted flowers for the house.

Since I was very young, I have loved picking flowers, starting, like many children, with lawn and meadow flowers like daisies, buttercups and dandelions. It was a passion fostered by my father. He was an academic at the University of Cambridge, taught classics at King's College and was a passionate hobby naturalist, knowledgeable about butterflies and birds, but particularly about wildflowers. He loved all plants, with the modest sedges and hawkweeds among his favourites.

Above I loved picking flowers from an early age. Here I am picking dandelion clocks with my twin Jane, in an orchard/vineyard just outside Asolo, Italy, where we had family holidays.
Right Our children helping with the garden in the very early days.
Opposite, clockwise from top right
In Asolo, Italy aged 7 or 8 with a posy and flower crown made from garden and meadow/lawn flowers.
A hawkweed painted in watercolour by my father (this was one of his botanical specialisms).
From tail to mane on Henry the horse: two of my siblings, Hugh and Jane, and me.
My father, John Raven.
Perch Hill in the early days: we were laying out the paths in the Farmhouse Garden and, as always, we had to do a lot of clearing and moving around before we could go forwards creating the garden.
Botanising in Scotland in my early teens.

Above Making my first cut-flower garden 30 years ago. This area to the west of the house is now called The Trials or Westernmost Garden.
Opposite Tulips underplanted with biennials (wallflowers and forget-me-nots) in the Farmhouse Garden in 1997. Through the gate you can see that what is now the Cutting Garden does not yet exist.

His father, Charles Raven, a clergyman, was also an academic and naturalist and, between them, they painted every plant in the British Isles. Whenever they found a plant that was new to them, either my father or grandfather would take out their watercolour paper and paints and get to work. This visual documentation built up over 50 years to become 18 volumes of watercolour paintings, which I was given when my father died, when I was aged 17. I can now see that set my path.

I remember well, when I was maybe five years old, picking a bee orchid. This was the crucial moment my father taught me his one-in-one-hundred rule for wildflowers: only if I could see at least 100 flowers from where I stood, was I allowed to pick one stem. Many people would now disapprove of even this, but that connection bound me firmly to wildflowers. It also instilled in me a great love for botanising and walking in nature-rich places. I have returned to that as often as I can, and when I do I find I almost instantly tap into that sense of easy contentment I had as a child. My love of wildflowers soon extended to include garden varieties and, being brought up with a beautiful family garden, there was plenty for the picking.

Below Botanising on the Lizard Peninsula in Cornwall in 2010, when working with Jonathan Buckley on our book, *Wild Flowers*.

Opposite Harvesting from a cutting patch I made when creating an online course on growing cut flowers with Create Academy. It's the end of June, a peak time for hardy annuals moving on to half-hardy annuals.

Being in nature, whether the countryside or the garden, felt to me like the calmest and happiest place to be. And bringing even the smallest bit of it inside reminded me of that feeling. It still does. But I have to confess, it was clear from when I was very young that I loved things a little showier than a sedge. I'm mad about colour – the more of it the better – strong, saturated and brilliant. Tulips and dahlias are my two favourite flowers.

There was a small niggling doubt when we moved to Perch Hill. My father's one-in-one-hundred rule had left me with a sense of unease when I picked almost anything. Wouldn't it last longer and give more pleasure left growing and flowering outside? I know many gardeners share this feeling: cutting flowers is stealing the view and the flower, and that splendid delphinium, huge pompom peony, or lupin spear are best left growing outside. I understand that anxiety, but, as it turns out, with some plants that's simply not true.

If you select the right plants – annuals, biennials and dahlias, for example – and grow them correctly from the start, the very opposite is the case. If you pinch them out at the three-leaf stage and then pick them right – above a pair of leaves – you promote axillary bud formation, which then develop into flowers.

Opposite top June in the Cutting Garden, which sits on the south side of the farmhouse. *Cobaea scandens* is just starting to cover its supports with new growth, and plenty of hardy annuals (*Salvia viridis* blue-flowered, *Malope trifida*, calendula and echiums) are providing a harvest.

Opposite bottom Dawn over our dahlia trial beds. We now grow more than 200 different dahlia varieties, about 10 per cent bred with, for or by us.

Next page My first cutting patch in 1997. To stop the hose from crushing stems, I decorated stout gondola posts at the corner of every bed.

By picking one flower, you create the potential for at least two more in a week or ten days. And on and on it goes until the end of that plant's natural season. The more you pick, the more they flower. These truly are cut-and-come-again plants.

What this process achieves is two things. Firstly, by pinching out and removing the plant's tip, we're taking away apical dominance. Instead of the growth hormone in every cell working towards pushing the apex onwards and upwards (with the aim of seed production), it goes towards pushing out more root and side shoots or axillary buds below the pinched scar. This gives a much bushier and more productive plant – what I call stocky, not whippy plants. It's the stocky ones that go on to produce up to five times more flowers.

Secondly, with plants like sweet peas, annual scabious, *Malope trifida* or *Ammi majus* (just four of my favourites), by picking flowers in bud or early flower, we're removing the means of reproduction. By picking flowers from seed-spreading plants like these, seed is prevented from forming, and so the plant has to produce more flowers to pursue its quest to reproduce. When you cut near the top of the plant, you'll have the next flower within a couple of days; harvest lower, into the heart of the plant for a longer stem, and you may wait a week to ten days for another flower. But it *will* flower again!

I discovered this from trialling a range of plants during those early years at Perch Hill. It soon became clear which plants behave in this generous way and which don't. Within the first few seasons of trialling in the cutting patch, I felt like the conundrum was sorted and the vague cloud of guilt from picking was gone. Here was a simple life-enhancer – plants in the garden and in the home. It felt like a gift to me, and can be to us all.

This book is the story of 30 years at Perch Hill, of seeking out, growing and assessing a huge range of plants in order to understand which make the most productive, easy and stupendous cut flowers. We've trialled many thousands of plants, from velvety polyanthus for picking early in the year to a multitude of tulips for spring, along with sweet peas, dahlias and chrysanthemums, and every sort of annual and biennial.

I'll share the lessons I have learnt through my first cutting patch and the plants that should form the backbone of any cutting garden, large or small. I'll take you through the year and show you everything I know about growing, picking and arranging cut flowers, honed over three decades. You'll discover why having homegrown flowers in your house is an easy life-transformer. I heartily recommend it!

My First Cutting Patch

I had done a bit of gardening, alongside a career in medicine, in the two or three years before we moved to Perch Hill. In my sunny London garden, I'd grown shrubs, climbers and perennials, and I'd grown a few salads and herbs in window boxes. But I'd never grown flowers specifically for picking, and I didn't have a clue.

I searched for information on the best cut-flower varieties, but this being a time pre-internet, I found only a couple of books that seemed to require a Victorian walled garden and at least one gardener to go with it. I decided to just make a start and get stuck in.

All I had was an illustrated seed catalogue, which turned out to be an invaluable guide. It featured a scissor symbol alongside certain plants indicating they cut well. From the 50 or so cut-flower varieties (each with quite a good mugshot) I selected seven. As soon as they arrived in the post, I got sowing.

My first cutting patch was six metres square and I divided this into five equal blocks. In each block I sowed or planted one thing. I also added my favourite herbs: flat-leaved parsley around the edges, rosemary, some French tarragon and sage. The rest of the ground was devoted to cut flowers.

The annuals I included in that first year were *Cosmos bipinnatus* 'Purity' and 'Dazzler', the English marigold *Calendula officinalis* 'Indian Prince', the pink and blue forms of *Salvia viridis*, *Cerinthe major* (the seeds of which I had discovered on a wildflower trip to Spain) and *Ammi majus*, which I knew already as I always bought armfuls on trips to the wholesale flower market at Nine Elms in London. In late May, everything was sown direct, straight into their squares.

Opposite, clockwise from top right
Cerinthe major 'Purpurascens', *Euphorbia oblongata* and *Calendula officinalis* 'Indian Prince'. *Cosmos bipinnatus* 'Dazzler'. *Salvia viridis* blue-flowered and 'Pink' with *Euphorbia oblongata*. *Cerinthe major* 'Purpurascens'. *Calendula officinalis* 'Indian Prince' with *Salvia viridis* blue-flowered. Bee landing on *Cosmos bipinnatus* 'Purity' with *Ammi majus*.
Below left *Dahlia* 'Rip City'.
Below right *Dahlia* 'Bishop of Llandaff'.

I also included one first-year-flowering perennial, *Euphorbia oblongata*, which was to become a major love of mine. That had to be sown into a seed tray before being pricked out into pots and then planted into its designated square. It was my first attempt at doing this.

As well as plants grown from seed, I wanted a few perennials. I loved peonies, so I went off to the local garden centre and bought *Paeonia lactiflora* 'Duchesse de Nemours', already in bud. My parents had grown this deliciously scented, pure white form in their Cambridgeshire garden for decades. I knew it was stellar.

I filled out the rest of the patch with perennials I knew cut well as they were similarly ones I recognised from my parent's garden as a child. There was a patch of helenium (*Helenium* 'Moerheim Beauty', if I remember correctly), a couple of euphorbias (*Euphorbia palustris* for acid-green in spring and *E. sikkimensis* for summer), some *Eryngium* × *tripartitum* (which liked my parents' free-draining soil but struggled on my Perch Hill clay), and a swathe of *Phlox paniculata* hybrids in purple, pink and white. These late-summer phlox, with their sweet scent spiked with a dash of curry, remain full of nostalgia for me.

I added two dahlias. *Dahlia* 'Rip City' was the first, in a rich chocolate crimson. I'd fallen for this on a trip to Monet's garden in Giverny the previous autumn. I had brought five plants back with me and had been keeping the tubers protected from frost in a cold frame. I also had a couple of the well-known scarlet, semi-double *D.* 'Bishop of Llandaff', which were given to me by a friend. Thirty years ago, that was one

Below An August harvest placed in indestructible stainless steel buckets. The Cashmere Jersey palette (see p62), with *Helianthus annuus* 'ProCut Plum', *Rudbeckia hirta* 'Sahara' and *Thunbergia alata* 'African Sunset'.

Opposite top July in the cutting patch. Hardy annuals start to fade (*Ammi visnaga*, *Cerinthe major* 'Purpurascens' and *Malope trifida*), and the half-hardies (tagetes and antirrhinums) come out at the right moment, so production remains pretty constant.

Opposite bottom Dahlias lining the path in the Annual Cutting Garden ('Dalaya Aruna' in the dolly tub with 'Labyrinth' and 'Blue Bayou' in the border).

of the very few widely available dahlias in the UK, and it was grown in good clumps in the Cottage Garden at Sissinghurst Castle, as well as in the Red Border at the Regency house, Nymans. 'Rip City', it turns out, has a decent vase life for a dahlia; 'Bishop of Llandaff' less so. But I loved their differing shades of red and contrasting flower forms growing together.

Everything grew well and I sat back for a few weeks until they started to flower. Once summer began and the plants were fully grown, I then measured, bucket by bucket – or fraction of a bucket – how much I was harvesting. And I kept a record of everything I picked on a sheet of paper tacked up on the wall. I found it incredible how productivity varied.

The perennials I'd grown up with were disappointing. I picked only a few buckets from the heleniums and phlox, and literally a handful of stems from the peonies and eryngium in that first season, even though I had bought large, mature plants, or was given well-established clumps from my mother's garden. It didn't get much better in the second season. The perennials turned out to be a washout.

Yet, boy oh boy, I couldn't keep up with the annuals and dahlias. They pumped out flowers and I picked them by the

bucket-load, at least twice, but often three times a week. Our house was chock-full with flowers all summer and much of autumn. *Cosmos bipinnatus* 'Purity' was the record holder: 48 buckets within three months of planting! The dahlias, particularly 'Rip City', were covered in flowers for a good four-month stretch. And the euphorbia was also remarkable. From my May sowing, it took longer to get started, only getting into its flowering stride 16 weeks later, but I went on to pick it every week almost up until Christmas. And I loved it for its colour and its plateau structure, which was like a natural alternative to florist's foam or chicken wire. Used as a foliage base, it could hold everything in place in a vase. All euphorbias have a downside – their milky sap, which is an irritant. But, with care, I still pick it almost every day in the growing season.

So I had some failures, but some massive successes too. Here are the results I recorded.

	Peony	Cosmos 'Purity'	Dahlia 'Rip City'
Time from planting to harvest	3 years	12 weeks	16 weeks
Duration of harvest	3 weeks	20 weeks	22 weeks
Quantity of harvest (per square metre, per year)	Half a bucket	48 buckets	30 buckets
Vase life	10 days	7 days	4 days
Difficulty to grow	Easy	Easy	Easy
Remarkable characteristics	Scented	Pretty foliage	Velvet flowers
Cost	Expensive	Cheap	Average
Overall productivity	**Bad**	**Exceptional**	**Excellent**

Dahlia 'Rip City' was excellent rather than exceptional, simply because of its relatively short vase life. We've since worked on finding and breeding varieties that have a vase life of at least seven days, such as 'Molly Raven', 'Perch Hill' and 'Sissinghurst', but more on that in the September chapter.

Out went my plans for growing swathes of perennials and in came almost any annual and dahlia I could get hold of. And that's pretty much how I've carried on for three decades.

The best of the annuals led the race because they are all, to a degree, cut-and-come-again plants, whereas most perennials are not (and if they are, they're on a much slower growth curve). The reason for the difference is evolution.

Below An airy, ethereal mix of *Cosmos bipinnatus* 'Purity', 'Gloria' and 'Fizzy Rose Picotee'.
Next page Perch Hill from the air in April. The rusty red, tin-roofed building at the bottom is our 'compost palace'. The garden is organic, so making large volumes of our own organic matter is key.

Many annuals in the wild originate in grassland or scree, where flowers are routinely grazed off, forcing them to produce more in order to set seed. Perennials, on the other hand, have a complex root system that can usually outlast an annual bout of damage. (See p12 for more on cut-and-come-again plant characteristics.)

I was instantly hooked on the idea of cut-and-come-again annuals and their reliable productivity in a small space – it has been the driving force behind my work ever since. With these plants, you can literally pick armfuls, not just posies, without needing acres. And you can have a house full of flowers and a garden that looks better for it, always jam-packed with colour because of your harvest. For me, that discovery was miraculous. It's gardening for the optimist and the greedy flower lover, and for anyone who wants to fill their house with colour and scent without going shopping. That's me, and I hope it's many of you, as that's what this book is about.

Plant Succession

Before we get stuck into a month-by-month guide to growing, picking and arranging cut flowers, it's useful to look at the year as a whole. This chapter will give you the nuts and bolts of what we do at Perch Hill to ensure the largest possible harvest from every bit of space. It's quite detailed, but once you get your head around it, it is transformational. It should deliver an incredible volume of cut flowers, and barely a downturn in colour or flower harvest, between March and November.

In the first few years of growing cut flowers at Perch Hill, we would have some weeks where the place was bursting with flowers, making it hard to keep up, and other weeks (which frustratingly always seemed to coincide with an event or wedding for which we were supplying flowers), when stems were thin on the ground. As a result, we've evolved a system – a form of plant rotation – to keep flower production pretty constant from the start of the growing year to the end. This overarching plan helps to smooth out the peaks and troughs.

Cut-and-Come-Again Productivity

About 70 per cent of the cutting garden here is stocked with cut-and-come-again plants, but each one has a slightly varying degree of productivity. I find it useful to know – in a straightforward way – whether something is a high, medium or low producer. So over the years I've aimed to record the quantities that can be picked from a plant in one metre square.

I'd suggest sticking to the high productivity group if you have limited space, adding in some from the medium group if

Previous page Buckets of June annuals and biennials including Icelandic poppies (*Oreomecon nudicaulis*), nigella, sweet peas (*Lathyrus*), sweet Williams (*Dianthus barbatus*) and foxgloves (*Digitalis*).

Opposite top A swathe of flowers in our Annual Cutting Garden, including *Antirrhinum majus* 'Costa Apricot', *Zinnia elegans* 'Lilliput Mix' and 'Zinderella Peach'.

Opposite bottom Our north-facing, shady bed of hellebores, polyanthus and pulmonarias in the Perennial Cutting Garden

you have more room, and only go for a selection from the final group if space is no issue for you.

In the case of bulbs, I would always recommend growing some for picking regardless of garden size, because they make such splendid cut flowers. But try to select perennial varieties that come back year after year (see p175). And plant them in a lasagne (see p391), with other things planted over the top to maximise your space.

High Productivity

These are a few examples of the most hardworking cut-and-come-again plants. They need regular picking, they replenish with new flowers fast (within days) and give a large harvest.

Productivity rating 8–10 / 10
Hardy annuals Sweet pea (*Lathyrus*), *Salvia viridis* varieties, annual scabious
Half-hardy annuals Cosmos, zinnia, amaranth
Short-lived perennials *Euphorbia oblongata*, snapdragon (*Antirrhinum*)
Tender perennials Dahlia

Medium Productivity

These produce axillary buds when cut, but more slowly than those in the high productivity group. Flowering is prolonged if you pick or deadhead, and they replenish with new flowers in weeks rather than days. Here are a few of my favourites.

Productivity rating 5–7 / 10
Tender perennials Chrysanthemum, alstroemeria (particularly modern hybrids such as 'Blushing Bride')
Hardy annuals *Ammi majus* (produces axillary buds, but slowly)
Biennials Foxglove (*Digitalis*) (produces axillary buds, but slowly)
Herbaceous perennials Euphorbia (*E. palustris*, *E. sikkimensis*, *E. ceratocarpa*), helenium, phlox, polyanthus, rudbeckia, sunflower (*Helianthus*), hellebore, delphinium (if cut to the ground, leaves and all, most give a second flush)
Roses 'Champagne Moment', 'Chandos Beauty' 'Duchess of Cornwall' and many more (see p241)

Above The Annual Cutting Garden in April. *Narcissus* 'Precocious' alongside *Primula* 'Stella Champagne', making for an efficient use of space. A selection of highly scented narcissi (including 'Pipit', 'Moonlight Sensation' and 'Quail') in the foreground. Also naturalising is *Muscari armeniacum* below the sweet pea frames in the background, ideal for April table centrepieces and posies.

Low Productivity

These do not produce axillary buds and are not cut-and-come-again plants. But they are lovely, and so worth growing if you have the space. This group includes bulbs, which you can include for succession and layering, giving you flowers in early spring and maximising space beneath perennials and dahlias (see p391).

Productivity rating 1–4 / 10
Bulbs Tulip, narcissus, *Anemone coronaria*
Shrubs Hydrangea (the best producers in the shrub category, being the quickest to grow back)
Herbaceous perennials Peony, bearded irises, oriental poppy (*Papaver orientale*)

Next page Tulips, honesty (*Lunaria*) and blossom at their peak in late April in our Annual Cutting Garden. There are lots of different varieties of tulips in the ground, including 'Purple Heart', 'Istanbul', 'Time Out', 'Spryng Tide', 'Unique de France' and 'World's Favourite'. The tulips in pots are (from left to right): 'Black Hero', a mix of 'Hermitage' and 'Chato', 'Sarah Raven', and a repeat of 'Hermitage' and 'Chato' in the far right dolly tub.

Seasonal Succession

To make a garden work hard, I find it useful to divide the year into five seasons with a different (often overlapping) cast of plants. Once you have five seasons, each with its most productive plants mapped out, you can add in sowing/planting times, as well as when to lift and replace certain plants. With an organised plant rotation, you can't fail to have a garden jam-packed with colour that's also highly productive. Over the next few pages, I will share my five seasons and the charts that accompany them.

In the charts, there is a column for the percentage of ground given to each group of plants. This usually adds up to 95 per cent – the remaining percentage accounts for space elsewhere in the garden, in pots or under cover. You'll also see perennials, shrubs and trees included, which provide some garden bones, but overall the charts focus on the more temporary plantings, which we rely on to put on our colour and flower show. When these go-for-it plants go over, it's time to clear some space for a new, more energetic and colourful crop. This process of planting and removing makes cut-flower gardening more like kitchen gardening, and less like mixed border maintenance. It involves regular propagating or buying and planting of seedlings, as well as weeding and staking. It's not about planting it up and sitting back for five years, so it might not suit everyone, but for flowers inside and out, you can't beat this way of growing.

Harvest season 1: mid-March to mid-May

Here in Sussex, the start of the growing season is usually mid-March. It will be at least a couple of weeks later for those further north and at higher altitude, and two to three weeks earlier in the far south-west of England.

For us, this first season ends in the middle of May, when the last of the tulips drop their petals and the first alliums start to flower. The main things we're picking during this time are hardy annuals (autumn sown to ensure the earlies flower as early as they can), and early-flowering biennials, such as wallflowers and honesty (*Lunaria*), and if you have any space under cover, Icelandic poppies (*Oreomecon nudicaulis*). Then, of course, there is a great parade of bulbs, backed up by a few early-flowering perennials, and the emergent spring leaves and blossom of shrubs and trees.

Harvest season 1: mid-March to mid-May

Plants to harvest	When to sow/plant	Cut-and-come-again	Productivity	Percentage of ground given	When to take out
Early-flowering hardy annuals, such as cerinthe	September	Yes	High 8–10/10	30%	June–July, replace with some May-sown, half-hardy annuals or biennials
Early-flowering half-hardy annuals such as schizanthus. And early-flowering biennials such as Icelandic poppies (*Oreomecon nudicaulis*)	August	Yes	Medium 6/10	For harvest season 1, sow and grow under cover so they can be picked from pots protected from frost	June–July
Early-flowering biennials, such as honesty (*Lunaria*) and wallflowers (*Erysimum*)	June and July	Yes	Medium 6/10	25%	June, but leave honesty in place for seed pods
Early-flowering, short-lived perennials, such as *Euphorbia oblongata*	September	Yes	High 7/10	5%	October, or if not heavily picked, leave in the ground for another year
Early spring bulbs, such as *Anemone coronaria*	September	One corm produces many flowers over weeks	Low 4/10 These are one of the few repeat-flowering bulbs	5%	Never
Spring bulbs, such as narcissi and tulips	September–November	No, however narcissi with tazetta genes do continue to produce flowering stems over many weeks	Low 2/10	30%	Never
Perennials, shrubs and climbers, such as blossoming trees and early clematis	October–November	No (except hellebores)	Low (except hellebores, 6/10)	Harvest from the rest of the garden rather than a dedicated cutting patch	Never

Next page The Annual Cutting Garden in late June with *Cosmos bipinnatus* 'Rubenza' just coming out in the foreground, next to a row of *Salvia viridis* blue-flowered, *Antirrhinum majus* 'Chantilly Bronze' and one of the best June bridesmaid flowers, *Echium vulgare* 'Blue Bedder', which flowers prolifically from May to July and the bees are crazy for it. We allow a certain number of self-sown opium poppies (*Papaver somniferum*). Seared, they last a day or two in a vase and their seed pods are also good as an upper storey for any July bunch or vase.

Harvest season 2: mid-May to mid-July

In season two, around 50 per cent of our cutting garden is filled with hardy annuals. Alongside these, we also have later-flowering biennials such as sweet Williams (*Dianthus barbatus*) and foxgloves (*Digitalis*). These two groups of plants give us the majority of our harvest. Around 70 per cent of ground is cropping in this season, as we need plenty of space for planting out half-hardy plants.

Like us, you might decide to plant some alliums and peonies in other areas of your garden to supplement your harvest, but these don't make the grade in terms of volume of production.

Harvest season 2: mid-May to mid-July

Plants to harvest	When to sow/plant	Cut-and-come-again	Productivity	Percentage of ground given	When to take out
Main season of hardy annuals, such as calendula, nigella, sweet peas (*Lathyrus*), salvia and echium	September for most or February/March; January for sweet peas	Yes	High 8–10/10	55%	July–September, depending on flowering length. For example, nigella is over quickly, but salvia goes on flowering until September
Main crop of biennials, such as foxgloves (*Digitalis*) and Icelandic poppies (*Oreomecon nudicaulis*)	June–July	Yes	Medium 6/10 (except Icelandic poppy, 8/10)	35%	August
Early-flowering, short-lived perennials, such as *Euphorbia oblongata*	September and/or February–March	Yes	High 7/10	5%	October, or if not heavily picked, leave in the ground for another year
Spring-summer bulbs, such as alliums	September–October	No	Low 2/10	Harvest from the rest of the garden rather than from a dedicated cutting patch. Or layer under dahlia tubers	Never. Cut foliage back in May/June once browned
Perennials, shrubs and climbers such as *Alchemilla mollis* and clematis	Plant October–November and/or February–March	No (except Alchemilla)	Low (except Alchemilla, 6/10)	Harvest from the rest of the garden rather than a dedicated cutting patch	Never

Opposite Buckets of cut flowers in September, including lots of dahlias, the odd spike of gladioli, setaria, amaranth, sanguisorba, *Selinum wallichianum* and asters.

Harvest season 3: mid-July to mid-September

In season three, the patch transitions to half-hardy annuals with a few hardy annuals hanging in there. Dahlias now also come on stream. Between them, they'll provide 90 per cent of the harvest.

Harvest season 3: mid-July to mid-September

Plants to harvest	When to sow/plant	Cut-and-come-again	Productivity	Percentage of ground given	When to take out
Half-hardy annuals, such as cosmos	March–April	Yes	High 8–10/10	50%	October–November
Long-season hardy annuals, such as *Salvia viridis* blue-flowered	February or March	Yes	High 8–10/10	5%	September–October
Early-flowering, short-lived perennials, such as *Euphorbia oblongata*	September and/or February–March	Yes	High 7/10	5%	October, or if not heavily picked, leave in the ground for another year
Tender tubers, such as dahlias	March (for planting tubers under cover to plant out in May). And May (for planting young plants)	Yes	High 8–10/10	25%	Never. At Perch Hill we mulch deeply (about 15cm/6in) to get through the winter
Late-season bulbs, such as gladioli	April–June	No	Low 2/10	5%	Never, mulch with dahlias in autumn
Tender climbers, such as cobaea	January–February	Yes	High 8–10/10	5%	November–December
Perennials, shrubs and climbers, such as clematis, alstromeria, phlox and perennial helianthus	Plant October–November and/or February–March	No (except phlox and perennial helianthus)	Low (except phlox and perennial helianthus 6/10)	Harvest from the rest of the garden	Never

38 PLANT SUCCESSION

Below An October bunch of chrysanthemums and eucalyptus. The chrysanthemums are 'Avignon Pink', 'Bigoudi Purple', 'Pip Salmon' (the one with the darker eye) and the spiky-petalled 'Tula Purple' and 'Tula Carmella'. The bunch was a result of an October cut-flower trial, and the almost allium-like Tula varieties have become firm favourites (see p368).

Harvest season 4: mid-September to mid-November

This is the time of year when many gardens become a little colourless. To prevent this, we concentrate on cut-and-come-again plants that flower well into autumn: first and foremost, dahlias. These are now giving almost three quarters of the harvest.

And to ensure plenty of colour now, we do a second sowing of half-hardy annuals. For instance, if I sow half a packet of snapdragons (*Antirrhinum*) in February or March, and then the other half at the end of May or beginning of June, then these plants will be ready to go into the bed as soon as the previous season's plants – such as zinnias – are beginning to look tired.

Zinnia flower production starts to drop off when temperatures cool in early autumn. We take them out and will already have put in that second sowing of snapdragons. I also make sure to do the same with amaranth. As well as being a wonderful late-season cut flower, these plants are a great source of seed protein for birds just as other food sources become scarce.

Harvest season 4: mid-September to mid-November

Plants to harvest	When to sow/plant	Cut-and-come-again	Productivity	Percentage of ground given	When to take out
Long-flowering half-hardy annuals, such as cosmos	March–April	Yes	High 8–10/10	30%	October–November
Second sowing of some half-hardy annuals, such as snapdragons (*Antirrhinum*)	June	Yes	High 8–10/10	10%	November–December
Second sowing of hardy annuals, such as *Ammi visnaga*	June	Yes	High 8–10/10	5%	November–December
Early-flowering, short-lived perennials, such as *Euphorbia oblongata*	September and/or February–March	Yes	High 7–10/10	5%	October, or if not heavily picked, leave in the ground for another year
Tender tubers, such as dahlias	March (for planting tubers under cover to plant out in May). And May for planting young plants	Yes	High 8–10/10	30%	Never, mulch deeply to get through the winter
Late-season bulbs, such as gladioli	April–June	No	Low 2/10	5%	Never, mulch with dahlias in autumn
Tender climbers, such as cobaea	January–February	Yes	High 8–10/10	10%	November–December
Half-hardy perennials, such as chrysanthemums	Take cuttings in March; pot on cuttings in April; plant out in May	Yes	Medium 6–10/10	Move under cover in September–October if you have space	November–December
Perennials, shrubs and climbers, such as Japanese anemones (*Anemone × hybrida*) and hydrangea	Plant October–November and/or February–March	No	Low 5/10	Harvest from the rest of the garden	Never

Opposite top Picking *Cobaea scandens*, one of the last plants to give us an abundance of flowers as the year ends.

Opposite bottom *Anemone coronaria* is permanently planted in one of our earth beds in the greenhouse. We plant them quite deeply so we can overplant with wallflowers (*Erysimum*) in October, once our indoor zinnias and tomatoes are finished. The wallflowers fill the greenhouse with scent and we pick them with the anemones from mid-February.

Harvest season 5: mid-November to mid-March

There's not a huge amount to harvest during these months, but we usually carry on picking cobaea until mid-December, plus scented-leaf pelargoniums. We also pick *Primula* 'Stella Champagne' lightly through the winter. It's a permanent perennial planting here and has been in the ground for five years. Early-flowering hellebores (such as *Helleborus niger* and *H. × ballardiae* 'Maestro') are also key. The dahlias may last into the start of this season, but it depends on how wet the weather is.

A trick to extend the number of flowers you get in season five is to use a greenhouse. If you have some under cover space, it's possible to grow lots of paperwhite narcissus, as well as *Narcissus* 'Erlicheer', 'Cragford' and 'Avalanche' and *Anemone coronaria*, which has the power to bring spring closer. We aim to grow plenty of all these, planted in layers in the greenhouse beds (see p159).

Harvest season 5: mid-November to mid-March

Plants to harvest	When to sow/plant	Cut-and-come-again	Productivity	Percentage of ground given	When to take out
Late or quick-flowering hardy annuals, such as violas	July/August	Yes	High 8–10/10	10%	May–June
Second sowing of some hardy annuals, such as cerinthe	September under cover	Yes	High 8–10/10	5%	March
Tender climbers, such as cobaea	January–February	Yes	High 8–10/10	5%	December (if protected)
Half-hardy perennials, such as chrysanthemums and pelargoniums	Take cuttings in March, pot on in April, plant in May	Yes	Medium 6–10/10	Move under cover in September–October	December (if protected)
Perennials, shrubs and climbers, such as hazel (for catkins), hellebores, polyanthus and willow	Plant October–November and/or February–March	No	Low 3/10	Harvest from the rest of the garden	Never
Forced bulbs, such as *Anemone coronaria* and paperwhite narcissus	September	No	Low 3/10	Indoors, under cover in a cold frame, greenhouse	Plant in the garden once finished flowering
Very early spring bulbs, such as irises	September or October	No	Low 1/10	Harvest from the rest of the garden	Never. Cut foliage back in May/June once browned

Compact Cut Flower Patch

Depending on the size of your garden or the space you want to dedicate to cut flowers, you may not have the resources or inclination to take on a huge number of plants in rotation over five seasons.

If this is the case, there are a few plants I would recommend for maximum impact on a small scale. The selection focusses on prolific flower producers, but finds the right balance of true flowery-flowers (the ones I call Brides, see p47), some more background flowers (Bridesmaids, see p49) and then some good foliage-fillers – not just leaves, but flowers as well – that give beauty and structure.

With just these plants, you'll still get a bunch or two of flowers per week from April to October.

**Harvest season 1 and 2:
April to July**

Bride *Calendula officinalis* 'Indian Prince' or 'Sunset Buff' (depending on the palette you've gone for)
Gatecrasher *Salvia viridis* blue-flowered and/or *Cerinthe major* 'Purpurascens'
Flower foliage *Euphorbia oblongata*

**Harvest season 3 and 4:
July to October**

Bride *Salvia patens*
Bridesmaid *Salvia viridis*
blue-flowered and/or *Ageratum houstonianum* 'Blue Horizon'
Gatecrasher *Euphorbia oblongata* (still going) and *Nicotiana* 'Lime Green'.

Form

If you're growing your own flowers to cut, it makes sense to work backwards to ensure you are planting the right plants for the arrangements you want. And while it's true that there's often nothing nicer than a simple mass of one flower in a vase, it's sometimes great to be a bit showier and create a mixed arrangement.

To achieve this, I have an easy set of rules; a framework of six or seven ingredients that each play a distinct if sometimes overlapping role in creating a pleasing form in a bunch or vase of mixed flowers. These rules should help you to grow, and then cut, just what you need for a flamboyant arrangement, no more and no less.

Flowers

I usually choose three types of flowers. The balance isn't just about size and showiness, but also colour. I adhere to my rules of colour in almost every arrangement and planting scheme I devise (see p57 for more on colour). I love the simplicity of knowing which form and colour I need – it makes picking and arranging super easy and I know it works every time. Just about every picture of an arrangement, hand-tied or in a vase, throughout this book uses my colour/flower rules.

Bride

The star of the show is the first thing to decide on as you plan your planting, walk into the garden with snips, or enter a flower shop (if you're adding bought flowers). What is the

Previous page Just one foliage plant (*Euphorbia amygdaloides* var. *robbiae*) adds good zestiness among the flowers, which are all tulips. The Bride is 'Sarah Raven', the Bridesmaid is 'Black Parrot' and the Gatecrasher is the orange 'Annie Schilder'.

Opposite A classic hand-tied bunch using my tried-and-tested picking recipe of six to seven ingredients, which I use almost daily.

biggest, showiest flower you want to include? Whatever your choice, this is your central flower, all your other flowers will merely complement her, which is why I call it the bride.

Bridesmaid

This next flower is smaller and a bit less demonstrative, but crucially the same or a very similar colour to the bride. The bridesmaid backs up the bride but does not compete with her. If you're making a huge arrangement, you can select several bridesmaids, but they all need to be a very similar colour.

Gatecrasher

Finally, I pick a showy flower in a contrasting colour. This can be from the same palette, or from a different palette, if you prefer. It's like adding a squeeze of lemon to smoked salmon: it adds a zing and makes a simple arrangement greater than the sum of its parts.

Foliage

I think it's crucial to grow plenty of foliage plants. And, when I say foliage, I don't mean evergreens – the likes of bay, rosemary or pittosporum are fantastic picked from the rest of the garden, but they can be on the heavy side in a vase of ethereal annuals.

To achieve a light look and feel, your foliage needs to consist of filler and background flowers. You may not want a mass of these leafy filler flowers in a vase (although, this does work well with ammi), but, sitting in the background, they provide interesting structure and silhouettes, making a flower arrangement feel more complete.

It's also worth noting that an interesting range of foliage is hard to buy, so it's good to grow your own. This gives you plants in the garden, plenty of choice when it comes to arranging, and lots of foliage to do it with.

As a general guide, aim to fill at least half the vase with these quieter foliage flowers – it will give an immediate garden-like feel to your arrangement – and save the other half of the vase for the star flowers.

I divide my foliage into three groups: primary, secondary and upper storey. For a small, simple bunch, the aim is to showcase foliage from just one of these groups. For a medium arrangement, two foliage types. And this increases to all three foliage types for a larger vase.

Opposite top left Dill (*Anethum graveolens*) is an invaluable aromatic, dazzling green umbellifer, which (as a hardy annual) self-sows from one year to the next.
Opposite top right I love all the amaranths (this one is 'Hot Biscuits') in crimson, copper and green and they make some of the best late-summer and autumn foliage plants.
Opposite bottom left *Ammi majus* remains one of my favourite primary foliage plants for a posy or vase, 30 years on.
Opposite bottom right *Euphorbia oblongata* is the best primary foliage plant in the world. And that's saying something!

Primary foliage

Plateau-like and umbel flowers are the best in this primary role because their flowers break from the main stem a few centimetres down and the stems tend to be quite strong and slightly woody, so they form a natural sieve, with holes in between each floret and stem. This forms an ideal structure that you can slot other stems into and it holds them just where you put them, stopping them from dropping down. It's like using natural chicken wire.

In the primary group, there is one plant that has been my favourite foliage choice for more than 30 years now: *Euphorbia oblongata*. Just one, acid-green, plateau-like flower instantly forms the base of almost any small or medium arrangement, while a handful of euphorbia stems make the ideal scaffolding for a large vase. Euphorbia is a favourite and one of the best foliage plants you can grow for the following reasons.

It has a robust, upstanding structure, which makes it an ideal base for any middle-sized arrangement. It has thin stems, but a generous, horizontal top, so you don't need much to create an effective plateau.

The intense colour of *Euphorbia oblongata* is also brightening, which is wonderful with almost any palette, apart from the very gentle and muted, where crimson or copper work better (in that case, I would use *Atriplex hortensis* var. *rubra* or an amaranth). I love euphorbia's sharp green with all the strong colours in spring and summer. By autumn, the shade has toned down and it fits with almost every dahlia.

Euphorbia oblongata is also hugely long-flowering, giving foliage from May to December in a good year. This is three or four times longer than most foliage plants we grow. In the right spot, it's perennial and gently self-sows – not so much as to become a weed, but enough that you can hunt around and dig up seedlings and transplant them to form a row or use them to edge a cut-flower bed.

The one downside with any euphorbia is its sticky, milky sap, which is allergenic. Wear gloves and take care not to wipe your face or eyes after handling stems. Sear the stem end in boiling water to seal the sap in.

Another primary foliage corker is *Ammi majus*. Several stems provide good scaffolding in a vase. With the airy look of cow parsley, but even prettier, this has a week-long vase life (it does drop its flowers in a cloud after day five). It is beautiful on its own, like a great powder puff, and equally good as a filler

Opposite top left Some of the very best filler foliage plants, including *Salvia viridis* blue-flowered growing with my number one primary foliage, *Euphorbia oblongata*.
Opposite top right *Cerinthe major* 'Purpurascens', its common name is honeywort and the bees love it as much as we do.
Opposite bottom left The spiky, green, pompom buds of the petal-less sweet William, *Dianthus barbutus* 'Green Trick', make the most brilliant filler foliage for almost any colourful vase.
Opposite bottom right A mini bunch picked on the go, with *Cerinthe major* 'Purpurascens', *Salvia viridis* and *Phlox drummondii* 'Blueberry Swirl'.

mixed with sweet peas, cosmos or wallflowers. I prefer the delicacy of *Ammi majus*, but *Ammi visnaga* is also excellent and flowers for twice as long. So if space is an issue, the latter is the one for you.

There are a few other primary foliage options. Dill (*Anethum graveolens*) is perfect for a bright-coloured vase – go for seven or nine main stems for a small or medium arrangement. And the puffy, airy flowers of *Thlaspi arvense* emerge in June and July and fulfil a structural role too. It's fashionable at the moment for its loose, natural wildness, but it can be a tricky plant to manage in the garden, as it sets seed willy-nilly and goes over pretty quickly.

Remember, foliage doesn't have to be green. Even in the primary role, foliage can provide additional colour. We use crimson and coppery amaranths and *Atriplex hortensis* var. *rubra* – these are substantial enough to give structure and have great shapes. Even the tassel-formers, such as the *Amaranthus caudatus* varieties, cascade over the side of a vase like velvet curtain tiebacks. I love them.

Secondary foliage / Filler foliage

Once I've selected my primary foliage, I move on to my secondary foliage. This foliage acts more like a filler, nestling in to fill the gaps in the structure in an airy way. Ideally the filler is a different colour and form to the primary foliage.

My go to secondary foliage is *Salvia viridis* blue-flowered, which is invaluable in this role. This hardy annual has a vertical shape, making it ideal for slotting in among the more plateau-shaped primary foliage. With wonderful rich blue spires, its colour goes with pretty much everything and it's a cinch to grow and happily self-sows. It is a brilliant garden plant for lining a path or edging a flower bed and is exceptional for picking, with a vase life of ten days. It is one of the first cut flowers I grew and I'd never go a year without it.

Again, green isn't the only colour you can go for here. I love using *Cerinthe major* 'Purpurascens' as a secondary foliage. With purple bells hanging below silver leaves, cerinthe is a wonderfully elegant filler. From a February sowing, cerinthe is over by July, so we do another sowing in April or May, which gives us stems at their peak from July for the rest of summer.

Dianthus barbatus 'Green Trick' also works, as do the flower buds of sweet Williams, particularly the dark-leaved forms such as *Dianthus barbatus* (Nigrescens Group) 'Sooty'.

Below Some of the very best upper storey foliage plants, including *Moluccella laevis*, which needs cold to spark germination. Sow in a tray and then place in the fridge or freezer for a week or two to break dormancy.

Upper storey foliage

The third ingredient is what I call the upper storey. This foliage plant is one with an interesting architectural shape. The idea of this is to break up any rigidity in the arrangement by introducing plenty of ups and downs and a sense of 'messiness' to create an overall shape that is as three-dimensional as it can be.

The vertical leaf spikes of bells of Ireland (*Moluccella laevis*) is ideal in this role. Rather like foxgloves, they give some of the best twists and turns to a summer vase. As soon as you pick them, strip off almost all of the leaves (as these wilt quickly) and reveal the brilliant green flower calyx.

Other options in this third group include annual and perennial grasses, which often have great shapes. I love the paintbrush-like grass, foxtail (*Setaria viridis*), with its flower and top leaf providing a good vertical line and great curves. There is a slight word of warning here: it is a prolific self-sower, so cut it back hard once it begins turning brown, or whip it out, otherwise you'll have a thousand seedlings to contend with next year.

Below left You'll see this grass called lots of things, including *Panicum capillare* 'Frosted Explosion' and *Panicum* 'Sparkling Fountain', or simply, 'Sprinkles'.
Below right I made this arrangement after a holiday in Sicily. I was trying to recreate the feel of the Sicilian meadow flowers we'd seen. As the Bride, I've used *Cosmos bipinnatus* 'Apricotta', the Bridesmaid is *Phlox drummondii* 'Crème Brûlée', and there are two crimson Gatecrashers: *Nicotiana langsdorffii* 'Bronze Queen' and *Scabiosa atropurpurea* 'Black Cat'. The only foliage here is the elegant meadow-like grass, *Setaria viridis* 'Caramel'.

Briza maxima and *Chasmanthium latifolium* are favourites here, nodding and swaying in a bunch or vase. Briza can be picked from May to July, and chasmanthium from July to November. They serve the same architectural, airy, upper storey role. Also great are *Wangenheimia lima* and *Panicum capillare* 'Frosted Explosion'. Sometimes called 'Sprinkles', this panicum looks like the finest spun sugar in a French patisserie and is perfect when it forms a halo around and above more substantial flowery flowers, particularly dahlias. And it dries brilliantly, too. 'Frosted Explosion' is unusual among grasses in that it is cut-and-come-again. By picking the leader, more panicles develop. It is stacked with seed for garden birds, which gives us one of the great sights of autumn: a patch of the grass covered in goldfinches. Do note, it does self-sow.

Spiller foliage

The fourth foliage element is an optional but valuable ingredient: a vine. Vines cascade down and give a loose, elegant, relaxed shape to a vase arrangement. I love growing and picking trailers – things like perennial sweet peas, *Cobaea scandens*, cardiospermum, honeysuckle and clematis – to fulfil this role.

Colour Palettes

Opposite Hand-tied bunch with *Tagetes patula* 'Burning Embers', *Salvia viridis* blue-flowered and *Euphorbia ceratocarpa*.
Below My four colour palettes, from left to right: Cashmere Jersey, Boiled Sweet, Champs-Élysées and Venetian Velvet. Between them they cover all the loveliest colours you can grow to pick.

After a few years of growing (and arranging) flowers in every colour, cheek by jowl, I felt that my planning needed some refinement. Like many of us, I was putting cohesive arrangements together instinctively, but I wanted to analyse why I made the choices I did, so I could coach others who might not be as confident with colour.

I wanted to break the rainbow down into families of colour that worked well together, both in the garden and in a vase. Not only did these families make picking flowers to a recipe (see p47) quicker and easier, it became increasingly apparent that it was fundamental to how well an arrangement works.

So, over the years, I have created four distinct colour palettes. Each works well as a group and, with care, can be mixed across groups.

Palette 1: Venetian Velvet

This palette is my first love, made up of dark, organic colours that are naturally rich in pigment. Featuring deep reds and dark purples, as well as coppery bronzes, mustard, gold and earthy browns, this palette holds the colours that suck up the light. They are like the colours of Venetian velvet, and I just want to wrap myself in them. By planting these shades together, and then picking flowers from within the palette, you can create sumptuous-looking arrangements that are earthy yet refined.

Right, clockwise from top right
Tulipa 'Sarah Raven'
Calceolaria 'Kentish Hero'
Dahlia 'Schipper's Bronze'
Dahlia 'Manoa'
Helianthus annuus 'Sonja'
Iris 'Red Ember'
Cosmos bipinnatus 'Rubenza'.

Opposite, clockwise from top right
Hand-tied bunch of Breeder tulips at Hortus Bulborum in the Netherlands. Our Rusty Dahlia Collection, including two of our own dahlias, bred with/for us – 'Schipper's Bronze' and 'Adam's Choice' – together with 'Copperboy', which has a great vase life.
Hand-tied bunch of the scented tulip 'Request' along with tulips 'Arjuna' and 'Sarah Raven'; the foliage is a self-sown crimson hellebore, already run to seed, so reliable as a cut flower. A few stems of the fringed *Tulipa* 'Bastia' and cut-petalled 'Black Parrot'.

Palette 2: Boiled Sweet

This palette is full of bright and bold shades, like classic boiled sweets – blackcurrant, raspberry, strawberry, orange, lemon and lime. It is really uplifting and impactful, particularly when picked for the vase. When you add in cobalt blue, the mix becomes reminiscent of stained glass, vibrant and luminous.

With so many primary colours involved, you need to take care not to get carried away. To avoid too much razzmatazz, select just a couple of colours and stick to them. The first colour should dominate and the second should be used sparingly, filling no more than a third of the overall design.

For example, you can grow or arrange a mass of orange flowers, with a smattering of blackcurrant. Orange is also great with cobalt, as is raspberry or fuchsia with lime.

Right, clockwise from top right
Euphorbia palustris
Gladiolus 'Magma'
Tulipa 'Mariette'
Centaurea cyanus 'Blue Boy'
Tulipa 'Golden Apeldoorn'
Tulipa 'Royal Acres'
Tulipa 'Prinses Irene'.

Opposite, clockwise from top right
A bold hand-tied bunch of the whopper tulips 'Queensday' and 'Perestroyka', along with 'Doll's Minuet' threaded through lime-green *Euphorbia characias* subsp. *wulfenii* 'John Tomlinson' as the foliage base.
A citrus mix of *Cosmos sulphureus* 'Bright Lights', *Zinnia* 'Cactus Orange' and 'Cactus Yellow' with zingy-green, *Nicotiana* 'Lime Green' and dill (*Anethum graveolens*).
Another hand-tied bunch with *Viburnum opulus* 'Roseum' providing the foliage frame, with pink tulips 'Pretty Princess' and 'Candy Cane', plus the orange 'Arjuna' for contrast.
A purple bunch of dahlias, 'Urchin', 'Purple Flame' and 'Downham Royal', with agapanthus seedheads for sparklers of brilliant green.

Palette 3: Cashmere Jersey

The third family of colours has plenty of white within the shades, so that orange, brown, gold or crimson become peach, milky coffee, ivory, faded coral and smoky pink. This palette is fashionable at the moment, with a vintage 1970s vibe. I think of these as cashmere jersey colours, and just like a luxurious jumper, they are warm, soft and comforting. They're so easy on the eye, they're often used in bridal displays.

You don't want too much of a good thing – cashmere top-to-toe would be overkill – so this palette needs an injection of white or ivory to break up the pinky, peachy shades.

This palette also benefits from a splash of sobriety – copper or bronze, or crimson from palette 1, which is ideal if it can be found in the centre of one of the flowers (see *Helianthus annuus* 'ProCut Plum' on p74 and *Phlox drummondii* 'Cherry Caramel' on p75).

Right, clockwise from top right
Tulipa 'La Belle Epoque'
Tulipa 'Apricot Foxx'
Dahlia 'Jowey Winnie'
Ammi majus
Chrysanthemum 'Avignon Pink'
Tulipa 'Blushing Lady'
Tulipa 'Charming Lady'
Crocus chrysanthus 'Cream Beauty'.

Opposite, clockwise from top right
Hand-tied bunch with foxgloves (*Digitalis*), peonies and white *Gladiolus colvillei* 'The Bride'.
The epitome of the Cashmere Jersey palette: dahlias 'Café au Lait', 'Labyrinth', Linda's Baby' and 'Wine Eyed Jill'.
Tulips 'Groenland', 'Mistress Mystic', 'Spring Green' and 'Apricot Beauty' with the crepe paper, saucer flowers of *Oreomecon nudicaulis* 'Meadow Pastels'.
A summer hand-tied bunch of *Ammi majus* threaded through with the snapdragons, *Antirrhinum majus* 'Chantilly Light Salmon', 'Chantilly Bronze' and 'Chantilly White'.
A peony-like bunch of tulips, 'Pink Star' and 'Verona Sunrise'.

Palette 4: Champs-Élysées

The final palette is light and cool, with mauves, soft blues, blue-pinks, primrose yellows and off-whites that can become so pale they can reach the purest bright white. This is what I think of as the chicest palette, crisp and smart, like well-pressed clothes and elegant stilettos, hence its Parisian name. These colours are also often used to make bridal displays.

Right, clockwise from top right
Allium hollandicum
Petunia 'Sophistica Lime Green'
Cynara cardunculus
Cosmos bipinnatus 'Purity' with *Malope trifida* 'Alba'
Lavatera trimestris 'Dwarf Pink Blush'
Echinops ritro
Dahlia 'Platinum 'Blonde'
Fritillaria raddeana.

Opposite, clockwise from top right
Hand-tied bunch with *Orlaya grandiflora*, *Nigella damascena* 'Double White' and *Ammi visnaga*.
Euphorbia marginata 'Summer Icicle' as the foliage base, with *Ageratum* 'Giant White', *Malope trifida* 'Alba', *Oenothera lindheimeri* 'The Bride' and *Malva moschata* f. *alba*.
Nigella damascena 'Persian Rose', *Phacelia tanacetifolia* and *Orlaya grandiflora* in a clear, pumpkin-shaped vase. Dahlias 'Wizard of Oz' and 'Melody Harmony' and *Cleome spinosa* 'Colour Mix' with *Panicum capillare* 'Frosted Explosion' as a light, airy froth above and between the flowers.
Hand-tied bunch with the elegant ivory *Tulipa* 'Sapporo', along with the *T.* 'Shirley', plus wallflowers (*Erysimum*) and stocks (*Matthiola*) for perfume.
Didiscus caeruleus in all its soft, cool forms.

Opposite A muted, gentle colour mix of the cool Champs-Élysées palette featuring *Cerinthe major* 'Purpurascens' and *Linaria maroccana* 'Licilia Azure', with *Calendula officinalis* 'Sunset Buff' as a warm splash of contrast.
Below When I'm working out colours for a bunch or planting, I often use coloured candles to help me. They're invaluable for resembling the mass and density you get with a flower, and so much better than paint colour swatches, where the white paper also influences the overall tones. I have my four colour palettes as a starting point and then play around with adding a splash of contrast, borrowing one candle from another palette until I find a beautiful mix. Then I select flowers to match.

Mixing Palettes

Borrowing colours from one palette to use in another can work to brighten up a bouquet or calm one down. However, not every colour is a good palette hopper. I think it's good to have some rules to follow, which you can experiment with to find what looks good to you in the garden and the vase.

I've spent many happy times playing around with colours when I have an event to design arrangements for, swapping swatches of one orange with, say, one with more brown in it (from the Venetian Velvet palette) or more luminosity to it (Boiled Sweet). I recommend spending some time with the four palettes before taking it one step further and mixing them up, juggling different colours to find a good balance.

Play around with flower photographs cut out from catalogues or paint colour swatches, or, as I do, use coloured candles. Once you decide on your favourite mix of colours, take that as the basis for selecting what to grow.

Here I'm sharing colour recipes I use all the time. Some of the accompanying photographs are of arrangements I made more than 20 years ago, but I feel the same colour rules apply, even as my tastes have evolved.

Venetian Velvet with Boiled Sweet

One downside to be aware of with the Venetian Velvet palette is that you can create a bit of a black hole if you use only the dark shades. That's why the copper tones and richer oranges and golds are needed for balance. But maybe even better is to mix this palette with a splash from Boiled Sweet. Combining the high saturation colours of Venetian Velvet with just one colour from Boiled Sweet works well – I use acid green and orange all the time in this mix. They can really perk up an arrangement of the dark velvets if you find that your display is starting to look a bit sombre. If you choose to stick with the crimsons, don't add bronze or coppery colours, but go for one of the sharper, citrus shades. This creates a wonderful depth, but with a good dash of acidity.

Right, clockwise from top right
Tulipa 'Sarah Raven'
Dahlia 'Totally Tangerine'
Smyrnium perfoliatum
Dahlia 'Manoa'
Euphorbia oblongata
Dahlia 'Schipper's Bronze'
Iris 'Red Ember'
Cosmos bipinnatus 'Rubenza'.

Opposite, clockwise from top right
A rich collection of pelargoniums, including 'Lord Bute', 'April Hamilton', 'Mystery' and *Pelargonium sidoides*. The foliage of *Pelargonium* 'Charity' gives the sharp green lift to cut through the richness of the flowers.

A predominantly rich-toned bunch of dahlias, 'Sarah Raven' and 'Darkarin', with *Rudbeckia hirta* 'Cherry Brandy'. *Cyperus eragrostis*, *Panicum capillare* 'Frosted Explosion' and *Dahlia* 'Totally Tangerine' to add a brightness and lightness, preventing the combination from being too dark and heavy. Dark, rich, crimson tulips 'Antraciet', 'Sarah Raven' and 'Wow' all threaded through the invaluable acid-green *Smyrnium perfoliatum* for contrast and structure, with the odd *Tulipa* 'Evergreen' to supplement the green.

Boiled Sweet with Venetian Velvet

Another favourite colour recipe of mine involves the same two palettes, but mixed the other way around: the emphasis is on the bright colours of Boiled Sweet, given a touch of calm sobriety with the use of a dark and rich crimson or mahogany from the Venetian palette. This calms it all down and gives some depth to the mix.

Right, clockwise from top right
Euphorbia palustris
Tulipa 'Royal Acres'
Tulipa 'Mariette'
Dahlia 'Manoa'
Malope trifida 'Vulcan'
Tulipa 'Sarah Raven'
Tagetes patula 'Burning Embers'
Tulipa 'Prinses Irene'.

Opposite, clockwise from top right
Hand-tied bunch of zinnias, 'Deep Red' and 'Benary's Giant Lime', with *Nicotiana* 'Lime Green', calmed by the scattering of rich velvet *Rudbeckia hirta* 'Cherry Brandy'.
Purple and orange wallflowers: *Erysimum cheiri* 'Vulcan' and 'Fire King', with crimson velvet 'Sunset Red' between. The classic six ingredient recipe for a hand-tied bunch (see p289) in the Boiled Sweet palette, with the addition of the crimson-black *Dianthus barbatus* buds to calm down and root this mix. Here, *Lunaria annua* seed pods are the structural primary foliage, with the dark buds of *Dianthus barbatus* (Nigrescens Group) 'Sooty' acting as the filler foliage and, *Dianthus barbatus* 'Green Trick' the upper storey. *Ranunculus* 'Elegance Clementine' is the Bride, *Calendula officinalis* 'Indian Prince' the Bridesmaid and finally *Dianthus barbatus* 'Oeschberg' with its magenta-pink flowers the Gatecrasher.
A purple and orange hand-tied bunch of dahlias including 'Purple Flame' and 'Waltzing Mathilda', with the almost-black velvet flowers of 'Soulman' (along with my velvet coat) adding rich and sober calm.
Zingy pink *Malope trifida* 'Vulcan', *Lathyrus odoratus* 'Zorija Rose' and acid-green dill, all settled by the rich crimson flowers and leaves of atriplex and *Scabiosa atropurpurea* 'Black Cat'.

Venetian Velvet with Cashmere Jersey

Here, the Venetian palette is softened, rather than sharpened, with a dash of café au lait from the Cashmere Jersey crew. This is a current favourite combination and we've recently been involved in breeding a dahlia, which we've named 'Sissinghurst' that has just this combination: crimson flowers with a milky coffee petal edge (you can see it in the bowl pictured opposite).

Right, clockwise from top right
Tagetes patula 'Burning Embers'
Tulipa 'Sarah Raven'
Calceolaria 'Kentish Hero'
Dahlia 'Schipper's Bronze'
Tulipa 'Vovos'
Iris 'Red Ember'
Tulipa 'La Belle Epoque'
Cosmos bipinnatus 'Rubenza'.

Opposite top
Hand-tied bunch of the rich and luscious tulips 'Ridgedale', 'Recreado' and 'Queen of Night', with the buds and flowers of the exceptionally beautiful milky coffee tulip 'Vovos' to add some brightness and lightness to the mix.

Opposite bottom
A bowl of three of the best dahlias bred for, and named by, us: the crimson 'Sissinghurst', gold 'Tom's Choice' and the soft putty-pink 'Jonathan Buckley'.

Cashmere Jersey with Venetian Velvet

In this mix, the Cashmere Jersey shades are dominant, and a dash of sobriety is provided by the Venetian Velvet palette, which prevents it from becoming too cloying. The centre of certain flowers can often perform exactly this function, for example, *Calendula officinalis* 'Sunset Buff', *Helianthus annuus* 'ProCut Plum' and *Phlox drummondii* 'Cherry Caramel' all have a rich, dark centre. At the other end of the saturation spectrum, pure white is also a good addition to this mix, and one I particularly love.

Right, clockwise from top right
Calendula officinalis 'Sunset Buff'
Tulipa 'Charming Lady'
Orlaya grandiflora
Tulipa 'Blushing Lady'
Helianthus annuus 'ProCut Plum'
Tulipa 'Apricot Foxx'
Iris 'Red Ember'
Crocus chrysanthus 'Cream Beauty'.

Opposite, first column from top to bottom
Dahlia 'Jowey Winnie'
Helleborus × *ballardiae* 'Merlin'
Rudbeckia hirta 'Enchanted Velvet Flame'
Dahlia 'Manoa'.

Opposite, second column from top to bottom
Chrysanthemum 'Avignon Pink'
Phlox drummondii 'Cherry Caramel'.

Opposite, third column from top to bottom
Hand-tied bunch using *Ammi visnaga* as a base, with *Rudbeckia hirta* 'Sahara' and *Scabiosa atropurpurea* 'Black Cat' as a dark, rich contrast picking up on the centres of the rudbeckia flowers. Another hand-tied bunch: the centre of *Phlox drummondii* 'Cherry Caramel' and *Calendula officinalis* 'Sunset Buff' provide the dark, rich contrast to the soft, warm mix of flowers, threaded through with *Orlaya grandiflora* as the foliage base. One of my favourite dahlia colour mixes with the lovely, single 'Hawaiian Sunrise', 'Café au Lait' and 'Rhubarb and Custard' giving the main soft tones, with the dark 'Manoa' providing the splash of rich contrast to prevent the bunch from becoming too sickly.

White With A Dash

White is such a strong colour in the garden and vase, I think it almost deserves to be in a category of its own. Gardeners tend to think of white as an easy colour to work with, but I believe the opposite. If you walk into a garden featuring lots of strong colour (as with our Oast Garden at Perch Hill) and one white campanula or foxglove has self-sown among the rest, your eye goes straight to that one plant – it dominates.

In my view, white is best with a scattering of another colour, such as greens and silvers. For me, the perfect real-life version of the white end of the Champs-Élysées palette is the White Garden at Sissinghurst Castle Garden in June, when clouds of white flowers are joined by bold, silver leaves from plants like cardoons (*Cynara cardunculus*) and the giant thistle, *Onopordum acanthium*.

All the bunches shown here follow the same principle: white is the main story, with the smallest splash of another colour, ideally just a coloured petal edge or flower centre.

Right, clockwise from top right
Nigella papillosa 'African Bride'
Cosmos bipinnatus 'Fizzy Rose Picotee'
Cosmos bipinnatus 'Purity'
Narcissus 'Actaea'
Malope trifida 'Alba'.

Opposite, clockwise from top right
The orange centre of *Narcissus* 'Actaea' provides the splash of contrast in this bunch of *Narcissus* 'Thalia' and spring blossom.
The elegant, starry black centres of *Nigella papillosa* 'African Bride' give the contrast here, with a splash of yellow from *Cosmos bipinnatus* 'Purity', spritzing colour through the pure white *Orlaya grandiflora* and *Ammi majus*.
The pink buds and stems of *Oenothera lindheimeri* 'The Bride' along with the carmine petal edges of *Cosmos bipinnatus* 'Candy Stripe' give the all-important splash of contrast to this mainly white bunch of *Malope trifida* 'Alba' and *Cosmos bipinnatus* 'Purity'.
A classic white mix of spring flowers with a splash of blue from muscari and the yellow, pollen-rich centres of *Helleborus niger*, along with *Leucojum aestivum* 'Gravetye Giant'.

Vase Life

Opposite Our scented daffodils trial in 2006, testing for length of flowering, stem productivity, scent, volume and vase life. *Narcissus* 'Actaea' won with 'Avalanche', 'Geranium', 'Silver Chimes', and *N*. 'Canaliculatus' (foreground) close behind.
Above Our pinks (*Dianthus*) trial in 2005, testing for the same characteristics as the daffs.

I have never liked the idea of picking a fresh flower, only for it to wilt and be chucked into the compost the next day. From day one, maximising vase life has been as important to me as discovering the most productive plants to grow. From my first vase-life trial (we tested the maximum vase life of various chrysanthemums in 2005) to a trial of 62 roses in 2023, I have worked on narrowing down the flowers that cut best and experimented with conditioning stems to understand which plants need a simple treatment to ensure longevity and which are fine without, as well as whether flower food makes a difference.

As you move through this book, you'll find specifics on conditioning certain seasonal plants, for example, getting the most out of famously floppy hellebores (p106) or managing tulips as they continue to grow in the vase (p178). But a broad brushstroke is also helpful.

The cardinal rule is: don't pick and plonk. Instead: pick, condition, rest and then arrange. That's the order to do things. You'll find a full breakdown of how to do that on the following pages. But one thing to note is that the focus is on natural and cost-effective treatments for homegrown flowers.

Homegrown flowers behave differently to some commercially grown and imported flowers you find in shops. Grown out of their natural season, these have often been forced into growth with higher than natural temperatures and large volumes of water, which makes flopping more likely. They often last significantly shorter durations of time than stems grown naturally

Above A chrysanthemum trial at Perch Hill in 2005 including 'Barnardo's Hope', 'Kate Harding', 'Tom Pearce' and 'Allouise Orange'. Sadly, chrysanthemums come and go, so many trialled are no longer available.
Below Zinnias cut and placed into water with a separate bucket for stripped leaves.

in the garden. If properly conditioned, homegrown is best! Commercially grown flowers can also be subject to toxic chemicals as a pre-vase treatment. You'll be able to tell which shop-bought flowers have been treated in this way by how long they take to break down in a wormery or compost bin.

The tips I share will give your homegrown flowers a vase life that is better than any you can buy. Another great reason to grow your own.

Picking

I recommend taking two buckets out to the garden when picking flowers; the first should be empty (to place the leaves stripped from the stems) and the second should be one third full of water (to place your flowers). At Perch Hill we use milk pails rather than florists' buckets because they have handles, which makes it easy to carry two or more into the garden. And we use zinc, or even better, stainless steel (Champagne or chandler's buckets) as these last for decades – expensive initially, but worth it.

- Don't pick flowers in the heat of the day. Pick first thing in the morning, or if you miss your moment, last thing at night. Plant cells are turgid (full of water) after a period of darkness when levels of transpiration and photosynthesis are low. The stomata close at night to save transpiration and water loss, so early morning picking is ideal. Turgid cells mean flowers don't flop as easily.
- Wear gloves. Ideally wear washable, thin, breathable garden gloves. This tip is crucial if picking hyacinths (which irritate many people's skin) and most of all euphorbia – its milky sap is highly allergenic.
- Using florists' snips (lighter than secateurs and stronger than kitchen scissors) cut the stems at an angle so they don't form a flat seal at the bottom of the bucket or vase.
- Strip the stem of leaves. Remove the leaves from the bottom two-thirds of the stem (at least) as soon as it has been picked and place the stripped leaves into a bucket. Pick, strip, plop into water, pick, strip, plop. There are really four reasons for doing this. Firstly, it saves lots of time and mess in the house later. Secondly, you don't want the leaves right in the middle of the arrangement, as these just clog it up. Thirdly, any leaves below water level will eventually rot. And finally, the fewer the leaves, the less water demands there are on the stem and the less likely it is to flop.
- Particularly in hot and bright weather, cut stems straight into cool water, not into a pretty basket or into your hand. This makes a difference to the eventual vase life.

Opposite Alliums 'Spider', 'Purple Rain' and 'Lucy Ball' picked straight into a bucket and placed in the shade on a hot June morning.

- Even if they're in water, don't leave flowers in direct sun. Find a spot in the shade.
- When you pick annuals and biennials, don't cut them to the ground. It's a waste of lots of potential flowers and may wipe them out. Take out the leading shoot, cutting just above a pair of leaves or better still, to a side-branch with a bud, which will grow and produce more flowers.
- Bear in mind the size of the arrangement/vase you're picking for and aim to cut to that scale. If you pick a longer stem than you need and end up only using the top two thirds of it, you waste lots of axillary buds below the cut (this is particularly the case with lots of annuals and dahlias). These would-be flowers just end up on the compost heap. The lower you cut the stem, the slower the plant is to flower again.
- When picking bulbs such as tulips, Imperial fritillaries and lilies, which have leaves up the flowering stem, you must leave a portion of stem and leaves behind. If you steal too much of its photosynthetic food factory – its leaves – the bulb will not be able to produce enough food to survive and flower well the following year. This does not apply to alliums, narcissi and hyacinths, which all have their leaves at the base; the flowering stems of these can be cut to the ground without affecting the bulbs' chances of survival, because the basal leaves are left behind when you take the flower.
- With perennials and shrubs, it's important to pick sensitively; stand back and look at the plant in its entirety to see how you could improve, or at least not damage, its overall shape. Don't pick stems all in one place; take one here, one there. You want to thin out, not decimate.

Conditioning

Conditioning refers to the treatment of the stems and flowers that will ensure the longest vase life. This process is done before arranging and techniques differ depending on the type of plant you're working with.

Searing

This is the technique we use most at Perch Hill and involves plunging stem ends into boiling water to maximise a flower's longevity. Rarely a day goes by without someone putting the kettle on for some searing. If I am worried about any plant flopping, I sear it.

I sear much more frequently in the late winter and spring than I do in the summer and autumn. Later in the year, a stem's cell walls have more lignin in them and are tougher, woodier and more upstanding. In the spring, there is lots of fleshy, new growth, which is more likely to sag. I even sear rosemary in spring. If you just pick and plonk it into a vase, the growth tips tend to bend double and don't look great. As a general rule, in winter into spring I sear 75 per cent of what I pick, in summer and autumn, only about 25 per cent.

The rule for searing throughout the whole year is that the time in the boiling water is proportional to the texture of the stem. Soft stems need just a few seconds, woody stems more like 30 seconds. So bluebells are seared for only 2–3 seconds, whereas lilac needs 30 seconds. Don't leave soft stems in too long, or they'll cook and disintegrate.

Put 2.5–5cm (1–2in) of boiling water into a mug and plunge the stems in. The length of stem you sear is proportional to the length of stem you've cut. I sear about 10 per cent of the overall length, which means if it's one metre long, sear 10cm. If it's 30cm, sear 3cm. With short-stemmed plants, take care to keep the flower heads away from the steam. Enclose the flowers in a sheet of newspaper if you need to.

Searing is easier and works better than burning the stem ends with a match or on the hotplate (although, oddly, in our

Opposite Searing stems in a cup of boiling water. This bunch includes *Papaver rhoeas* 'Amazing Grey', *Nicotiana* 'Whisper Mixed', *Ammi majus* and *Orlaya grandiflora*.

Opposite top left Searing a selection of flowers that all get five seconds in boiling water before being placed in cold water to stop them cooking.
Opposite top right Searing *Helleborus foetidus* Wester Flisk Group (the red-stemmed, so-called stinking hellebore). This picks well, as do its leaves.
Opposite bottom Searing *Lupinus* 'Blue Javelin', *Orlaya grandiflora* and *Cerinthe major* 'Purpurascens'.

experiments, this is the best treatment for poppies). And you get better results searing woody shrubs than you do hammering their stem ends.

My theory is that searing works by increasing the surface area for water absorption; searing softens the tough, impermeable layer on the outside of the stem. This is just what hammering the stem end does, exposing more of the xylem, the capillary network of the stem, to the water. But you destroy lots of cells in the process through hammering, which results in bacterial build-up. The searing technique has the same effect, but the stem end is (at least for a while) sterile, avoiding such a dramatic bacterial build-up and the production of slime.

Searing has a miraculous effect on vase life. Even if they have flopped already, many flowers will make a total recovery. I had three large buckets of snapdragons in a prominent place on a stand at a trade fair when I first started selling seeds decades ago. By the end of the first day, all the flowers I'd grown were fine, except the snapdragons. Every stem had collapsed under the heat of the spotlights. I took them off the stand and, that evening, seared the stem ends and shoved them in a deep bucket of water in the back of the cool van. By morning, every stem had completely recovered and was standing bolt upright. It was incredible.

So, I always say, if in doubt, sear. You won't do any harm and you'll do lots of things a lot of good. If you're not sure what to do and what not to do – go for it and do the lot!

Plants that need searing
- All wildflowers, such as buttercups
- Angelica
- Atriplex
- Bluebell (the only bulb that I know of that benefits from searing)
- Cerinthe
- Cobaea
- Poppy
- Euphorbia
- Fern
- *Helleborus orientalis* hybrids will only last if you sear them and all hellebores benefit
- Herbs, such as sage, rosemary and lavender in spring
- Plants that drop their petals readily, such as *Verbena bonariensis*
- Rose
- Sunflower
- Wallflower
- Woody plants, such as lilac, philadelphus, *Viburnum opulus* 'Roseum' and the best white, single-flowered cherry, *Prunus* 'Tai-haku'; you will double their vase life

Plants that don't need searing
- Bulbs (apart from bluebells)
- Sweet pea
- Dahlia

Submerging

There are a few flowers that benefit from submersion. Float the flowers in a large bowl, sink or bath of tepid water, pushing them below water level – the whole flower head as well as the stem. A few hours will do, but if you can, leave them overnight. Even if you've left the flowers in the car or in a basket in the garden, and they have seriously flopped, they'll recover fully in the bath. I used to worry about submerging white peonies as I thought the flowers would turn brown, but even seemingly delicate things like these really benefit from submersion. If you use the submersion technique, you don't need to sear the stem ends.

Plants to submerge

All of these plants (which have complex structures) have evolved to absorb water over their whole leaf or petal surface area. Submerging them under water gives them much more of a chance to absorb the water they need compared with merely sucking up fluid through a narrow stem.

- Hellebore
- Hosta
- Hydrangea
- Ivy
- Parsley (flat- and curly-leaved)
- Peony
- Some shrubby foliage plants, including cotinus and cornus

Right *Paeonia lactiflora* 'Duchesse de Nemours' floating in a bath of cool water for a few hours. This hugely enhances vase life.

Resting

Resting means giving the cut flowers a few hours, or best of all a full night, in a bucket of water sat in a cool, dark place. This resting comes after conditioning. Fill the buckets with tepid (not ice-cold) water; the plants absorb tepid water better. Be sure to rest your flowers somewhere cool. Being kept cold, but not freezing, makes a huge difference to the vase life of any flower.

Everything we pick, we aim to give this rest period. I don't really know why it works, but it does! If you're arranging things into a vase sitting in a coolish, darkish place (such as a church), you can skip the rest time, but if your flowers are heading to a hot marquee, it's crucial.

A note on temperature

In winter in particular, with the central heating going at full tilt, it's a good idea to move your flowers to a cool place until you need them. If you have an easily portable table centrepiece, put it outside overnight and bring it in come the morning. Don't do this if a hard frost is forecast – go for the larder or a cool place in the house instead. Doing this can literally double the amount of time you'll enjoy the flowers, so it's worth the hassle.

Right *Salvia viridis* blue-flowered picked for a family wedding and resting in our barn.

Next page We use our open-fronted barn – which is cool and dark – to store flowers as we harvest. Here a mix of June peonies, roses, honeysuckle and hardy annuals along with biennials stand in water overnight before arranging. Pick, condition, rest, arrange. That's the order to do things.

Opposite On shorter stems than many plants we grow, sweet peas can get crushed or drowned in deep buckets, so we have special shallow, double-sided zinc buckets for harvesting.

Flower Food

Your flowers are now all set, as good as they can be, ready for arranging. The final thing to bear in mind is flower food. Adding flower food to the vase water is important. You can buy it in sachets to sprinkle into the vase or make your own; either way, the preservative needs to contain certain ingredients.

The most important of these is bleach or an acidifying agent, such as vinegar or lemon juice, to reduce the proliferation of bacteria. Tap water is alkaline and many bacteria prefer this. By adding a weak acid, you create a hostile environment for bacteria reproduction. Bacteria create the slime at the stem ends that makes the vase water stink. It also blocks the stems and stops them taking up water. This is the basis of the old wives' tales of adding an aspirin, or half a glass of lemonade, to your cut flower water. Aspirin contains salicylic acid; lemonade contains sugar and citric acid, and its bubbles are created by carbon dioxide, which forms carbonic acid in water.

In a 30cm (12in) high vase, use half a teaspoon of bleach or a good slurp (about 5 tablespoons) of clear, cheap, distilled malt vinegar. I also put a drop of bleach in water with strong-smelling plants such as alliums, cleomes and any brassicas to prevent their characteristic pong developing.

Some shop-bought sachets of flower food includes sugar. The sugar feeds the flowers, but in my view, it feeds the bugs too. In our experiments it seems to add to the vase life of sweet peas, but nothing else.

A note on ethylene gas
Bananas give off ethylene gas. Don't put flowers near bananas or they will age more quickly. Delphiniums and sweet peas are very susceptible.

January & February

I love flowers in the house. So much so that since my late twenties, bunches of flowers were what I hoped to get for my birthday, which is at the beginning of February. It's a grim time of year in the UK, particularly as there is so little to pick in the garden; so from the first year I was with Adam, his birthday present to me was cash, which I was to spend on flowers.

At the crack of dawn, we'd drive to the wholesale flower market in Nine Elms, London and spend the lot. I'd fill my arms with tall pussy willow, scented branches of mimosa, paperwhite daffs, bunches of asparagus-like hyacinth buds only just starting to show their colour, and saucer-sized *Anemone coronaria* in velvet red, blue, and if we were lucky, a deep crimson variety called 'Bordeaux'.

After a whopping full English breakfast in the market café, we'd head home and I would pack every vase, glass, jug and jam jar we had with flowers. For the next few days, I'd feel like an old-fashioned opera diva staying at the Ritz. How nice!

As you can imagine, once we moved away from London and had a decent garden space, growing (a room-filling quantity of) my own flowers was at the top of my priority list. I'm still at it, 30 years on.

In January and February, garden flowers may not grow in great abundance, but they are there. With a bit of planning and planting with the start of the year in mind, and then consciously seeking flowers to harvest, you'll discover there are real beauties out there.

I find at this time of year some flowers draw you in, but others wait to be found. I love the perfumed wands of sweet

Opposite A classic, mid-January cut flower harvest of hellebores, *Salix gracilistyla* 'Mount Aso' and *Leucojum aestivum* (forced in pots), arranged on a side table in our kitchen/living room.
Below A bowl of mixed snowdrops, including the whopper sycamore seedhead-like, *Galanthus* 'Atkinsii' and the simple, species, *G. nivalis*. They are threaded through a lichen-covered twig support, balanced on my favourite turquoise bowl.

box (*Sarcococca*) that we have growing against a north-facing wall, as well as winter-flowering viburnums (such as *Viburnum × bodnantense* 'Dawn' or 'Charles Lamont', which flowers from November to March). Sarcococca is ideal for any shady spot – it's non-descript for most of the year, but its winter scent provision is gargantuan and it is the first shrub in the year to truly deliver.

By February, daphne flowers start to open and create a strong perfume cloud. *Daphne bholua* 'Jacqueline Postill' will fill a sunny corner with scent for weeks at a stretch and one mere sprig of the more compact, *D. odora* 'Aureomarginata' will suffuse a room with its spicy, gingery, warm and delicious fragrance.

Very early blossom is rare, which makes growing it all the more worthwhile. If you have room for a tree or flowering shrub, I think February blossom should be a priority. Almond tree blossom comes first and there's nothing better than its huge, honey-scented, white flowers with stained pink centres that arrive just as the glossy leaves are starting to unravel. This is more glamorous than any of the winter-flowering prunus (such as *Prunus × subhirtella* 'Autumnalis Rosea') in

Opposite **Spanish jugs filled with olive branches and white wax flower *Chamelaucium uncinatum* taking us through Christmas and well into the New Year. These flowers lasted three weeks; I changed the water and washed the jugs every four days, recutting the stem ends at the same time and adding a good slurp of vinegar to the fresh water.**

my view. But, sadly, its flowers come so early they often get frosted, turn brown and then drop. We've just planted the beautiful *Prunus mume* 'Beni-chidori' for just this reason: it should provide delicate yet glamorous blossom very early in the year. In London, I also grew mimosa; it thrived in the protected environment of a city. It starts to flower in February, but needs a sheltered position. I love both these blossom providers, and if you have a very sheltered spot in your garden, do consider one of these.

Many of the willows, hazels or alders are lovely at this moment, with the pink willow, *Salix gracilistyla* 'Mount Aso', my favourite among them. All are super hardy and early to produce catkins, making them ideal for picking in January and February.

It's well worth growing a few elegant evergreens for winter picking, too. I love rosemary and I routinely turn to one or two of these to add to vases. The first is the very upright *Salvia rosmarinus* 'Foxtail', which has a distinctive silver underside to every leaf, making it reminiscent of a fox's bushy brush. I also love *S. r.* 'Vatican Blue', which often starts to show its dark blue flowers in February. And then there's the cascading *S. r.* Prostrata Group. There's no better plant for softening the edge of a terrace or giving instant elegance to a pot. We pick it pretty copiously at this time of year.

I also love olive for winter picking. I planted an olive tree in the Farmhouse Garden 20 years ago and it's still happy there, although I must confess it doesn't bear fruit. Olive trees require two months of cold weather (below 10°C/50°F) and they obviously get that in the UK, but to get them to fruit you need another cultivar close by, as they are wind pollinated.

Even if we don't get an olive harvest, I love the way its evergreen leaves catch the light and the simplicity of a large vase of olive leaves, studded through with white wax flower (*Chamelaucium uncinatum*), or some early hellebores. We have a wax flower plant in a large pot in the greenhouse and it flowers now and on through spring. It has a vase life of well over a fortnight if it is kept cool.

As well as these tall, upper storey plants, we are building up our clumps of snowdrops and cyclamen into carpets at Perch Hill. These seasonal beauties are joined by winter aconites (*Eranthis hyemalis*) and early crocus (*Crocus tommasinianus*) from the end of January. This and *C. sieberi* subsp. *atticus* 'Firefly' are the first to flower at Perch Hill and are worth spotting and cutting to bring in. More will open

Opposite top Snowdrops, crocus and winter aconites in a spot of dappled shade in mid-February. Little, delicate stems like these are a joy to pick at this time of year – just remember to sear stem ends for one second to maximise vase life.

Opposite bottom Three snowdrops, *Galanthus* 'S. Arnott' for height and whopper flowers, the double *G. nivalis* f. *pleniflorus* 'Flore Pleno' and single, species *G. nivalis*. Even with snowdrops, you want a heart and a horizon to your arrangement, so use varying stem lengths for that breadth and height.

week by week, but in the first part of January they're rather hidden under general winter garden chaos and leaf litter.

One can become a bit of a nerd about crocuses and even more about snowdrops. There are hundreds of sought-after cultivars, one being *Galanthus elwesii* 'Grumpy', with markings that look like a mouth turned down at the edges. This makes me smile, but the rarities like this can be expensive and slow to spread. Instead, start off with the species, *G. nivalis* and the frilly, tutu-like double, *G. n.* f. *pleniflorus* 'Flore Pleno'. The straight up, wild (or naturalised) snowdrop has silvery-green leaves and neat, slim flowers. If lifted and divided in the green (when it is in active growth or even flowering), it's quick to get established on almost any soil, in sun or partial shade, and usually flowers from early February. 'Flore Pleno' is also happy to spread. Within three years you can divide it and replant it to create massive carpets. I love and pick lots of both to bring inside.

It's also worth having one of the long-stemmed, bumper-flowered snowdrops such as *Galanthus* 'S. Arnott' or 'Atkinsii'. 'S. Arnott' is one of the largest and most impressive, with beautiful pure white, light bulb flowers. They open up to look like sycamore seedheads and smell deliciously of honey. The bees adore it. 'Atkinsii' is a quick clump former, with finer petals than 'S. Arnott', but still lush and lovely. It's easy to grow, looks good bringing light under a tree, bulks up easily and is ideal standing with 'S. Arnott', towering above the rest in the general snowdrop garden party each February. Both have good oomph in a bowl or vase. The recently bred 'Mount Everest' comes a little later, but is equally statuesque and very long flowering.

From the middle of February, the crocuses start to form swathes and the miniature *Iris reticulata* and *I. histrioides* emerge. I usually grow these in pots and pick the odd flower, which I've discovered lasts better in the house with the flower left on the bulb. The bulbs can then be stored for replanting in the autumn.

If you have a sharply draining spot in full sun (or can create one), go for one of the *Iris unguicularis* crowd. My parents had this Algerian iris on their doorstep, and the clump is still thriving some 60 years on, flowering all winter. My mother has since added the rich, velvety purple 'Mary Barnard' and the delicate mauve 'Walter Butt' – both scented.

Fritillaria raddeana give these irises a run for their money in the glamour stakes. It's always the first fritillary to flower

Opposite top **Our dwarf iris trial from 2025. Left to right: 'Pauline', 'Painted Lady', 'Angela', 'Katherine's Gold' and 'Clairette'. I love them all for their intricate delicacy *and* that they flower from the middle of February (or earlier if grown in pots under cover). I found that with bulbs left on, they last better inside: give them barely half an inch of water in a vase. Once the flowers are over, dry out the bulbs, leaves left on, in an onion bag (or similar). Hang them somewhere cool and dry for replanting in the autumn.**

Opposite bottom **Adam's grandmother's cup, from a market in Mexico 100 years ago, filled with a miniature arrangement of irises 'Purple Hill' and 'Fabiola', *Anemone coronaria* 'Double Mauve', polyanthus and pulmonarias.**

in the garden here and by far the most reliably perennial. We learnt last spring – on a trip to the Netherlands to see fritillaries being farmed – that *F. raddeana*, together with many of the imperial cultivars, make the best garden plants. They reappear reliably without the need for summer heat, something the wild, Syrian *Fritillaria persica* really does need. *F. raddeana* is the one to go for, super early and splendid; just one stem in a narrow-necked bottle, in pride of place, looks fantastic and lasts two weeks.

Miniature, and perfect for collections of petite vases and bottles, are any member of the polyanthus and primrose troupe, which flower lightly from the very start of the year, but by the middle to the end of February, get into their blooming stride (more on these in March from p122).

Hellebores are a key winter-into-spring cut flower, even if they are hellishly temperamental. There are some varieties such as the Christmas rose (*Helleborus niger*), which cut well. And I find the autumn-to-spring flowering *H.* × *ballardiae* 'Maestro' good; its later-flowering brother 'Merlin', and also *H.* × *nigercors* 'Emma', make excellent cut flowers.

Then there's the apple-green Corsican variety, *H. argutifolius* and our native hellebore, *H. foetidus*, of which the Wester Flisk Group is the loveliest, with strong crimson staining to the heart of the leaves and down the stems, as well as edging the green bell flowers. With 10 per cent of their stem ends seared, these are both super robust and easy to grow and last up to three weeks in a vase. Many of the others, including the Lenten rose (*Helleborus* × *hyrbidus*), or so-called garden hybrid forms, are real floppers, unless you condition them meticulously.

If you don't have a few of these stalwart early-flowerers in your garden, then think of adding some. They bring spring forward in a brilliant and spirit-lifting way at a much-needed time. And there isn't a single one that, with a bit of conditioning, doesn't make a great cut flower.

Picking and Arranging

Opposite One of my favourite picking baskets which I found in a market in Copenhagen. Here it's filled with a February flower harvest. Picking into water is not always necessary when it's cool.
Below Searing snowdrops in heat-proof Moroccan tea glasses. Just a second in boiling water, in and out. Alternatively, place the snowdrops into empty tea glasses, add a splash of boiling water, and then fill the tea glass with cold water pretty instantly. This works well and is quicker if you're doing loads.

As the weeks go by, more and more lovely things start to emerge, many of them petite and delicate.

The weather here is pretty much guaranteed to be cold and wet at the start of the year, so cutting and placing stems straight into water is not necessary. I tend to carry elastic bands around my wrists and, as I pick, I bind a bunch together and place it in a basket or trug. This stops them getting muddled and bruised as you add things in. Pick, bunch with elastic, plop into a basket, and on you go.

Conditioning cut flowers at this time of year is not as essential as it is on a hot, sunny day. But some brief prep of almost every stem is still needed. All the early, delicate bulbs (such as snowdrops and scilla), as well as polyanthus, last longer if their stem ends are seared, but their stem texture is not robust, so they should be dipped quickly in and out of boiling water and then straight into cold water to disperse the heat. That's enough to add several days to their vase life.

Cutting and Conditioning Hellebores

Hellebore flower heads can be beautiful floating in a bowl. But if you want to use whole hellebore stems in an arrangement, they need careful conditioning; just searing them isn't sufficient for a good vase life. This conditioning routine has five steps, which together increase the chances of hellebores staying upright.

1. Careful harvesting Harvest only the stems which have a good percentage of flowers that have already dropped their yellow anthers and are starting to run to seed. At this stage in their life cycle, they are more mature and have had time to lay down a little more lignin in the cell walls, making them more upstanding.

2. Score the stem Score all the way down both sides of the stem, top to bottom, using the very tip of a sharp knife. Scoring means creating a very light groove – not cutting – along the outer stem surface. This allows water to access the stem when it is submerged.

3. Splice the stem Once scored, use the knife to splice the very end of stem.

4. Sear the stem ends Dip the ends in boiling water for 10 seconds.

5. Submerge Finally, place them in a bowl, sink or bath filled with cold water and leave them overnight. This encourages maximum hydration and an upright stem.

After all that, if any flop in the vase, repeat step five, the cold water treatment, and you'll find they often resurrect miraculously. It's worth doing.

Making A Flower Grid

A flower grid is an ingenious structure for arrangements that I use throughout the year, but particularly in the early months. It sits on top of a bowl or deep dish and creates a support that holds the flower heads out of the water.

You can simply float flower heads in water (see p138), but keeping them just out of the water slows down their decomposition and therefore lengthens their vase life. It's also a sustainable alternative to florist's foam (or oasis, as it's known), which is made from plastic and next to impossible to recycle.

Creating a flower grid for a bowl makes a ideal table centrepiece for dinners and parties, as it is low enough for people to easily see across, but it looks generous, never mean. The arrangement can involve stray stems – vines, climbers and trailers – twisting and turning over the table surface, and these can link one low bowl with another further down the table, or even a row of trestle tables. It's very effective.

At this time of year, I use this flower grid technique for hellebores, winter aconites, wood anemones and snowdrops – for all of these, sear stem ends briefly before arranging.

In spring, a flower grid works well with heavy-headed Parrot tulips, which tend to hang their flowers, as well as cherry or apple blossom and Icelandic poppies, with the backing of *Smyrnium perfoliatum* or euphorbia. A grid is also how I often arrange huge-headed flowers such as magnolias and camellias.

In summer, use the grid arrangements for fragile flowers such as the huge *Rosa* 'Madame Grégoire Staechelin'. Or for the Mexican sunflower (*Tithonia rotundifolia*) whose stems

are hollow just below the flower head and break all too easily.

For autumn, this arranging system is perfect for the cup and saucer vine (*Cobaea scandens*) sunflowers, dahlias, particularly the huge-headed ones (see p352) and spidery chrysanthemums (see p373).

Select twigs Hazel, cornus or willow provide ideal material – straight, and about the thickness of your little finger (or a bit less). If you are creating a small grid, go for finer stems; and for a large structure, look for chunkier twigs.

Cut the twigs Do this so that they hang over the bowl by about 2–3cm (1in) on both sides. Lay the twigs in a grid formation.

Secure the twigs Secure at each crossing point with a reef knot. I often use flexi-tie rather than string, as you can pull it very taught and it has some elasticity. As the branches age and dry, the flexi-tie then relaxes and keeps the branches held tight. Ensure the knots are all tied in the same direction. Tied like this, the grid will concertina and can be folded away, making it easy to store. If you tie just one knot in the wrong direction, it prevents the grid folding away.

Tie a reef knot To tie this knot, bring two ends of string together, putting right over left. Tie a half knot, then bring the two ends back together, but this time left over right. Tie a second half knot. I tie all the knots loosely first, and then, one by one, pull each knot really tight.

Add a pin holder If I'm planning to use taller stems threaded through, I also add a pin holder. You need to stick this firmly to the bottom of the container using waterproof florist's tape. Place the grid over the bowl and fill the bowl with water.

Arrange the flowers Begin with a good basic structure of stems poked into the pin holder (if using). Then you're away, and you can slot the rest of the flowers in easily.

Add flowers to each square For delicate and small flowers like snowdrops, place a bunch of several stems through each square in the grid. For larger flowers, add one to each square. You can keep it super simple and use just one or two flowers or do a full mixed arrangement using the structure and colour rules outlined in Form (p46) and Colour Palettes (p56).

Opposite *Galanthus nivalis* bunches being threaded through a small grid.

Below A few sprigs of silver birch create an upper storey to the arrangement.

Party Wreath

Christmas wreaths decorate many of our doors in the run up to December festivities, but I like making them at other times of the year, too. Dried flower wreaths can hang on an inside wall (and last for months or even years) and fresh flowers naturally keep cool on an outside door in the autumn and winter months. Scent is important to me when selecting ingredients for the wreath; I tend to pick with my nose as well as my eyes, scouting with all my senses at this lean time of year.

My preference is for a wreath to be as natural and sustainable as possible, so florist's foam, or even a wire base, is out of the question; instead I use stems of salix, which can be easily bent. If everything is biodegradable, so much the better; once the flowers are over, you can remove the odd water vial (essential for keeping the live flowers hydrated), strip the plants off and add them to the compost heap. The wreath base can be used for kindling or shredded and put on the compost heap.

I was born in February, and some years have a party, and that's what this fresh wreath was originally designed for. Hanging on a door or entranceway, it's the first sign for guests that this is *not* just any old day, but time to have a party! I like that signal. For me, the bigger and more generous the wreath, the more I love it. Its volume lifts it out of the ordinary. Use the ingredients as a guide and make use of what you have growing around you.

For festive party wreaths, see p416–421 in November/December.

Wreath base, 3 branched stems
Look for branched stems, around 1m (40in) long. This makes a whopper wreath, 60cm (24in) in diameter, but you can make one half the size if you prefer.

Willow 'Nancy Saunders' (*Salix purpurea*)

Main plants, 10 stems each
You need good, long stems, around 60cm (24in), which you can then cut down when forming bunches to around 20–30cm (8–12in).

Rosemary (*Salvia Rosmarinus*)
Sweet box (*Sarcococca*)
Hazel (*Corylus*)
Euphorbia
Winter-flowering honeysuckle (*Lonicera fragrantissima*)

Finer touches, 30 flowers each
Hellebore (*Helleborus*)
Snowdrop (*Galanthus*)

Condition
Ensure your flowers are conditioned using the guide from p84. Bear in mind the flowers should be prepped the day before you want to make your wreath. For these ingredients, euphorbia needs its stems seared in boiling water for 15 seconds, then plunged into cold water. Snowdrops need searing for just 2 seconds. For hellebores, see p106 and give them the full treatment.

1. Make a base Twist the branched willow stems and secure together to form a hoop. Do this by bending each branch of willow, twisting it to and fro, to encourage a circular form. At about one third of the length of the first branch, secure a second branch with twine, twisting the remaining lengths together. Do the same with the final branch, securing it to the second branch and twisting them together until you reach the first branch. The twiggy ends of each stem are very pliable and easy to bend and weave into the thicker parts of the branches. Tie in any twigs that stick out and ensure it is secure at all points.

2. Create bunches With the main plant ingredients to hand, start arranging them into individual bunches, using around 5–6 stems in each bunch. You should end up with around 10 bunches.

3. Tie the bunches To tie the ends of each bunch, take a length of twine and double it over and lay it on the table. Place the bunch on top of the twine, take the two loose ends of twine and place them through the loop on the other side. Pick the bunch up and pull one end around the bunch to the left and the other end around the bunch to the right. Tie and cut off the excess twine.

4. Add the bunches Attach the individual bunches onto the wreath base, one by one, with the flower heads all pointing in the same direction. Use the same knot as in step 3.

5. Add delicate flowers Place the snowdrops and hellebores into water vials. Add a few stems to each vial to maximise impact. It's helpful to hang the wreath in place, step back and decide where the flowers should go. Tuck the vials in so they are secure and hidden well.

PRACTICAL
January & February

Opposite Sowing sweet pea seeds into root trainers.

January and February are the quietest months of the year in the cut flower garden. Apart from sowing a few things that are slow growing, there's little that needs attending to. That applies to the rest of the garden, although roses and shrubs will need pruning (if that wasn't done at the end of last year, see p426).

This temporary lull in activity makes it the ideal moment to design your cutting patch and work out what you want to sow and grow, and where to put everything once it's ready to be planted.

The word 'design' makes it sound elaborate, but I think of the planning and design of a cutting patch as a five-stage process that everyone can achieve.

1. First decide on which colours you like best (see p56 for guidance). Which is your favourite palette or combination of palettes?
2. Decide what you most want to grow. Have a look through seed catalogues and do some online research (and, of course, consult this book) to choose your favourite plants within your palette/palettes. Select plants that are predominantly cut-and-come-again.
3. Consider succession. Ensure that you have selected plants that will be in flower throughout as much of the year as possible, without a flower feast or flower famine at any particular time of year. Find more advice from p26.
4. Create a sowing plan. You only need to complete this step if you have tons of seeds to sow (rather than plants to plant out).
5. Draw out your plot. Once you have the dimensions and space locked in, use tracing paper overlaid onto the drawing, with a sheet for each of the growing seasons. You can then plan your plot on the tracing paper to ensure you use the space as efficiently as you can (see p117).

Preparing a Patch

All gardeners are working within parameters of space, time and money. As a rough guide a 3.5m x 1.5m (11ft x 5ft) patch will give three to four bunches a week between July and October. Most households won't need or want more flowers than that, so don't overdo it. But whether you have a cut flower patch, a whole cutting garden or a flower field, there are a few overarching principles it's worth bearing in mind before you start to plot and plan.

Choosing a spot

Sun and shelter from strong winds are both important factors in this sort of gardening. There are a few cut flowers that grow well in shade (such as nicotiana and foxgloves), but not many. Annuals, which fill most of my cutting patch, make their food from the sun. They also have a steep growth curve, reaching full size in only a few weeks, so they need all the nourishment they can get. Full sun it has to be. Almost all plants, but particularly annuals, rarely thrive in a windy place where their roots get rocked as they establish, and their buds and flowers get trashed or wind burnt. A sheltered spot is ideal.

Practical

Below Our heavy clay soil at Perch Hill, before it was improved. The yellow is the clay; the black-brown, our very minimal topsoil. Where we live, it's hard work to garden!

Paths

Paths are key and you need to factor them in. If flowers are out of reach, you can't pick them. If they're not harvested, they will run to seed and that's their season done for. The simplest way to make sure you've got paths in the right place is to measure the length of your arm – i.e. how far you can reach. If you are able to have paths on either side of your bed, then the bed's width can be double the length of your arm. If you are only able to have one path, then the bed should be no wider than the length of one arm. Putting a stepping stone within your bed is also a great idea if you want to maximise your space, as it extends your reach into the bed and means you can have more planting space and less path.

Soil

The soil at Perch Hill is clay, and very heavy with it, but the whole garden has had tons of organic matter and grit added to it over the last 30 years, so the soil is easier to plant into and maintain than the slab of yellowish-brown butter I remember having to contend with when I began.

While the no-dig method is better for the structure of the soil, we weren't able to implement that method from day one due to the heaviness of the clay. These days, it's straightforward to create no-dig beds as our soil has become very workable. We still mulch regularly, but now we leave it up to the worms to draw it down into the soil below.

If you're lucky enough to have a rich, loamy soil then you won't have to do much soil improvement, but if your soil is heavy clay or chalk, you will have to put in some groundwork. See p199 for guidance on soil improvement and mulch.

To discover more about your soil, dig a hole in your garden and see if you can visually identify what type of soil you have. If you can see chalk, sand or heavy clay below the dark brown top soil, then this is a clear indication of your soil type.

If it is less clear cut, pick up your soil and feel it. Does it feel gritty or slimy? If it's gritty, then your soil is sand based, if it's slimy then you probably have a clay base.

If you have tricky clay, sand or chalk soil, consider a raised bed. Raising the level of your beds means you can add in more organic matter, and it allows you to plant into lighter topsoil, composed of organic matter.

Below Laying out a garden with a drawing below sheets of baking parchment. Here I am deciding what's going into the pots that line the path.

Creating a Planting Plan

I've included in this book a few recommendations for exceptional shrubs, roses, perennials and bulbs that can be planted and harvested from other parts of the garden, not strictly the cutting patch. This is a supplement to your patch, and the suggestions are based on over 30 years of plant trials. If you have the space, do add at least some of these. Then you can have fun with planning the planting for your designated cut-flower patch.

I have a master black-and-white line drawing of the cutting garden at Perch Hill, with the paths (and any other significant features) clearly marked on. I'd recommend making this sort of basic drawing of your plot (with dimensions and features), even if it's rough.

I can then overlay the master garden plan with tracing paper or even baking parchment and mark everything out. I cut out round shapes representing frames for climbers and stripes for a line of plants. I tack these on and, in pencil, mark what's going in the circle or stripe, along with photographs cut out from catalogues, if I need a reminder.

I then hang this on the wall to live with and think about until I'm 100 per cent happy with the plan before final sign off. Having a plan like this will ensure you get a bumper crop of exactly the cut flowers you love and want to fill your house with, so it's worth it!

Sowing / Planting Calendar

After working on your design and deciding where you are going to place your plants, it's time to get down to the nitty-gritty and create a sowing and planting out calendar. The simplest way to do this is on a large sheet of paper, divided into blocks of months with a column for the plants you need to sow and another for the ones you need to plant out. Organising your planning like this makes the whole year seem much more manageable and ensures you give yourself a balanced amount of work throughout the year.

PRACTICAL

Below Our seed filing system – store in a cool, dry place, or even better in the fridge.

Organising Seeds

Many of the plants I recommend are annuals and biennials, grown from seed, which means you'll need to be organised. Don't just shove your seed packets in a drawer, devise a quick and easy filing system.

I create a serial sowing box using a shoe box or an old box designed to store CDs. I divide this into nine compartments, which I label with months starting with January/February through to October.

When the seed packets start to arrive through the winter, I put them in the slot corresponding to the month they are best first sown. If the packet has a generous quantity of seeds, I never sow them all at once. If they are plants that I want to repeat sow – such as *Ammi majus*, snapdragons or zinnias – I sow some, and then put the packet in a slot a couple of months on. With this system, I don't forget that these flowers need to be sown again and when.

Keep the box cold and dry and the seeds will be fine from one year to the next.

Sowing

As far as the cutting patch is concerned, there's very little that needs sowing this early in the year, but sweet peas, the climber cobaea and snapdragons are the exceptions. All of them are excellent cut flowers that benefit from having that bit longer to get growing before the summer. Sowing them now gives them plenty of time to germinate and develop their roots to ensure the maximum length of flowering.

Sowing sweet peas (*Lathyrus*)
If we know we have a big event coming up in spring, we will sow our sweet peas earlier in November or December, but generally, we will sow at the beginning of January. For the best varieties, see p241.

- I never bother to soak sweet pea seeds. They'll germinate without soaking within 10–14 days.
- Sow one seed to each cell of a root trainer. We always use these as they help to form stronger roots. The legume family, of which the sweet pea is a member, has a long root and if it is allowed to grow to its full

Below left Sowing sweet peas into a root trainer.

Below right Opening a block of root trainer cells to show the straight root run to the base of the pot, which then quickly promotes branching and lateral root formation.

capacity then it will produce lateral side shoots, which will make it even stronger. Root trainers also have channels in them, which will direct the roots to the bottom of the pot so that they will grow vertically instead of spiralling. Root trainers speed up the whole process of root development. The roots grow stronger and at three or four times the speed of a sweet pea that has been put in a standard seed tray.
- Use a peat-free, loam-less compost with an open structure (such as a multi-purpose potting compost). The plant roots need air, as well as moisture and nutrients.
- Dampen the surface and then, with your finger, push each seed in about 2.5cm (1in) below the surface of the compost. Water.
- Label and put in a cold greenhouse or cold frame. Don't mollycoddle them – that's the most common mistake. Heat can inhibit germination and, with it, you're likely to get more seed rot. So put the trays somewhere cold. They're frost tolerant to about −5°C (23°F). A bit of frost seems to do them good.
- Guard against mice. Mice love sweet pea seed and your whole crop may disappear in one go. If you have the trays in a cold greenhouse, put them on a sheet of wood or ply (not hardboard), and place them on empty, upturned pots; make sure that there's a good overhang so that mice can't climb up on to the plants. Or you can soak the seeds in liquid seaweed fertiliser overnight to make them unpalatable. That seems to work too.

- After a week, begin to check for germination every day. Don't water until you see seedlings start to come through, usually in 10–14 days.
- Once the seedlings appear, keep them cool at about 5°C (41°F). This promotes root growth, rather than stem growth, which is exactly what you want. A cold greenhouse or cold frame is ideal. When I started growing sweet peas, I just used a couple of straw bales with a reclaimed window over the top: that gave enough shelter.
- Once they've started shooting well and maybe have 2 or 3 pairs of leaves, we usually pot on 2 seedings together. Don't let them get pot-bound, they will never be quite the same again. A slim, deep, 1-litre-pot is ideal. Use a good compost and water them in.
- After a couple of weeks when there are three or four pairs of leaves, pinch out the leaders – just squeeze off the growing tip between your finger and thumb. This promotes vigorous side shoot formation, directing the energy of the plant and roots toward growing out.
- Every week, check your plants. Water them lightly if they are dry. If they have started to shoot again, pinch out any spindly tips.
- See p149 in March for planting out your sweet peas.

Sowing cup and saucer vine (*Cobaea scandens*)
Cobaea scandens also needs to be sown early in the year. It won't flower until it reaches about 2m (6½ft). Sown late, it tends to reach this height just when we get our first hard frost of the winter, meaning you'll never see flowers. Sown early, it will fill your autumn with cups and saucers.

- Each seed has a large surface area and is a round, wafer-thin saucer shape: sow vertically (any end up), not flat, into their own individual small pots.
- Put them in a propagator. They'll germinate in this warm and moist environment within 2–3 weeks.
- *Cobaea scandens* is a half-hardy annual in this country, so it can't be planted out until mid-May. As this is a climber, you need to start training it while it is still in the greenhouse, otherwise it will turn into a messy bird's nest. Once the seedlings start to grow, after about 3–4 weeks, they need a climbing frame to clamber over – don't leave them sprawling. Pot them on, and in their new pot, create a simple support frame using silver birch pea sticks (see p148 for instructions).
- Keep your plants in a light and frost-free environment until ready to plant out.

Sowing snapdragons (*Antirrhinum*)
I'm crazy about snapdragons. They flower on and on in the garden for months, and if you don't get around to picking every flower spike, they're quick and easy to deadhead, which should encourage more flower production. We tend to do two – or even three – sowings in February and also May or June. We have under cover space, so we sow again in September or October. Snapdragons can

Below left **Sowing** *Cobaea scandens* seeds.

Below right **Sowing** tiny, dust-like *Antirrhinum majus* seeds into a half-sized seed tray.

take moderately cold nights, and in the right place, can survive a light frost.

- Do your first sowing of snapdragons in February. As short-lived perennials (we treat them as half-hardy annuals), they have a slower growth curve than a true annual and take up to 20 weeks from seed to flower, so get going with them early.
- Snapdragons have tiny seed, so are best sown in a half-size seed tray. The seedlings should appear within 10–14 days from sowing, but can take anything up to three weeks, so don't lose heart. In a month or so from sowing, the seedlings will need pricking out into 9cm (3½in) pots (see p148).
- Like us, you can sow again in May or June to provide a flower harvest until November or December.
- If you have a greenhouse and cold frames, sow once more in September/October. Prick out 6 weeks later into 9cm (3½in) pots. Store the potted seedlings in cold frames throughout winter and pot on in February or March. These give you flowers from May or even late April, if you're lucky.

Early tulips   Muscari
Fritillaries   Narcissi
Euphorbia   Hyacinths
Polyanthus

March

There are five main harvests at Perch Hill at this moment in the year. The super-early tulips, narcissi and hyacinths. Then there's what I call the petite and delicate things, such as *Iris reticulata* (which will be over soon), scilla, polyanthus, cyclamen, crocuses, winter aconites, snowdrops and miniature narcissi. And finally, the last of the harvest from the greenhouse, before the garden takes over. There's nothing better than a good bunch or vase of *Anemone coronaria* that go on to last well over a week in water.

The very early tulips are the ones I always yearn for – a sign that winter is properly over and something to be celebrated. That's why we grow plenty of these harbingers of spring. *Tulipa* 'Ice Stick' is the first to flower, followed by 'Apricot Delight', 'Purissima' and 'Exotic Emperor' (syn. 'White Valley'). All guaranteed to be there for picking by the middle of the month, whatever the weather. And in a warm spring, the perfumed 'Orca' and 'Orange Emperor' or 'Apricot Emperor' will also be out, plus any in the Impression series. I'd be bereft without at least one or two of these to pick for arranging; I do this simply, with single stems in a series of narrow-necked vases, or a few stems in a small jug on the kitchen table.

To me, hyacinths are a little too chunky for growing in a border. I prefer to grow them in pots, though I must admit, the longer they're in the garden, from one year to the next, the finer and prettier they become. They are a must-grow, because I love to pick them for their perfume.

My favourite is *Hyacinthus orientalis* 'Anastasia'. It is closely related to the species hyacinth, *H. orientalis*, from the southern Mediterranean. It has plenty of air between each floret, which

Opposite A scented collection of *Narcissus* 'Prinses Amalia' and the orange-peel scented 'Kedron', with the soft pink *Hyacinthus orientalis* 'China Pink' and white hellebores.

Below Three excellent hyacinths for picking: *Hyacinthus orientalis* 'Woodstock', the bluebell-like 'Anastasia' and 'Peter Stuyvesant'. Blue hyacinths have the strongest scent of all.

gives it grace and elegance. Also, as a blue-flowered form, it has the strongest fragrance. We have some soft pink hyacinths which have been coming back in the garden for over a decade, and I relish picking them in the middle of March. I didn't used to be a soft pink person, but everyone can change! I love this colour now, particularly in a March vase mixed with narcissi and hellebores.

I also love *H. o.* 'Woodstock' for its rich, saturated beetroot shade, as well as the airy, open flowers of multi-flowered 'White Festival'. In a sunny spot, these flower in March, or you can extend their season by planting a few in dappled shade to flower a little later.

Equally invaluable are the March-flowering narcissi, many of them powerfully fragrant. As a cut flower crop, narcissi have become more and more important at Perch Hill. They are the key bulb in our cut flower lasagnes (see p391) for the following reasons.

Super perennial Narcissi are perennial, much more so than even species tulips. We spend a few weeks every year in a cottage on the west coast of Scotland and there's a walled

garden next door – it once provided food and flowers for the residents of a house that burnt down in the mid-nineteenth century. That's the last time it was actively gardened, yet every spring, the place becomes a carpet of *Narcissus poeticus* 'Albus Plenus'. These bulbs have been there in a very wet climate for nearly 200 years, gradually spreading, quietly thriving. I love that. So, once planted in sun or dappled shade, you can forget about them, knowing they will come back in bigger and better clumps in 10, 50 or even 100 years.

Even though individual narcissus varieties don't need planting every year, we always have interesting new ones to trial from our trips to the Netherlands, Cornwall and the Isles of Scilly, where they have breeding programmes, so we create a new lasagne bed every few years.

Super healthy With the wet springs of recent years, tulip blight has become more of an issue, whereas narcissi don't suffer from an equivalent disease. In fact, most do well in moist soil.

Scent Lots of daffodils also have fragrance, although how we perceive the scent is down to genetics. I love the smell of them all – including the paperwhites, which some people find almost unbearable. But any with tazetta genes tend to have a cleaner, sharper fragrance that everyone seems to enjoy.

Length of flowering The final characteristic that makes them invaluable as a cut flower crop is the long season some varieties provide. It's something I realised on a winter trip to Crete, to a valley below the island's highest mountain, Psiloritis. I spent three months there with my husband, Adam, and every day we walked with our dogs, exploring the stony paths running across the valley. Week by week, more flowers emerged: muscari, crocuses, miniature irises and carpets of *Anemone coronaria*. But for me, the highlight was a metre-wide clump of the wild *Narcissus tazetta*, which was just starting to flower on our first walk at the start of the holiday and still flowering on our last. The clump never had more than ten flowers at any one time, but its length of flowering was remarkable. I look for that stamina in the varieties we trial. *Narcissus* 'Avalanche', 'Cragford', *N. fernandesii* var. *cordubensis* and a couple of newer ones, 'Polar Hunter' and 'Starlight Sensation', provide a season that's almost as long.

Now you're convinced by the merits of daffodils, on to the best to grow. I love the trendy new ones with pink grapefruit trumpets (such as Narcissus 'Pink Charm', 'Carice' and the older 'Bell Song' and 'Katie Heath'). The idea of a pink daff might seem challenging, but they're glamorous and many of them have a spicy, exotic perfume.

But if I had to name just three favourite daffodils for picking now it would be 'Actaea', 'Starlight Sensation' and 'Polar Hunter'. 'Actaea' is a traditional variety, a Narcissus poeticus, or pheasant's eye daffodil. The other two are newcomers and each a winner in our picking trials of 2023 and 2024. 'Actaea' came out on top in terms of scent and vase life in our original, 2006 narcissus trial. We have repeated that trial many times since and it still reigns supreme.

I planted 20 bulbs of 'Actaea' more than 15 years ago, on a west-facing bank on our drive. They've gradually merged into a solid carpet producing some 500 flower heads every spring. They've naturalised so comprehensively, I can pick to my heart's content without feeling guilt. That's all to the good, but more important than productivity is just how lovely they are. 'Actaea' is simple and chic, has fantastic perfume

Below A classic Cashmere Jersey palette (see p62) with the early Tulipa 'Apricot Delight' and scented Narcissus 'Bell Song', 'Actaea', 'Pink Charm' and 'Beautiful Eyes'.

Right I've used a white hyacinth as the structure through which I've threaded the earliest tulip in our garden, 'Ice Stick', along with Narcissus 'Carice' and 'Prinses Amalia'. I made this as I walked in the garden and then slotted it straight into a vase for my bedroom.
Opposite Narcissus 'Actaea' naturalised on our grass-edged drive.

and a vase life of a week if kept cool. I think these look their loveliest piled into a large vase or urn, as many stems as you can pick, with a few of their leaves on the stems to break up the flowery whiteness.

My other two favourites seem to have everything going for them, several varieties rolled into one in terms of what they offer. 'Starlight Sensation', new to us in 2023, is exceptional. It flowers from March for five or six weeks, it's multi-headed so gives a great show in a pot or vase and it has wonderful perfume and a vase life of over a week. Like 'Actaea', it's a robust grower, happy naturalising, which means we can plant and pick it from areas of rough grass and save on border space.

Finally, 'Polar Hunter', hot off the breeding bench, is one we first grew for spring 2024. It's similar to 'Starlight Sensation', but with more pointed petals and comes into flower earlier. It flowers reliably from late February, all the way through March. Many of the varieties that put on an early show are on the coarse side, but not this one. It's fine, with delicate stems topped with a clutch of ivory flowers that have a distinctive green hue to the centre of the trumpets and a green wash over the petal hearts.

Opposite The narcissus trials bed in the Cutting Garden in 2006. Included here, and still growing 20 years later, are *Narcissus* 'Trevithian' (in the foreground) with 'Avalanche' and 'Geranium' behind. We have dahlias planted over the top in one of our bulb lasagne beds (see p391).

Below left I love the delicacy and elegance of March flowers, epitomised here by the ice-blue *Scilla mischtschenkoana* and *Scilla* 'Pink Giant', with *Leucojum aestivum* and *Narcissus* 'Winter Waltz' threaded through.

Below right A scented bunch with a succession of March into April flowers, including *Narcissus* 'Actaea', joined by 'Polar Ice'. All these Pheasant's eye daffs have excelled in our trials with wonderful scent and good vase lives.

They look good for two weeks once cut, if kept cool. And the fragrance of 'Polar Hunter' is unbelievable. Even people who can't bear the smell of paperwhites find their perfume delicious. I try to have a pot on my window ledge or doorstep through the first weeks of spring so I can pick the odd stem to put beside my bed.

March is also the time for miniature narcissi, some of the best plants of all, with flowers the size of a ring on your finger. I love *Narcissus* 'Canaliculatus' (a favourite of Dad's), and the similar 'Pipit', along with the species *N. fernandesii* var. *cordubensis*, which has a scent so powerful, it's hard to believe it's produced by those tiny flowers. And there are the hooped petticoat daffodils such as *Narcissus romieuxii* 'Julia Jane' and *N. bulbocodium* 'White Petticoat'. These have a vase life of at least a week, are excellent for naturalising and look great in a pot. They're also guaranteed to be in flower this month.

Perhaps the most emotionally resonant flowers for March picking are, for me, these very petite and delicate things – the narcissi, but also the mini polyanthus, irises, cyclamen, crocuses, winter aconites, snowdrops, scilla and miniature daffs. All with tiny flowers, they're at their best arranged in

Opposite A true coincidence: the scarf I was wearing perfectly matched a mini bunch of spontaneously picked *Primula* 'Stella Champagne' and *P. vulgaris* 'Avondale'. With stem ends seared, both last ten days in a vase.

a sherry glass, mini bottle or teacup, something I've done since I was a child.

During the winter and early spring of 1970, when I was seven, my father had a duodenal ulcer. These were not then treated with the relatively painless drug regime they are now, so he had to undergo a major operation. Already frail from heavy smoking, he was confined to bed in a spare room at home for many weeks. Every Saturday during February and March, I would wake up and go straight into the garden to pick him bunches of flowers to put by his bed.

For the first few weeks, there wasn't much out there, but I'd find double snowdrops with their ballerina tutu flowers and early-flowering, pink *Cyclamen coum*, surrounded by the elegant, marbled leaves of the autumn-flowering *C. hederifolium*. I'd pick mini bunches, their short stems fiddly but worth it. I also hunted for winter aconites (*Eranthis hyemalis*), which I transformed into golden waterlilies to take up to my father in a breakfast bowl filled with water.

I'd pick fistfuls of early crocus, with the finest crimson-black feathering on the outer petals, to mix with primulas from the Gold-laced group and scilla, which had seeded all round my parent's garden. I still grow the blue *Scilla forbesii* and soft pink 'Pink Giant'. These are perfect flowers, simply arranged.

Looking back at that time, when I felt so upset about my father being ill and confined to his bed, unable to go to the place he loved – his garden – I realise how deeply this experience of picking small, early, jewel-like treasures became so important to me and my sense of wellbeing.

Early spring remains my favourite flower season, and these delicate arrangements are a prized way of having flowers inside at this moment in the year. Polyanthus, muscari, dwarf daffs, early fritillaries – every one of them a gift for a miniature vase. And florists tend not to sell flowers on this sort of scale, so they are always a priority on my growing list. I'd recommend everyone making room for a few, planting them in the autumn to ensure you have plenty to pick before the rest of the year's cut flowers are in full swing.

Picking and Arranging

Opposite A trug of mid-March flowers including early-flowering tulips and main-season narcissi. The tulips are 'Orca', 'Apricot Delight' and 'Exotic Emperor'; and the daffodils are 'Starlight Sensation', 'Precocious' and 'Actaea'. This harvest also includes fritillaries (*Fritillaria meleagris* and *F. imperialis*), euphorbia, polyanthus, hellebores, cardoon foliage, rosemary and muscari.
Right A mini cup of flowers, including *Iris reticulata* 'Scent Sational', *Muscari aucheri* 'Blue Magic', *Scilla siberica* and *Fritillaria michailovskyi*, with rosemary, *Viola* 'Aquarelle Flambé' and *Primula* 'Stella Neon Violet'.

March is the moment in the cutting garden when things change radically from the start of the month to the end. The first days can feel like winter, whereas towards the end of March, there's a mountain of lovely flowers to be cut, with the added bonus that lots of them are scented. Many of these early flowers have evolved fragrance as a means of drawing in the pollinators, which are still few and far between in March. Scent is key to the plant's survival, but also to its beauty.

Miniature Vases

I love a vase of flowers beside the bath, bed, or on my desk: something quiet and fine, something to live with as spring emerges. March is the time to celebrate this style of arrangement.

What are the rules? Not many. This is simple stuff. Just remember the smaller the better – and don't cram too many different ingredients into one vase. If you want to make these tiny arrangements into something showier, group a few together on a mat, tile or tray.

Above A March vase no more than a few centimetres high, with delicate, feathered Crocus 'Advance', 'Gipsy Girl' and C. chrysanthus 'Zwanenburg Bronze', plus Primula 'Gold-laced Group'.
Below In early spring, I love picking a mix of blue flowers. Here we have three grape hyacinths (Muscari 'Baby's Breath', M. latifolium and M. 'Siberian Tiger'), with the blue Anemone blanda and Scilla mischtschenkoana. The latter often flowers from February and continues all through March.

Above Here, again, it's grape hyacinths, which give such great small-scale vases. *Muscari armeniacum* 'Valerie Finnis' and *M. armeniacum* with the super-long flowering, *Ipheion uniflorum* providing ice-blue stars. All of these are reliably perennial, reappearing with us for well over a decade.

Mini Floating Flowers

I talk about floating flowers with major brouhaha, perfect for a party on p352. But in early spring, I also love this way of arranging quieter, more delicate flowers. Placing them in water in this way means you really see the form, the texture and colours of each flower.

It's ideal for snowdrops and primroses, and it's the quickest and easiest way of arranging hellebores, as they don't need the careful conditioning I talk about on p106, which you must do when arranging them on a stem.

One of my favourite arrangements, which I create every year at just this time, makes special use of a 30cm (12in) diameter bowl given to me by my husband, Adam, which he found in an antique ceramic shop in Seville, Spain. In it I float the saucer-like flowers of the rich-coloured polyanthus, such as *Primula* 'Stella Champagne' and 'Gold Nugget Apricot'.

But even with a simple arrangement like this, I stick to my rules (see p47). The Bride (the velvety *Primula* 'Stella Victoriana Lilac Lace'), Bridesmaid (matching, but more delicate, 'Gold-laced Group') and Gatecrasher (the dominant 'Stella Champagne'). With this recipe up my sleeve, I go out into the garden and pick exactly what I need: four stems of the first two ingredients and six of the Gatecrasher. They last three or four days and it takes two minutes to do. Perfect!

Below The simplest arrangement of the crimson *Primula* 'Stella Victoriana Lilac Lace' with matching 'Gold-laced Group', plus scented 'Stella Champagne' and peachy 'Gold Nugget Apricot'.

Above left With a large surface area, the ballerina tutu, double snowdrop *Galanthus nivalis* f. *pleniflorus* 'Flore Pleno' is ideal for floating in a bowl. You can look straight down and really admire the intricacy of each flower. Above right A mix of single, semi-double and double hellebores floating in a contrasting-coloured bowl.

Left I remember doing the flowers for a friend's birthday in February about 35 years ago, and with almost nothing out there to pick, I discovered winter aconites (*Eranthis hyemalis*) make great mini waterlilies. I filled the dining table with 20 bowls, just like this, and scattered candles in between.

PRACTICAL

March

Opposite Pricking out February-sown seedlings.

Below A selection of my favourite seeds to sow in March.

When you walk out into the garden, particularly after a warm day and a bit of rain, you'll find it has changed. Where it looked tidy last week, suddenly the soil is starting to fill with weed seedlings – hairy bittercress, groundsel and chickweed are the earliest here. Spring is off, and that's the signal for us cut-flower gardeners to get going too.

As well as keeping on top of the weeds (see p229) with a hoe, we should all be thinking of sowing the bulk of our seeds. With a cutting patch or garden, when you're mostly growing cut-and-come-again annuals, this is a major job. So, there's tons of sowing to do, plus a bit of pinching out of sweet pea growing tips and pricking out of snapdragons and possibly cobaea.

All these jobs are absorbing, constructive and calming, yet quick and easy. It's also warm! It's always a few degrees warmer in our propagator tunnel, and I get to be out of the wind and rain.

Whatever is happening in your world or the general world, it's cheering and optimistic to spend time doing these jobs. I love the feeling that a whole wealth of new life is being created that wasn't there before, which will enhance the cutting garden through the summer and autumn.

Seeds to Sow Now

Sowing is one of my favourite pastimes. As I set off for the polytunnel with my packets of seeds, I love imagining what these black and brown specks are going to turn into. I love the simple kit, the lack of paraphernalia. Yes, you need a few seed trays, some peat-free compost, some labels, ideally a watering can and perhaps a tamper, but you could always improvise if you don't have at least the last three.

If you sow early in the morning, the dawn chorus is reaching its operatic peak at this time of year, and for me that's a fitting accompaniment. Then there's the actual sowing, the work of a minute for each

PRACTICAL

Below **Checking germination in the polytunnel, which is starting to kick off.**

variety: water, sow, usually cover lightly with compost, label, and it's done. A positive act and a peaceful moment.

Hardy annuals

Sow these now, if you didn't get around to sowing them in February, or last autumn. Or in some cases, this will be a second sowing, for example, we sow our calendulas twice a year, once in March and once in September.

Cerinthe we sow three times a year, and if we miss a sowing, we carefully look out for self-sown garden seedlings and transplant them. The first sowing is in March, with seedlings planted out six weeks later in April. We sow again in July to give us flowers through to autumn. And we sow again in September for planting out in a sheltered place before winter sets in, for flowers the following spring.

Salvia viridis blue-flowered is sown in March for planting out six weeks later. It usually flowers well until at least September. As with all hardy annuals, you'll find this will self-sow, so may not need to be resown every spring.

Sow sunflowers (*Helianthus*) toward the end of the month as they are quick growing.

- *Ammi majus* and *A. visnaga* (in root trainers)
- *Calendula officinalis* 'Indian Prince' and 'Sunset Buff' (in a seed tray)
- *Cerinthe major* 'Purpurascens' (in a gutter)
- *Papaver rhoeas* 'Amazing Grey' or other annual poppies (in Jiffy 7s)
- *Salvia viridis* blue-flowered (in a gutter)
- Sunflowers (*Helianthus*) (in individual pots)

Half-hardy annuals (slow)

These are the slow-growing half-hardy annuals. For the amaranth, sow from mid-March and prick out quite quickly. They have tiny seeds and the seedlings will soon starting competing with each other. Plant out in May.

- *Amaranthus* 'Red Army' and *A. cruentus* 'Hot Biscuits' (in a seed tray)
- Snapdragons (*Antirrhinum*), if not done last month (in a seed tray)
- Tobacco plants (*Nicotiana*) (in a seed tray)
- *Phlox drummondii* (in a seed tray)

Half-hardy annuals (fast)

These are the fast-growing half-hardy annuals.

Cosmos is really simple to sow in Jiffy 7s or modular trays, as each seed is large, long and can be separated easily (add two to each cell). With basal heat, they may appear within 24 hours, but most will be up and germinated within three to four days, so don't sow these too early. Cosmos seedlings then grow very quickly, so the best way to work out when to sow them is to think about when you expect the last frost. Here, the last frost is around early May, so we need to sow our cosmos seeds four or five weeks before then, which usually means the last week of March. If you're in the north and your last frost is later, then sow your seeds around mid-April. If you sow your cosmos too early, you'll end up having to pot them on before planting them out, which just creates more work as well as taking up more valuable space in your greenhouse or on your windowsill. We start planting out our cosmos in early May, if the weather is mild.

Don't miss out on *Panicum capillare* 'Sparkling Fountain'. This is currently my favourite grass. It produces new buds at each stem node, so is cut-and-come-again. It looks good for months and keeps going even longer, with a bit of picking or deadheading. Like spun sugar, this is the prettiest, frothiest addition to a vase. Sow anytime in spring into a seed tray. It will germinate quickly and soon need pricking out.

- *Cosmos bipinnatus* 'Apricotta', 'Purity' and 'Rubenza' (in Jiffy 7s)
- *Panicum capillare* 'Sparkling Fountain' and other grasses (in a seed tray)

Sowing Systems

Compost

If you visit your local garden centre you will find an almost overwhelming selection of compost, from seed to potting mixes and general multi-purpose compost. From our research, we have found that it doesn't matter what type you use, because your seedlings are only spending about six weeks in this compost. Just ensure it is peat-free.

We have trialled many different bagged composts and have concluded that they vary rather too much from one year to the next to settle on one brand. Although we've had consistently good results from Biochar, as well as our own brand of compost, which has had more than seven years extensive trialling across thousands of plant types and propagation processes.

PRACTICE

Below left Sowing hardy annuals into a seed tray.

Below right At the end of the month, we start sowing the modern hybrid zinnias (such as 'Queen Lime Red', which I'm sowing here).

These have been bred to be well-adapted to our colder, greyer climate. With other varieties such as *Zinnia elegans* 'Envy', I'd wait a few

more weeks before sowing. They tend to damp off and/or get botrytis if sown before light and temperature levels rise.

Note that bagged, peat-free composts can have twigs and larger bits within them, so sieve these out. At Perch Hill we tend to make our own compost consisting of equal parts molehills, leaf mould and sifted homemade compost. Of course, you may not have access to these ingredients. But whatever you go for, my advice is: don't over think it!

Seed trays

Seed trays are the only viable system for small to dust-like seeds such as tobacco plants (*Nicotiana*), panicum, amaranth and foxgloves (*Digitalis*). They're just too tiny to individually place. If we don't have huge numbers of varieties to sow, or for valuable seeds (like snapdragon), we sow into seed trays, often dividing them into two or four sections with

green canes. Or we use half-sized trays to discourage us from getting carried away and sowing more than we need.

- Fill the tray with peat-free compost, breaking up any lumps as you go.
- Water the trays before, not after sowing. This avoids displacing any tiny seeds. Or you can place the tray in a watertight container to soak from the base.
- We use a clean, empty seed tray to gently press down the compost. The underside ridges leave slight indentations in the compost, which is helpful for sowing in straight lines and remembering where you have sown.
- I sow quickly, from a height, in a sweep from one end of the tray and then back

144 MARCH

again, rather than close to the compost, slowly to and fro. If you do the latter, you get seed clumped closely, which is a pain to prick out.
- Sow only a small pinch, not a palmful. Treat the seed like gold dust, sowing as thinly as possible. Save the leftover seed for the next sowing.
- Cover with a dusting of sieved compost (unless the packet instructions advise not to) and label.
- A bit of basal heat will encourage most seeds to germinate quickly. Use a propagator or heated bench (see p146) at 18–20°C (64–68°F).

Jiffy 7s

Jiffy 7s are small pellets of compost that can be rehydrated and then used as a medium for sowing and growing. Traditionally made up of a peat mix, you can now buy peat-free Jiffy 7s made of coir. Simply pop them in their tray into a shallow container of water for 10 minutes to let them plump up. Then sow your seed directly into the middle of each pellet.

We use Jiffy 7s for plants that hate root disturbance, such as zinnias and poppies, and for plants that germinate quickly and reliably, such as cosmos. This is because there is no need for pricking out or potting on. The Jiffy 7 can simply be planted out straight into the ground. You should remove the teabag-like net before planting. It is biodegradable, but it takes a while to break down and from our trials we have found that it holds the roots back and delays the seedlings establishing quickly.

For cosmos and zinnia, add two seeds to each cell, and for poppies, just the meanest pinch. For poppies, we have also trialled sowing a pinch of seeds into an ice-cube tray and leaving them in the freezer for a week to break dormancy. Plant each cube spaced apart. This works well too.

Root trainers

We use root trainers for most of our legumes, including sweet peas (sow in January/February, see p118) and annual lupins (sow in March or September).

Gutter pipes

I first read about using a guttering for sowing seeds in a book by the late gardener Geoff Hamilton, who advised using one for growing

Below Sowing calendula into a gutter pipe. I individually place the seed about 2.5cm (1in) apart. I can then push out the seedlings into their flowering position, one by one, with minimal root disturbance.

peas. Sowing seeds this way is incredibly efficient as there's no need for pricking out or potting on and you get maximum productivity from minimal time and space.

With this method of sowing, you are likely to get a high germination rate, even upwards of 90 per cent, which you would be unlikely to get with direct sowing, especially this early in the year. I generally use metre-long gutter pipes to sow my seeds, and focus on larger seeds such as *Cerinthe major* 'Purpurascens' and calendula. The gutter pipe acts as a ready-made row, so that when your seedlings are big enough, all you have to do is push them out into your planting bed at suitable intervals (see p194).

Pots

We use individual, 9cm (3½in) pots for plants with large seeds that rot easily, such as sunflowers and cobaea.

Storing open seed packets

Once you've done your sowing, if you have leftover seed, store it in an airtight box in the fridge or somewhere cool (see p118 for more on creating a seed organising system).

Where to Grow

Wherever you decide to start off your plants, I recommend finding a way to provide heat, ideally basal heat, to your seeds, which gives them a growing boost.

Cold frame

A cold frame is the one bit of kit that I recommend for any gardener. Ideally, the cold frame should have a heated cable or a horticultural electric blanket (heat mat) at the base. That's how I started over 30 years ago, when I wrote *The Cutting Garden*. It makes a huge difference to the speed of germination and root formation of seedlings and rooted cuttings, as it encourages basal rather than top growth (top growth is what you get if you heat the air). If there is no electricity source near to your cold frame, you could seek a solar-powered option or opt for a frame with insulated roof lights.

All-round light, or as near to that as is possible, is the other key. That's why the seeds in our polytunnel grow better than those in the greenhouse, which has a solid wall along the longest side. A cold frame with a heat source is cheap to run and gives the best possible results.

Making a heated bench

For those with a source of electricity in a greenhouse or other under cover space, it's worth having a heated propagator bench. You don't have to spend lots of money on this; we have made a heated bench Heath Robinson would be proud of. It is easy to do and very effective.

On top of all our wooden workbenches, we've added a layer of polystyrene insulating tiles. These tiles push the heat back up into our plants and ensure that it doesn't leach out through the wood. The next layer is a horticultural electric blanket (heat mat). And on top of that, a layer of capillary matting, which is a water-absorbent fabric used to evenly distribute water to plants. We put our seed trays on top.

Below Our homemade propagator bench, which we've had for 25 years. It still works brilliantly.

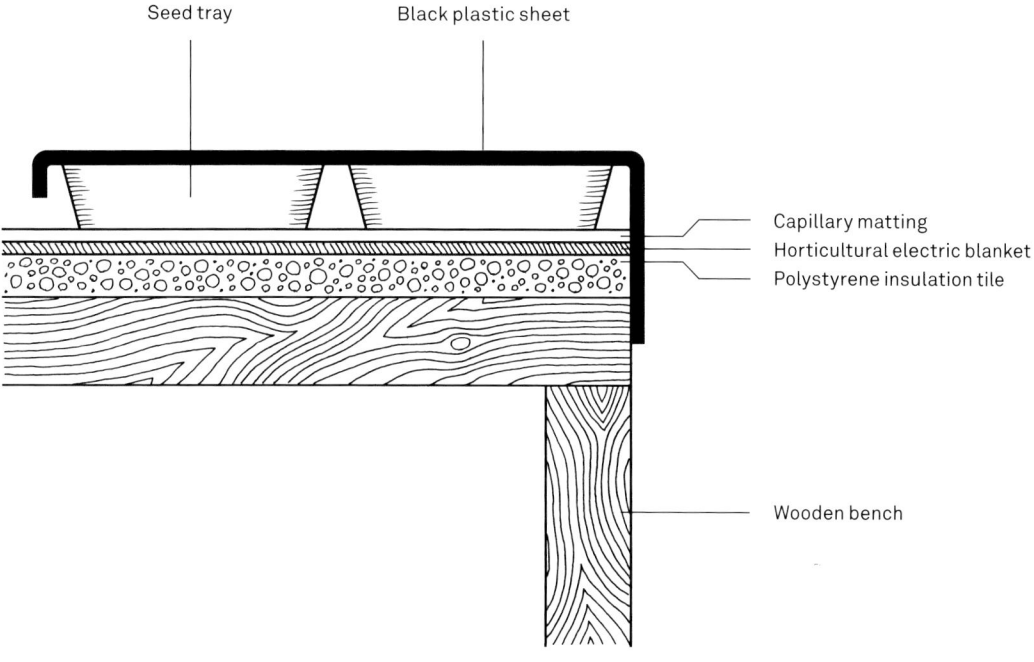

Of course, your seedlings will still germinate without a horticultural electric blanket, but providing a heat source will ensure they develop strong root systems.

We place a black plastic sheet (or recycle empty compost bags, cut open and turned inside out) over the seed trays for 48 hours after sowing to speed up germination. This helps to maintain heat and moisture in the seed tray. However, you must be careful to check for germination, roughly every 12 hours, and move anything showing a shoot of green out into the light.

Watering

Remember, lots of annuals come from warmer and drier climates than ours, so they do not need lots of water to thrive. Generally speaking, you will do more harm if you over water a plant, than if you slightly under water it. At this time of year, you only need to water your seedlings three times a week at the most, but it is a good idea to check in on them as often as you can to see whether they are germinating.

We put our Jiffy 7s on capillary matting. Water one end of the matting and the water then spreads across the surface area of your bench, watering all of your plants evenly.

Pricking Out

Once the seedlings are growing well, they'll be ready to move on to the next stage.

- Prepare an individual 9cm (3½in) pot with peat-free potting compost. Use a dibber or pencil to create a small dimple (not a channel) for the seedling.
- To lift out each seedling, get as much root as you can by pushing a dibber (or you can use a pencil or rigid label) right down to the base of the tray and lift the seedling from there. Avoid touching the stem and instead lift the seedling out by the leaves. You may need to tear the roots of one seedling from another a little, but don't worry, as long as they're left with some, they will be fine. You can be firm not tentative.
- Sink it into its new pot, almost up to its seed leaves.
- Firm it into its new pot and water. Label.
- Place the pot back on the heated propagator until it's time to harden off.

Cobaea scandens

Once your seedlings reach 10cm (4in), pot them on into deep 1-litre pots. You need to create mini frames to support them (see below for instructions).

Small pot frame

For tender perennial climbers, such as cobaea, you'll need to encourage them to grow up a frame as seedlings. Left trailing, both top and root growth slows.

Below Making a pot frame for *Cobaea scandens*.

- Push birch or hazel twigs that are about 60cm (24in) tall firmly into the compost around the perimeter of the pot.
- Gather the ends and tie them in a bundle at the top using twine or a flexi-tie. The climber can then scramble over this twiggy mini teepee.
- As soon as the risk of frost has passed, plant out alongside a frame (see p231).

Dahlia Tubers

If you only have a few tubers to grow, plant them individually into their own pots from mid-March, with the tuber just below the compost or soil surface. Place the pot under cover, in a light place. Water very sparingly.

Below top **Filling a sweet pea trench with well-rotted farmyard manure – essential for happy, healthy sweet peas.**

Below bottom **Planting sweet pea plants next to silver birch frames. Again, fill the holes with organic matter before planting. It makes all the difference to how they grow and flower.**

They can then grow on happily until the risk of frost has passed and they can be planted out.

If you have lots of dahlia tubers, lay them out, packed tight, in a shallow tray and cover the tubers with moist compost. They'll start to sprout in a few weeks and you can then take cuttings (see p192 in April) before planting the mother tuber out into the garden once the risk of frost has passed.

Planting Out Sweet Peas

It's too early for all but sweet peas to go out now, but they really benefit from March planting. They need to get their roots down deep before the demands of flowering, and they seem to do this best before the soil starts to warm in April. You can still plant sweet peas out then, but their stems are likely to be shorter and they have a tendency to be blighted with mildew on their lower leaves while still in full flower.

Planting in a row
1. Create a good climbing aisle (see p151).
2. Dig a generous trench and add plenty of well-rotted organic farmyard manure (or similar) to the base. Fork it in and cover it back over with the soil.
3. Dig holes around 5–7cm (2–3in) away from the support. The plants need to be spaced at 15cm (6in), but you can alternate either side of the frame.
4. Remove your plants from their pots and pop them into the holes. Firm in each plant.
5. Water and label.

PRACTICAL

Planting around a frame

We plant ten sweet pea plants around a 1m (3ft) diameter, homemade frame.

1. Dig the right number of holes around the base of your sweet pea frame.
2. Fill each hole with some compost and a handful of well-rotted farmyard manure, which will feed your sweet pea plant and help with water retention.
3. Remove your plants from their pots and pop them into the holes. Firm in each plant.
4. If your plants are a little too far away from the frame to be tied in, wait until they are a bit taller and tie them to the very base when they reach the right height.
5. If you are growing several varieties around your frame, then always put the label back in by each individual plant.
6. Water.

Making Frames

We make frames for our sweet peas and climbers like cobaea using silver birch (*Betula pendula*) or hazel (*Corylus*), which gives them something lovely to climb over. You can also use bamboo or shop-bought frames, if you prefer. We usually create climbing frames for *Ipomoea lobata* and thunbergias, too, although we do leave some to find their way up through dahlias, which results in good shapes and curves that break up the formality of our dahlia beds.

If the birch or hazel wood is harvested in February or early March, the sap is rising, which means the branches will be pliable and not yet in leaf – ideal. These supporting canes or branches are referred to as 'uprights'.

For the larger structures, the uprights need to be at least 2m (6½ft) tall. You can supplement these with smaller sticks pushed in between each upright, around the base. The twiggy nature of the thinner birch branches make them the best climbing supports, with plenty of handholds on which the plants can climb.

With bamboo canes, you need to add a network of twine between the uprights to create an efficient climbing frame, which doesn't look so good, but does the job.

Standalone frame

- Start by marking out a circle about 1m (3ft) diameter onto the surface of the soil.
- Push a circle of 6–8 uprights into the ground, sinking them a good 20cm (8in) deep. It's key to secure the structure well into the ground.
- Gather the uprights together and tie with a robust flexi-tie or piece of twine at the top.
- If using birch or hazel, then weave the smaller side branches around the structure. Start at one upright in the circle, gather all the thinner side branches about 45cm (18in) from the ground and hold them together in your right hand. Twist horizontally. Carry on twisting, moving up a little all the time, until you get to the next upright and twist the second bundle, binding and weaving it in with the next. Carry on creating a helter-skelter, round and round, moving up a little as you go, until you reach the top. Tuck in any loose ends.

Below top Finishing off a silver birch frame for our sweet peas.
Below bottom We also grow our sweet peas up an aisle frame made from hazel posts clad with jute netting. We follow the sweet peas with climbing beans (such as the delicious 'Monte Gusto') or *Cobaea scandens*.

Aisle climbing frame

We create attractive fence-like structures for the sweet peas to climb up.

- We use hazel. Go for branches that are 3–4cm (1½in) diameter and about 2m (6½ft) tall.
- Uprights are placed at 1m (3ft) intervals and hammered a good 30cm (12in) into the ground – we do this from a ladder using a rubber mallet.
- Shorter hazel struts are added to strengthen the frame at each corner.
- Jute netting is then attached, stretched taught over the hazel frame and tied on securely.

April

Opening the gate to the cutting garden in April is like walking into a sweet shop. You can hardly see the ground for the drifts and rows of colour. And there's *so* much to pick, making April one of the great moments in the cut-flower-garden year.

I love January and February for their scarcity of flowers. In those weeks before the growing season starts, it's possible to treasure the smallest, most delicate things: just a few stems can bring life to a room. I also love March for its bounty of blues, yellows, whites and crimsons, from narcissi, hellebores and early amelanchier and pear blossom. But it's in April that the carnival flower floats truly arrive at Perch Hill.

Just as important as the vast array of bulbs in flower, are the trees and shrubs that form their backdrop. It's powder puff central with many of our fruit trees starting to blossom, their pastel flowers accompanied by emerging green leaves, zingy as they unfurl. We have plenty of euphorbias in the perennial picking beds echoing spring's leaf colour. If you love vibrancy and colour saturation, acid-green is the perfect accompaniment to tulips in dark and rich shades, as well as the boiled-sweet hues. There are plenty of both palettes right now.

Towards the end of the month, one of my long-standing favourite shrubs for picking starts to bloom. The stems of *Viburnum opulus* 'Roseum' (known as guelder rose or snowball tree), these last ten days in a vase if the ends are seared. Try to find room for it in your flower patch if you can, as it plays such an important role in many a vase in spring. It's ripe for harvesting this month and next, when its flowers gradually turn ivory.

Above We often plant swathes of tulips from our pot plantings into the cutting garden for picking. This was a really successful chance mix of a new tulip 'Flevo Passion', along with 'Slawa', 'Sarah Raven' and 'Amazing Parrot'. And it's been coming back now for several years.
Opposite My favourite jade glass vase full of tulips 'La Belle Epoque', 'Recreado' and 'Copex Cairo', filled out with the purple and scented *Matthiola incana*.
Next page March into April tulips that reappear reliably each year, including 'Spryng Tide' (foreground), 'World's Favourite' and the elegant pointy-petalled, red 'Istanbul'. You'll see autumn-planted *Cerinthe major* 'Purpurascens' and several polyanthus, including *Primula* 'Stella Champagne' forming a peach carpet in the far bed and 'Stella Neon Violet' in front of the shed.

All this makes for a great backdrop to rows and rows of tulips: tall ones with stems up to my knee and miniature ones that hardly fill the palm of my hand. It's tulips, tulips, tulips, together with late-flowering narcissi, that fill our buckets now.

But let's not forget muscari and their fragrant cousins, the garden hybrid hyacinths, which are usually still around for the picking, particularly if planted in dappled shade. These are perfect for putting in vases beside the bed.

Having seen it grow in swathes in the wild, *Anemone coronaria* is a spring flower I also love. Adam and I spent a winter in the Amari Valley in Crete and these anemones were flowering away all through the olive groves in February. I picked bunches every week. They were such a highlight, along with the wild, delicate and hugely fragrant species daffodil, *Narcissus tazetta*, which was being sold by the bucketful in the markets of Rethymno and Chania.

Anemone coronaria usually bloom in April in the UK. We grow them in brilliant pink ('Sylphide'), white ('Die Braut', which translates as 'The Bride'), burgundy ('Bordeaux') and with single or double petals (from the Saint Brigid Group), as well as the classic Mediterranean forms in blue and scarlet.

Opposite top A mass of buckets filled with tulips at Perch Hill. Opposite bottom left *Anemone coronaria* 'Mistral Plus Vinato' and 'Mistral Plus Blu' growing up through an autumn-planted carpet of *Cerinthe major* 'Purpurascens'. Opposite bottom right A clutch of *Anemone coronaria* in a green, pumpkin-shaped vase. The anemones here are 'Israeli Pink', 'Bordeaux' and 'Israeli Red'. Below A blue palette for April, including viola, muscari, pulmonaria, rosemary, *Anemone coronaria* 'Mister Fokker' and *A. nemorosa* 'Blue Shades'.

And it's not just the depth of the colour or the richness of the petal's texture that makes garden anemones so good: they last an impressive ten days in a vase.

We either plant them to grow up through wallflowers (*Erysimum*) or with the hardy annual *Cerinthe major* 'Purpurascens'. If cerinthe is sown in autumn or February, it's guaranteed to flower at the same time as the garden anemones. And we have *Anemone coronaria* planted in the greenhouse as well, to force them into flower six weeks earlier. They produce longer stems under cover, but out in the garden they look more like their wild selves. They are reliably perennial at Perch Hill, in a sheltered spot.

We now have a permanent lasagne of bulbs in the greenhouse earth beds (where tomatoes grow through the summer). *Ranunculus* Butterfly forms the top layer (flowering April), followed by garden anemone corms (they flower first, with early narcissus such as 'Erlicheer' and 'Cragford'). The next and deepest layer is tulips that are reliable for early forcing (such as 'Orca'). It gives us an early burst of glamour from a space that is not fully utilised through winter.

Opposite A vase featuring the final April harvest from the greenhouse bulb lasagne, picked just before the tomatoes go in. I've arranged a mix of highly fragrant stocks (*Matthiola*) with *Ranunculus* Butterfly 'Ariadne'.

The claw-like corms of ranunculus seem to survive better and flower more prolifically under cover, so if you have a greenhouse, I'd recommend using it for a layer cake of bulbs similar to the one I just described. This whole bulb lasagne has become perennial here, reappearing every spring, so we just forget about them for the rest of the year. They are planted right at the edge of the beds, so we know where they are (and know not to dig them up), and there is still room for summer crops such as tomatoes.

The single ranunculus are, to me, more beautiful than the fully double, button forms, with *Ranunculus* Butterfly 'Lycia' and Butterfly 'Ariadne' my two current favourites. They look ethereal, but in fact are robust, with a vase life of two weeks. They're one of the best April cut flowers.

Ranunculus has a tendency to suffer from mildew, particularly when grown in the greenhouse. To counter this, we give them a fortnightly dose of a homemade remedy – and it works. To make the mixture, add one teaspoon each of bicarbonate of soda, vegetable oil and liquid soap (such as a non-toxic washing-up liquid) to one litre of water. Pour this into a water atomiser/spray bottle and shake before spraying on to the plant. It's a great preventative organic treatment for any plant fungal disease, which does no harm to the key mycorrhizae or invertebrate life in the soil.

There are other beauties out in the garden now. Stellar, of course, is the snake's head fritillary (*Fritillaria meleagris*), and the pasqueflower (*Pulsatilla vulgaris*). These are like treasures and should be treated as such, though in fact they are easy and reliable to grow. The pasqueflower likes an open site, on well-drained soil, so we have them right by the edge of a path and they do fine. On our heavy clay, the fritillaries spread better in a border than in grass. They have come up in the same place, right on the edge of a bed in the Annual Cutting Garden, for some 15 years now. We often place a frame for sweet peas just near this spot, so they are in dappled shade for much of summer, and they thrive. Plant the bulbs in September or October and you'll be enjoying them for decades.

The statuesque crown imperial (*Fritillaria imperialis*) and Persian lilies (*Fritillaria persica*) are very impressive, but imperials have a strange, slightly foxy smell. Better for bringing into the house are the newly bred hybrids, such as *F. persica* 'Green Dreams'. We have found these reliably perennial. The species, *Fritillaria raddeana*, has been used in some of these hybrids to make them more successful in our

Opposite top right *Fritillaria persica* 'Green Dreams'.
Opposite bottom right I love a vase of spring-flowering biennials, here honesty (*Lunaria*), forget-me-nots and the wallflowers, *Erysimum cheiri* 'Purple' and 'Sunset Apricot'.
Opposite bottom left *Pulsatilla vulgaris*.
Opposite top left A hand-tied bunch of the early-flowering tulips 'Apricot Pride' and the slightly deeper toned 'Salmon Van Eijk' with *Narcissus* 'Cosmopolitan' – all soft and warm Cashmere Jersey shades with *Fritillaria meleagris* providing the contrast.
Next page Our Terracotta Tulip Collection (tulips 'Request', 'National Velvet', 'Slawa' and 'Brownie') in a spring border with swathes of highly scented wallflowers, *Erysimum cheiri* 'Sunset Orange' in the foreground.

climate, as they don't require intense summer heat to induce flowering. *Fritillaria raddeana* flowers from late February with us in a mild year. But we find the Persian lilies need that intense sun. After a heat wave in June and July, they reappear and flower well the following spring, but if we have a summer of cold and rain, they often come up blind. 'Green Dreams', in contrast, has flowered every year since we planted it, more than five years ago. They are highly glamorous stalwarts, but as with lilies, they seem so precious, I only want to pick one or two.

April is a key time for early-flowering biennials, an invaluable and unmissable group of plants for any cutting garden. They're cheap and easy to grow from seed, and many are cut-and-come-again, so you can pick them by the bucket-load and they'll be back in flower in no time. Light and airy, they're also perfect fillers, providing background and structure for the chunkier bulbs both in the garden and the vase.

We harvest tons of wallflowers (*Erysimum*) in different colours, with their sweet, old-fashioned perfume. And we always aim to have plenty of black-leaved cow parsley, *Anthriscus sylvestris* 'Ravenswing'. The dark-leaved form gives greater presence than the wild cow parsley. It self-sows a little in one of our cutting garden beds, so it's always there for picking in April and May, without needing attention.

Another biennial, honesty (*Lunaria annua*), is also hugely useful now and we return to its rows in June and July to harvest its elegant green seed pods. And we're picking it again in autumn, as it provides one of the best and most reliable bases for our large, dried flower arrangements. We make sure we sow plenty of both the purple species and its black-leaved cultivar 'Chedglow', as well as white-flowered honesty (*L. a.* var. *albiflora*) each June, so that there's never a shortage. We also grow a few forget-me-nots (*Myosotis sylvatica*), but they are massive self-sowers, so take care to whip them out before they run to seed.

To me, April means abundance and optimism. Walk out into the cutting garden this month and it's hard not to feel uplifted.

Opposite Our Opal Fruits Tulip Collection with great double varieties, including 'Icoon' (the orange), 'Jinan' (purple-crimson) and 'Green Power' (single green).
Below left The peony-flowered *Tulipa* 'La Belle Epoque'.
Below right Tulips looking more like peonies, including a long-standing favourite, 'Exotic Emperor' with 'Foxtrot', 'Dreamer' and 'Peptalk'.

Tulip Categories

There are 15 official tulip groups, with categorisation based on shape, flowering time and breeding history. For the cutting garden, many of these groups are not particularly relevant. So instead of summarising the groups, I've listed the characteristics that are important and make different tulips stand out as cut flowers. Out of the one hundred or so cultivars we grow, I have mentioned a few favourites.

Long vase life
Tulips in the Double Early and Double Late groups, often called peony-flowered, tend to have the longest vase lives. Their nectaries have been bred into the extra petals, so the flowers are sterile. With less possibility of being fertilised, the blooms just keep going, trying to bring in a pollinator. I think the extra petals also make the flowers more robust. These can last over a week in the vase. The milky coffee 'La Belle Epoque' is an outstanding member of this clan, and I love the long-flowering crimsons, 'Jinan' and 'Palmyra'.

Scented

It tends to be the yellow, orange and coppery tulips that have scent. One of the strongest scents can be found in the Lily-flowered *Tulipa* 'Ballerina', which has a perfume like a freesia. There is also the hybrid, 'Campbell', which has retained the 'Ballerina' scent, although it's not quite as strong and sweet. 'Campbell', as a double, has the added attribute of a vase life of ten days. I also love the early-flowering Triumph tulip, 'Brown Sugar' – it has a freesia-like scent with a pinch of garam masala – and the self-sowing, wild *Tulipa sylvestris*.

Multi-headed

Having a few heads at the top of a stem, will, of course make a tulip good value in a vase. *Tulipa* 'Blue Heaven' is my favourite for its unique, coppery, verdigris colour. I also like the white-and-red-striped 'Flaming Club'.

Opposite left The best scented tulips: 'Orca' and 'Brown Sugar' in the front vase; 'Ballerina' and 'Request' in the acid-green vase in the middle; and, the fragrant *Tulipa sylvestris* behind.
Opposite right A double version of 'Ballerina' with almost the scent to match, *Tulipa* 'Campbell' with *Amelanchier lamarckii*.
Above Like the vintage chintz curtains behind, I love the quiet flamboyance of these multi-headed tulips, 'Flaming Club' and 'Candy Club', here arranged with brand-new 'Sarana', which we discovered in the Netherlands in 2025.
Left The multi-headed *Tulipa* 'Blue Heaven' changes colour as you look. It's sometimes blue, sometimes brown, it can seem silver or almost pink. Incredible!

Opposite top A pretty vase of delicate species tulips and fritillaries, including *Tulipa* 'Little Beauty', *T. clusiana* 'Peppermintstick' and *Fritillaria meleagris*.

Opposite bottom After coming across a field of *Tulipa clusiana* forms in the Netherlands in 2024, I came back determined to grow and arrange them more. Here I've showcased *Tulipa clusiana* 'Lady Jane', 'Cynthia' and *T. c.* var. *chrysantha* 'Tubergen's Gem'. Grown in a pot, grass or border, they are super perennial.

Below A flamboyant, tapestry-like mix of tulips 'Black Parrot', 'Victoria's Secret', 'Ballerina', 'Sarah Raven', 'Flaming Parrot', 'Bastia' and wallflowers (*Erysimum*).

Delicate

Species tulips and their hybrids are gaining popularity because they're so perennial, they're happy in grass and invaluable for naturalising. They also seem to have good blight resistance. The fungal disease blight has become more of an issue as our springs become wetter. Tulips in the Species group tend to be smaller, about a third of the size of the garden hybrids, which gives them a different look and feel. I love them. *Tulipa* 'Little Beauty' is a favourite here, as are any of the *T. clusiana* clan, which have delicate and beautiful verdigris-toned leaves.

Flamboyant

As well as the delicate forms, I love to have plenty of flamboyant and OTT tulips for picking. These work perfectly as single stems, each in a different vase running down a table or lined up on a mantelpiece. And, on mass or in a large arrangement, they can look like a Dutch still life masterpiece. Tulips in the Fringed group work in this category, their petal edges look as though they have been cut with crimping shears. And I'm crazy about *Tulipa acuminata*, with it pointy petals like dancing flames.

Below The very early tulip 'Light and Dreamy' arranged with the purple-washed foliage of leek 'St Victor', with which we plant it.
Opposite These are some of the last spring-flowering bulbs to pick in our garden – the double lilac and green *Tulipa* 'Katinka', classic green, pink and white *T.* 'Green Wave' and the wonderfully elegant *Fritillaria acmopetala*.

Flowering season

When I started gardening at Perch Hill, I ordered tulips just because I liked the look of them in a catalogue, paying no attention to their flowering time. We had a massive colour bonanza for about three weeks in late April, but it was a very short burst. It's worth choosing your tulips carefully to extend the flowering season, selecting some early and some late.

Those in the Kaufmanniana group are early, reliably flowering in the middle of March. I particularly love 'Ice Stick' (pictured on p128). Fosteriana group tulips flower next, such as 'Exotic Emperor' and 'Chato', as well as the Double Early 'Orca'. Then any in the Impression series and Emperor series, plus 'Light and Dreamy', which is the loveliest soft pink.

If you want late tulips for May, go for the ones in the Parrot group. I love *Tulipa* 'Green Wave' – a huge, green and pink, wavy-edged Parrot with extreme glamour. But sadly supplies are drying up; it's a hybrid that has become vulnerable to disease. The green tulips, such as the Viridiflora 'Green King' or the Double Late 'Boa Vista', are also late to arrive. 'Boa Vista' looks more like an artichoke than a tulip, and is one of the last to flower with us, hanging on into June.

Opposite White tulips 'Purissima' and 'Green Star' with brunnera to light up the shade at the back of the barn. This mix returns reliably each year.

Below left We call this our Trooper Tulip Collection because each of these have been reappearing in the garden for more than ten years. 'Mistress Mystic', 'Spring Green', 'Green Wave' and 'Groenland'.

Below right The perennial tulips 'Spring Green' and 'Green Wave' in our artichoke bed – they last almost two weeks in a vase.

Perenniality

Tulips in the Viridiflora group are famously perennial and they also have a long vase life. I think it must be the green pigment within their petals that makes their structure more robust. Even in a wet spring, these pick well. *Tulipa saxatilis*, *T. turkestanica* and *T. clusiana* varieties are also exceptionally perennial. We have also had great comebacks from 'Mistress Mystic', which is in flower for as long as any tulip we grow. Where you plant them impacts perenniality (see p430).

Good for shade

White and pale colours work best in shade, so if your garden is shady, but you still want to grow tulips for picking, these are the ones for you. Soft primrose yellows work well in dappled shade. I love early *Tulipa* 'Purissima' planted with the late 'Spring Green' – we have this duo planted in a water trough on the north side of our barn. They radiate from the shadows and last well from year to year. 'White Triumphator' looks elegant and statuesque against a dark hedge.

Picking and Arranging

April is the month when it becomes easy to fill your house with homegrown flowers.

At the beginning of the month, narcissi provide the bulk of the harvest, but by the second or third week, there's a feast of tulips. Tulips are – equal with dahlias – my favourite cut flowers. They both offer such a goliath range, from very simple singles to huge and heavy-headed flowers the size of plates. With tulips, it's their presence in a vase that wins me over, one spectacular stem or a clutch on their own with no padding from other spring foliage and flowers. They are simply the queens of spring. Some years when it's wet and, with light levels still low, they can suffer from blight. This makes us think perhaps we should move away from growing so many. Then, the following year, its sunny and bright and they amaze from one day to the next, winning the glamour prize every single day. They are unbeatable garden plants and stellar cut flowers. We just *have* to grow them.

Opposite Here I'm holding a bucket of tulips starring 'Dom Pedro' and 'Copex Cairo', with tulips 'Merlot', 'Louvre Orange' and 'Labrador' in the pot beside me.

Right I love picking tulips at varying stages of bloom, some almost blown with others in tight bud. This gives you more interesting and varied shapes as well as longevity in the vase. In this bucket, I've picked tulips 'Mystic van Eijk', 'Apricot Beauty', 'Slawa', 'Beachberry', 'Apricot Foxx' and 'Nightshade'.

Picking and Conditioning Tulips

There are a few things worth doing to make sure your tulip bulbs thrive from one year to the next and also that the flower stems last as long as possible once cut. All my general advice (see Vase Life from p78) still applies.

Support next year's growth When you cut the stem, don't cut too low to the ground – always leave a short section of foliage and stem behind. This enables photosynthesis and food storage, which the bulb needs in order to build up enough energy to flower again next spring.

Vase life and shape Once picked, strip almost all the leaves off the stem. This extends the flower's vase life. With all bulbs, including hyacinths and narcissi, place them in a narrow bucket full of water, to help keep stems straight.

Correct floppy stems If you pick (or buy) tulips and they are left out of water for a few hours, they may be floppy by the time you come to arrange them – not elegant, swan-neck floppy, but bent over double. If you then put them in water as they are, they set rigid in that flopped position, with the stems dangling over the edge of the vase.

To avoid this, bunch 10 or 20 stems together. Take a long length of string and wind it around the stems. The stems and flowers support each other while being held ramrod straight. Put the bunch into a bucket of water, and the stems will set straight.

An alternative method, which has the same effect, is to secure chicken wire (or a wooden grid) over the top of a tall, narrow bucket. Fill the bucket with water right to the brim. Place the tulips into the gridded slots, allowing the chicken wire or wooden grid to hold the heads out of water. Leave them there for a few hours. Their flowers will be held perfectly flat on top of the frame and the stems will be in deep water.

Disrupt the growth plate Tulips continue to grow after you've cut them; they have a 'growth plate' just below the flower. If this bothers you, pierce the tulip stem with a thick darning needle or a pin – poke it right through the stem about 2.5cm (1in) below the flower, and then remove it. This disrupts the growth plate and prevents new growth. I like the way tulips twist in a slightly chaotic fashion as they continue to grow, but with Parrot and Darwin Hybrid tulips, the new growth can't hold the weight of the flower head and they bend right over. For these whopper varieties, pierce the stems before arranging.

Opposite Conditioning tulips by tying stems and then swaddling them in brown paper to support them while in water.

Above Piercing the stem of a parrot tulip with a needle. This disrupts the growth plate and stops the stem bending over.

Sunrise Vase

I love tulips arranged en masse, on their own. It's an opportunity to celebrate each flower and the mix of colours you've chosen. This sunrise vase was inspired by a spring morning, when I was up at dawn with photographer Jonathan Buckley to capture the garden at its tulip peak. It features tulips 'Sanne', 'Apricot Delight', 'Apricot Beauty', 'Silver Cloud' and 'Mystic van Eijk'. But the structural advice I give here is relevant for any arrangement of tulips.

If you have a round, full-bellied vase like the one I've used in the picture, some engineering is needed to hold the stems in place and avoid them flopping. You could do this with tulip stems alone: you will need enough stems crossing in the vase to enable you to build up the structure, into which you can insert more stems. In my experience, this means you'll need about 30 per cent more tulips in the vase than you might otherwise have used. And, with that, you lose the all-important air between the flowers.

We stopped using florist's foam at Perch Hill more than ten years ago (its microplastics easily get into the water table), and these days we very rarely use chicken wire. I do use the odd bit of coated stub wire for adding fruit to wreaths at Christmas, but I am increasingly using twine threaded through a darning needle as an alternative. My aim is to use biodegradable materials.

To that end, I now use a system that works brilliantly. I bend a pliable silver birch (*Betula pendula*) branch – or willow (*Salix*) or cornus – into the belly of the vase before I start adding flowers. Just find a twiggy branch with no leaves on and push it in. The criss-crossing twigs support the stems as they are poked in, and it acts just like chicken wire, except it can be chucked on the compost heap with the flowers when they go over.

Opposite **Tulips 'Sanne', 'Apricot Delight', 'Apricot Beauty', 'Silver Cloud' and 'Mystic van Eijk' in a clear, pumpkin-shaped vase.**

Spring Party Flowers

If you want to go to town, you can cover a whole table surface with garden flowers.

I tend to arrange a larger vase for the centre, surrounded by lots of smaller arrangements using the same or similar flowers. It makes me think of the sun and the planets of the solar system.

For the central vase, I have used my favourite vase shape – it's shaped like a goblet, and we call it our Nero vase. There's hardly a day at Perch Hill when it's not in use. If you can find something similar, I recommend it. It has a generous, flared neck, which allows stems to fall naturally, rather than being held straight (as they would be in a cylindrical vase). A vase with a belly like this holds the stems well, wedged at the top, with a stable base on which to build. And I love the dimple in the base of this vase. It acts like a pin holder, the all-important initial engineering for your arrangement. See p314 in August for more ideas on how to use the Nero vase.

I have used my classic recipe (see p47) of Bride and Bridesmaids in the same tone (soft greens and almost matching yellows) with a Gatecrasher in a contrasting crimson.

It feels quite indulgent picking statuesque fritillaries, so I've restricted myself to three stems, but they do last nearly two weeks in a vase, almost as long as they do outside. When cutting any of these large fritillaries (related to the lily family, where the same rule applies), make sure you leave at least one third of the total stem height on the bulb, so that photosynthesis can continue and the bulb can create enough energy to flower the following year.

For the narcissi, pick buds and flowers of each. All four have a better-than-average vase life for daffs, but picking buds will help extend the shelf life of this arrangement.

Structure, 3 stems each
Silver birch (*Betula pendula*)
Willow 'Nancy Saunders' (*Salix purpurea*)

Foliage, 5–7 leaves each
Globe artichoke (*Cynara cardunculus*)
Mizuna 'Red Knight' (*Brassica rapa* subsp. *nipposinica* var. *laciniata*)

Bride, 3 stems
Fritillaria raddeana

Bridesmaids, 10–12 stems each
Narcissus 'Avalanche'
Narcissus 'Jack Snipe'
Narcissus 'Prinses Amalia'
For the mini vases, pick Narcissus 'Rip van Winkle'

Gatecrashers, 10–12 stems each
Wallflower 'Vulcan' (*Erysimum cheiri*)
Pittosporum tenuifolium Bannow Bay 'Breebay'
For the mini vases, pick *Viola × wittrockiana* 'Matrix Sangria'

Step 1

At this time of year, the stems of silver birch are pliable. To form the structure, take two or three branches, bending them as you push them below the water line in the vase. You're trying to create a sort of nest within the belly of the vase. Don't worry if it looks messy at this stage. It will be totally hidden.

Then add some vertical height. I've used the willow 'Nancy Saunders', which at this time of year has silver velvet flower buds and fine stems with red bark.

Step 2

I've used a few leaves of the cut-and-come-again Japanese leaf mizuna, 'Red Knight', which gives a splash of rich crimson. To condition, sear the stem ends and then float the leaf flat in a tray of water for a couple of hours.

Step 3

Globe artichokes have some of the biggest and showiest leaves in spring. Harvest the new growth for this arrangement. The older leaves are generally a bit battered by winter storms. Both artichokes and cardoons are very tolerant of having their leaves removed, so you can continue to take them throughout the year without compromising the vigour of the plant.

Sear their stem ends in boiling water for 10 seconds, plunging 10 per cent of the total stem length into the water. Cool them immediately in cold water. The seared section will discolour a bit, but this is nothing to worry about. Thread five to seven leaves evenly through your birch, willow and mizuna structure to create a great shape and silhouette.

Step 4

Add the green and yellow flowers. First the Bride (the fritillary stems) then the Bridesmaids (a mix of similar-coloured narcissi). Try to avoid creating a symmetrical dome; instead, work to create a high point on one side, to emphasise the fritillary.

Step 5

Next, add the Gatecrashers, for colour contrast. You have to work with what you've got: the stems of the wallflowers and pittosporum are not quite as tall as I'd like, so I've just wedged them into the neck of the vase. If this happens to you, it's important to top up the vase with water at least every day, but ideally morning and night, to make sure every stem remains in water. Some florists use vials on cones or sticks to add height to short stems. This works well too, but the vials will need topping up with water each day.

Step 6

Once the main vase is finished, I arrange the smaller flowers in mini vases to surround it. For this, I have used mini milk-bottle vases. These complement and add contrast to the central arrangement. The flowers should mirror and echo the main arrangement, and the whole group comes together for maximum impact.

Spring Harvest Table

I love to decorate our breakfast table with spring flowers for Easter, but you can create a flower-laden table like this for any spring party.

When picking, concentrate on perfume so that your whole room is full of scent for a few days. *Narcissus* 'Geranium', 'Avalanche' and 'Actaea' are all strongly scented, plus hyacinths, *Tulipa sylvestris* and, if squeezed (you need to bruise the leaves to properly release the scent), rosemary.

With people chatting over the table as they eat, it's good to keep the flowers low, so I don't use a tall central vase. Instead, I go for equal-sized bottles and small vases.

Think of the arrangement in layers. The highest layer, and the silhouette, is created with *Tulipa* 'Ice Stick' and the fragrant *Narcissus* 'Geranium'.

In the next layer down, add stems of rosemary, hellebore and hyacinth for perfume. Add mini jugs filled with *Narcissus* 'Actaea', their stems cut short to make them showy.

Quail eggs are beautiful and I love a rich brown Maran egg, so I've hard boiled a few of both and added them to bowls that sit down the length of table – this is the lowest layer.

That's it: super quick and easy, with no rules. Simply fill the table with cheerful, perfumed seasonal flowers and produce – it's the spring equivalent of a Harvest Festival table, and you can hardly go wrong.

PRACTICAL

April

Opposite The Annual Cutting Garden as narcissi hand over to tulips.

Below Pots of tender plants in the polytunnel.

By this time of year, you can direct sow hardy annual seed into your flower beds, although on our heavy clay, we get very patchy germination if we direct sow. You also run the risk of birds eating your seed or the seed rotting in wet weather. So for us, April is the month for planting out all the hardy annuals we've sown and grown, or the seedlings we get in the post.

Half-hardies sown last month may well need pricking out or potting on. Don't let things get pot bound. And in April we continue to make frames (see p150). The sweet pea frames were made in March, but lots of other plants need climbing and support frames before they can be planted out, such as cobaea.

Most of the herbaceous perennials we grow for picking (phlox, euphorbia, peonies) will need support (often we can reuse supports put in place the year before). We tend to do most of our annual staking in one go when the half-hardies go out in May to join the hardies, but you can get going now (see p265).

Greenhouse and Polytunnel Tasks

All our inside space – the greenhouse and polytunnel – is jam-packed in the month of April. We're bursting at the seams. Here is a list of jobs that we usually work through.

- Most of the half-hardy annuals sown in March (such as cosmos and amaranth) are ready for pricking out (see p148).
- A few half-hardy annuals such as zinnias benefit from April sowing. Sow these into Jiffy 7s now.
- Usually we plant all the dahlia tubers in March, but if we have any left over, they urgently need to be planted now.
- For the dahlias already growing well, it's possible they will be big enough to take some cuttings from towards the end of the month.
- Take chrysanthemum cuttings (see p193).
- Tender perennials for picking, such as scented-leaf pelargoniums, are putting on new foliage and may need potting on. If you've taken any cuttings in March, these will need to be potted on to individual pots.
- Hardy annuals are ready to go out. Wait for a mild spell and plant them in the garden (see p194).

PRACTICAL

Below top Taking basal cuttings from a dahlia.

Below bottom Putting the cuttings around the edge of a black plastic pot, which speeds up the rooting process.

The black plastic warms up readily and, as the new roots are drawn towards the warmth, they hit the pot edge, break, branch and form lateral roots. You get a virtuous circle of root development.

Taking Dahlia Cuttings

Flower farmers use cuttings to extend their dahlia season. This is because the cuttings you take will flower in the same year as the mother plants, just a little later – and they will continue a little longer, too.

At Perch Hill, we lift and divide the largest clumps in late spring as another means of propagation, but only every three to four years. Divide them into sections, each with one good stalk emerging or growing 'eye', before planting the clump elsewhere.

- To take a cutting, slice off short, stout shoots with a sharp knife, aiming to take a little off the tuber with the cutting.
- Remove any bottom leaves that may be below the compost level.
- Push the cuttings into a gritty mix of compost, spaced 2–3cm (1in) apart around the edge of a pot.
- Pinch out the tips – the growth hormone is then diverted from pushing the plant upwards and instead channels into strong root growth.
- They will root fast with a bit of basal heat, so put them in a propagator or on a heated mat, if you have one.
- These will need potting on into their own individual pots in 3–4 weeks, but will be established enough to plant out in the garden in about 6 weeks. They should grow so rapidly they'll be almost indistinguishable from the mother plant by the end of their first season.

Below left **Taking basal cuttings from a chrysanthemum.**

Below top right **Pinching out the tip aids rooting rather than shooting.**

Below bottom right **As with dahlias, we insert the cuttings around the edge of a pot.**

Taking Chrysanthemum Cuttings

In general, you should follow the same guidelines as for dahlias, but there are a few tips to bear in mind.

- Take your cutting, ideally 7cm (3in) tall, from the base of the plant, trying to get a little of the mother plant's root if you can.
- As with dahlias, insert these around the edge of a pot and, once rooted, pot them on. We pot on three cuttings of the same variety to a large (around 7-litre) pot.
- As with almost all plants you grow for picking, you want stocky, stout plants, not spindly ones. This gives you the best production later in the year. To achieve that, a couple of weeks after potting, pinch them out. Simply remove the top growth, down to 3 or 4 leaves (about 22cm/9in tall).
- If you have planted three cuttings to a large pot, you can do as we do: dig a hole in the flower bed and sink the whole pot into the ground. It stays there until autumn, and as the frosty weather threatens, we lift the pot out and bring them into the greenhouse to extend the flower-picking season.

PRACTICAL

Below Planting out a gutter of *Cerinthe major* 'Purpurascens', sliding seedlings out to their final position.

Planting Out Hardy Annuals

By the middle of April, it is usually the right temperature to begin planting out hardy annuals. At this time of year, the soil is beginning to warm up, hours of daylight are rising and you will notice that weed seeds have started to germinate. This is a sure sign that it is safe to plant out your hardy annuals. A tip: when planting out at the end of the year, plant a little clutch of seedlings at each end of the row. If any down the line fail, these can then be used as transplants.

From a gutter

A few of our key hardy annuals – including cerinthe and *Salvia viridis* blue-flowered – were sown in gutter pipes. The joy of growing plants in a gutter pipe is that they grow on with minimal root disturbance. This helps them develop a strong and healthy root system quickly. And it is simple and time-saving, just two stages – sow and plant – with no pricking out or potting on.

- Once the seedlings are a good 3–4cm (1in) tall and wide, we plant them out. First, water the plants in the gutter. Then make sure the base of the hole they're going into is well-watered too.
- Put your hand to the side of the first plant and push it and its root out of the mouth of the gutter straight into a pre-dug hole in the soil.
- Move the gutter along about 45cm (18in) and push the next seedling out, and so on.

Below Making sure the base of all the roots go in damp to ensure rapid settling in.

A full-size plant grows to this width, so spacing them 45cm (18in) apart gives the plants enough room to develop. People often overcrowd their plants, but if you want to give them the best chance in life, you need to give them adequate space.

- Do note, with cerinthe, a few seedlings in the gutter will be twins – that is, the seed will have split and two plants will have germinated. Dig these out with some soil and gently but firmly pull them apart. It should be easy to do as they will have separate root systems.

From a pot or tray

Our ammi plants, calendula and sunflowers were all sown in pots or seed trays and are ready to be planted out.

- Water the plants before planting out. It's better for plants to get water from the bottom up rather than the top down. By pre-soaking the plants, you're giving them the best start in their new home. I do this by submerging a plant tray full of pots or the whole seed tray in a bucket or barrow that's full of water. I leave it there for around 5 minutes before planting out.
- For a good, straight line (this looks better in a cutting patch), place a garden line to guide you. This can be as simple as a cane or length of twine placed on the ground.
- With a trowel, dig a hole, aiming at twice the depth and width of the root ball.
- You don't need to add any compost or manure to the base of the hole. In our experience, most annuals flower better in pretty poor soil. We noticed this acutely when the cerinthe was flowering better in the gravel paths than in the well-fed beds – so we stopped the double digging and have since moved to a no-dig policy with positive results.
- Water the hole so that the base roots go straight into damp soil.
- Knock the seedling out of its pot with a firm strike to the pot base, tease out the roots a little if they are knotted.
- Plant, cover and then water again to fill any air pockets left within the soil after planting.
- If your plants look like they are already about to flower, then pinch them out or cut them back. This will make them put lots of effort into root formation, which makes for a better, stronger plant in the long run.

PRACTICAL

Below top right Pinching out the tip of a sunflower at the three-leaf stage enhances branching rather than giant vertical growth.

Below bottom right The same plant five weeks later. You can see the scar that formed at the pinch.

Below bottom left This is the same plant, and many flower buds have now formed. With pinching, you won't win the 'giant sunflower competition', but you will multiply your harvest from every plant.

Pinching Out

As you plant, pinch out your seedlings to get them to branch. This even applies to sunflowers: pinch out the tip once three sets of true leaves have formed. Sometimes it can seem a bit cruel with sunflowers as they can look a bit thin and spindly when they first develop, but you must do it. Pinching out your plants will help them grow into strong and sturdy individuals, giving you many more flowers than you would get otherwise.

Planting Out Cut Flower Combinations

As you plant out your hardy annuals, you can get creative with combinations to enhance your garden and give yourself a long-flowering season from which to pick.

Cerinthe major 'Purpurascens', *Salvia viridis* blue-flowered and borage

These three make a great mixed row. The salvia will flower from the end of May until September. The cerinthe and borage, on the other hand, will reach the end of their life before this, but will self-seed. So by the time September rolls round, you may be onto another generation of plants. All are great for pollinators, especially butterflies and bees.

Ammi majus and *Scabiosa atropurpurea* 'Black Cat'

A classic duo of hardy annuals perfect for planting now. If we're organised, we'll have the ammi already in from an autumn planting and then we dot the scabious through in April. Ammi will survive outside in all but the worst winters, but we find scabious usually succumbs. These two are beautiful growing and arranged together.

PRACTICAL

Malope trifida and *Scabiosa atropurpurea* 'Black Cat'

This is one of our top duos for planting in a mixed row, and it is at its best in June and July. The malope goes over around the end of July, so we take it out and leave the scabious where it is. At this point, you can slot in some snapdragons (sown in May) to fill in any gaps. And both can go on flowering together until almost Christmas, if the autumn is a mild one.

Euphorbia, *Calendula* and *Cerinthe major* 'Purpurascens'

This trio is an absolute classic at Perch Hill. The three can be planted in early to mid-autumn, for flowering from now, or planted in April for flowering in summer (the euphorbia will go on through much of autumn too). They work beautifully planted side by side, they are highly productive and, with stem ends seared, make very long-lasting cut flowers (pictured on p44).

Below left A barrow of mulch sits at the ready for any planting out.

Below top right *Antirrhinum majus* 'White Giant' being planted out, watered and mulched.

Below bottom right Evenly applying mulch at least 5cm (2in) deep across the new planting.

Mulching

Laying a carpet of grit or organic material over your soil surface in April or May (and in October, too) enhances the general condition of your soil.

In spring, it helps to suppress the weeds and assists with water retention, firstly by decreasing levels of evaporation and also by adding a sponge-like layer to absorb water into the structure of your soil.

You can up your soil's fertility, too. In the autumn, we mulch with any dry, spent compost that we have knocking about, whereas in spring we mulch with a mix of our own organic farmyard manure and homemade compost. If we did this only in autumn, the nutrients would be long gone before they're needed for the growth spurt in May. Organic matter feeds the soil's invertebrates and microorganisms.

At any time of year, it adds nutrition and structure, so it is generally an excellent thing to do.

How to apply mulch

The key thing to remember when applying mulch is that you need to lay down a thick enough layer to make a difference. This means applying at least a 5cm (2in) layer of mulch to your beds. We use a 50:50 mix of organic farmyard manure with our homemade compost. But green waste (which you can usually buy from your local council) is also fine.

We also use grit on our beds to create paths. This acts as a natural weed suppressant and is useful in heavy clay soil as it helps with soil drainage, plus it looks good, adding structure and crispness.

A note on green waste
Green waste can form a crust on your bed, so look out for this. To make sure any water can penetrate, break this crust up with a trowel from time to time.

In recent years, we have also found a residual amount of a broad-spectrum herbicide called Aminopyralid present in some green waste and (even supposedly organic) farmyard manure.

This widely used herbicide is used to kill ragwort in fields and meadows, and is often used in stables and golf courses. And from there, it can get into the compost chain. The problem with Aminopyralid is that it can still be active up to three or four years after use, even when it's been through the digestive system of a horse or been sitting on a compost pile for a year or two. Unfortunately, even if you use farmyard manure that is labelled organic, you may still find it present.

After losing a whole dahlia patch to contaminated green waste, we now attempt to make all of our compost. But if we do need to buy in any green waste in bulk, we test it before using in the garden.

We do this by sowing some broad bean seeds in it. If the quick-to-germinate broad beans look normal, then we know the green waste is safe to use, but if they shrivel or have black markings on their leaves, then we know it's infected and we tell the suppliers.

Tulip Blight

Tulip blight (also known as tulip fire) is a fungal disease that can devastate tulip crops, and with the wet springs we've had in recent years, this has been an increasing problem (damp and low sunlight levels exacerbate the issue). The fungus initially infects the bulbs and then travels upwards and affects the leaves and flowers, causing holes and damaged petals.

As an organic garden, we don't use any sprays to kill off the fungus, but we are currently trialling a new biological fungicide that we hope will help us combat tulip blight.

As with potato or tomato blight, you must remove the infected plants as soon as you see them, to stop the fungus from infecting its neighbours. Sadly, if you have had a bad bout of tulip blight, you will have to plant your tulips somewhere else in the garden the following year and beyond. And you need to leave that patch of ground tulip-free for a few years. This is the only truly organic way to combat it.

To avoid getting blight in the first place, space bulbs well apart (at least twice the diameter of the bulb). Don't cram them in tight as this chokes air circulation and encourages a blight outbreak.

Below top We gather sheep's fleece when out for dog walks and split up skeins of horticultural wool to clad a willow wreath in March and April. That's when many garden birds are nesting and need any help we can give them.

Below bottom Making up a pail of Nemaslug, the biological slug control. It's safe for birds and pets and more effective than slug pellets, chemical or organic.

Controlling Slugs and Helping Birds

Birds are a major part of pest control at Perch Hill, and we make a lot of effort to take care of the birds, ensuring they have food (mainly garden plants), water and habitat, which draws them in and encourages them to stay and, importantly, to breed (see p295 and p343). It's when they're feeding their young in March and April that the adult garden birds are on the hunt for protein-rich slugs, snails and their eggs, as well as caterpillars and aphids to take back to the nest.

We do whatever we can to look after them, including hanging material out for their nests. At this time of year, poke clumps of horticultural wool into a woven willow wreath and hang it near feeders.

Prior to building a healthy population of small birds, we used biological control based on nematodes to keep our mollusc population under control. We would apply the first treatment in mid-April and a second in September (follow the instructions on the pack). We did this for three years, supplementing with an evening patrol with a head torch (when I could face it).

Cow parsley
Sweet rocket
Euphorbia Blossom
Lupins Clematis
Guelder rose
Early alliums
Geums Late tulips
Solomon's seal

May

In early May, we're still picking tulips (particularly those in the Parrot, Viridiflora and Double Late groups), as well as the odd, strongly perfumed *Narcissus poeticus* var. *recurvus* and the rare *N.* 'Felindre'. Then, as with most gardens, we're at risk of a flower lull. It's commonly known as the May colour gap, when the lanes and countryside are full of cow parsley and hawthorn blossom, but most gardens are noticeably bare of flowers.

With careful autumn planting and planning, this lull can be avoided. Key May players are early-flowering alliums, along with a few early season perennials. I'd include the splendid lupin, which flowers by the middle of May, and a clan of hardy annuals and biennials that are increasing in number day by day. You'll need a range of these plants to keep your May cut-flower harvest decent and varied.

Let's start with alliums. The first one I recommend as a cut flower is *Allium hollandicum* 'Purple Sensation', closely followed by the newish hybrid *A.* 'Purple Rain'. Both are excellent for picking from the middle of the month and grow happily here in sun or dappled shade. 'Purple Sensation' can lose its petals and transform into handsome seedheads in the vase, which can be stored for winter arrangements (see more on picking alliums on p219). And next come *Allium schubertii* and *A. cristophii* – both sensational – flowering from late May.

We have a corner in dapple shaded full of 'Purple Sensation', mixed with the invaluable shade-lovers, *Smyrnium perfoliatum*, Solomon's seal (*Polygonatum × hybridum*), honesty (*Lunaria*) and lily of the valley (*Convallaria majalis*). I often turn to the elegant, arching stems of Solomon's seal, along

Opposite My favourite vase (see more on the Nero vase on p182) with the invaluable, arching stems of Solomon's seal (*Polygonatum × hybridum*) and a mix of hellebores, filled out with the flamboyant tulips 'Vovos', 'Victoria's Secret', 'La Belle Epoque' and 'Apricot Foxx', plus the wallflowers, *Erysimum cheiri* 'Sunset Apricot' and 'Purple'.
Below left *Allium* 'Purple Rain' growing up through roses and bronze fennel (*Foeniculum vulgare* 'Purpureum').
Below right Soft and cool shades from *Allium* 'Purple Rain', and tulips 'Double Surprise', 'Green Glow' and 'Crunchy Cummins', with sweet rocket (*Hesperis matronalis*) and artichoke (*Cynara cardunculus*) foliage as the base.

with guelder rose (*Viburnum opulus*), to stylishly transform a vase. Add either to any mid-sized or large hand-tied or vase arrangement and it takes on an immediate beauty.

By the middle of the month, we can see waves of white flowers as we look out of our windows to the south. The Farmhouse Garden is chock-a-block with the biennial, white honesty (*Lunaria annua* var. *albiflora*), with white sweet rocket (*Hesperis matronalis* var. *albiflora*) taking up the baton as the honesty runs to seed. We also have the short-flowering but triumphant crab apple (*Malus hupehensis*), filling the air above the Farmhouse Garden.

Cresting the wave beyond, we have hawthorn (*Crataegus*) trees in full bloom lining the drive, one of the first things we planted when we arrived 30 years ago. And beyond that, there's three, well-established, 20-foot domes of guelder rose (*Viburnum opulus* 'Roseum'). The tennis-ball flowers open soft, eau-de-nil-green, and gradually turn cream as they mature.

There's more white froth to the east of the house by way of another great crab apple, *Malus* × *robusta* 'Red Sentinel', in the hedge line of the Perennial Cutting Garden. Its saucer-sized flowers emerge with pink on the outer petals, but these

Above Hawthorn (*Crataegus monogyna*) blossom and sweet rocket (*Hesperis matronalis*) growing along the hedge at Perch Hill.
Right Just a few stems of hawthorn blossom are enough in this elegant jade vase.

quickly whiten and the flowers become billowing clouds. They only last a couple of weeks, but we pick boughs while we can for large urn arrangements (see p224). Walk alongside this hedge in a moment of sunshine and you hear the low drone of bees feasting. And we – and the wildlife – return to harvest again in September and October when these trees (and the *Malus hupehensis*) are covered in fruit.

It's a joy to pick stems and flowers from climbers, particularly as so many of them are fragrant at this time of year. I always pick wisteria as I adore its heady, exotic fragrance, which takes me back to many childhood holidays spent in a town called Asolo in the Veneto region of northern Italy. There, almost every wall, loggia and balcony is covered in wisteria, which suffuses the whole place with scent in April into May.

In May, we also enjoy the banksia rose (*Rosa banksiae*), its white form more fragrant than the yellow. And in the centre of the Perennial Cutting Garden, we have a couple of arches clad in *Clematis montana* hybrids, *C. m.* var. *wilsonii* and *C.* 'Elizabeth'. They're pale and ethereal and the former in particular fills the air with delicious perfume. They're a fiddle to untangle, but I cut single stems for small vases and arrange

Below left A vase of apple tree blossom makes the ideal bathroom or bedroom arrangement.
Below right It's all about the curves – and the scent – here, with *Clematis* 'Elizabeth'.
Next page Overhead view of the Farmhouse Garden in May with *Euphorbia characias* subsp. *wulfenii* and the blossom of crab apple (*Malus* × *robusta* 'Red Sentinel') and hawthorn (*Crataegus monogyna*).

Below Lupins (here 'Terracotta', 'Beefeater' and 'Masterpiece') are the queens of our May Perennial Cutting garden, once the tulips are over. They are truly spectacular!
Opposite A feather-duster-like vase of lupins (again, 'Terracotta', 'Beefeater' and 'Masterpiece').

them down the length of the kitchen table or threaded through a grid (see p107) as a table centrepiece – they create great shapes. Sear the stem ends of all clematis to give them a longer vase life.

Lupins are stellar perennials for picking in May and often offer a second flush of flowers in August and September. I'm crazy about pretty much every form, both seed-grown and the specially bred West Country hybrids, which have denser and long-lasting spires. They have a strange, peppery fragrance. And their ostrich feather plumes lift our Perennial Cutting Garden to one of its finest moments, just as the main spring bulbs fade. With stem ends seared, they hold their flowers for five to six days. They are best arranged alone, with their own clear, green, finger-like foliage in a large vase.

Just as wonderful – some would say more so – are the irises, particularly the velvet, bearded forms, many of which flower in May. In terms of a cut flower crop, these are super luxurious because most give you a peak picking season of about a week to ten days, and most don't give a second flush. But these are the Rolls-Royce of cut flowers, with texture, colour range and scent to draw you in. I tend to pick almost every one we have

Opposite Bearded irises flower for such a short time, but when they do, I love to pick a mass of them to bring inside. Individual flowers go over fast, but more continue to open on the stem in a vase, just as they do in the garden. In the vase on the left, *Iris germanica* 'Dusky Challenger', 'Black Tie Affair', 'Benton Old Madrid', 'Jane Phillips' and 'Benton Menace'. In the middle vase, *I. × hollandica* 'Midnight Passion', 'Tigereye', 'Lion King' and 'Red Embers'. And the vase on the right features *I. germanica* 'Sultan's Palace', 'War Chief', 'Carnival Time' and 'Devil May Care'.

Below A perennial mix of *Tulipa* 'Ballerina' and *Geum* 'Totally Tangerine' under hawthorn trees. The tulips kick off the show, the geum overlaps. They flower for ten weeks between them in dappled shade.

and then luxuriate in them – enjoying these is like sitting back and admiring a catwalk show.

Then there's *Phuopsis stylosa*, often noted for its cannabis-like scent. This looks okay in the garden, and looks five times better once picked and put in a vase (much like carnations, chrysanthemums and frilly, flamboyant Parrot tulips), and they last well, too. When I first saw *Phuopsis stylosa* as a cut flower, I thought they were miniature alliums – they share the same pompom jollity, but at a quarter of the size. They're a late-May and June boon here, and they bloom again if cut back after flowering.

I also love the flowers of geums now, they are like hovering butterflies and last for over a week in water once the stem ends are seared. And *Alchemilla mollis*, that classic acid-green plant with powder puff foliage, comes into bloom towards the end of May. There's also shade-loving astrantia and aquilegia, both self-seeding, short-lived perennials that scatter themselves about pretty reliably, bringing colour to the May and June garden.

For those fond of pastels, one of the loveliest May perennials is *Veronica gentianoides*. It's supremely pretty and

Below These three sweet peas – *Lathyrus* × *hammettii* 'Erewhon', *L. odoratus* 'Painted Lady' and 'Matucana' – are often the earliest to flower with us. Sown in January, we're picking them by Chelsea (the third week of May).

Opposite Flowers you see growing together along many a Cretan roadside in spring: *Lupinus* 'Blue Javelin', *Briza maxima*, *Orlaya grandiflora* and *Cerinthe major* 'Purpurascens'.

delicate, with the softest blue flowers arranged all the way up its spires. I love a few arching stems in a narrow-necked bottle or piercing through a jug filled with Icelandic poppies in similarly soft-toned, pastel pinks and creams.

We pick all or any of these perennials if we want to fill our tables with flowers for a May event and they're all invaluable for decorating our stand at the RHS Chelsea Flower Show.

Last but not least are two groups of plants that are cut-and-come-again. Autumn-sown hardy annuals are starting to come on stream, and biennials are also having their moment. Among these you'll find a harvest for the next few months.

Autumn-sown cerinthe is a prolific flower producer for these leaner weeks. With its stem ends seared, it is elegant in a vase on its own or mixed with orlaya and greater quaking grass (*Briza maxima*).

If we sow our sweet peas early, in the first week or two of the year, we'll have a few emerging now to take with us to Chelsea. At this time we love *Lathyrus* × *hammettii* 'Erewhon' and *L. odoratus* 'Wiltshire Ripple' and 'Painted Lady', which are just beginning their eight to ten weeks of production.

Opposite top Armfuls of biennials – Icelandic poppies (*Oreomecon nudicaulis*) and the tall-stemmed sweet William, *Dianthus barbatus* 'Electron Auricula-eyed Mix'.
Opposite bottom May Stalwarts, *Erysimum cheiri* 'Blood Red Covent Garden', 'Vulcan' and 'Sunset Orange' with Icelandic poppies.

And ignore biennials at your peril! Many gardeners don't have time for this group of plants because they have to be sown from seed, which can seem a hassle, especially if you don't have the space, and then they don't flower for a year. But don't be put off. You get a hell of a lot of flowers for the cost of one packet of seed.

For a cutting garden – or any garden – biennials provide frothy abundance and horizontal drifts and clouds of colour. They provide all-important mortar that bonds together the garden's colour highlights into a beautiful and cohesive whole. We grow masses of early-flowering biennials: wallflowers (*Erysimum*), honesty (*Lunaria*) and a scattering of forget-me-nots (*Myosotis sylvatica*) – don't get carried away with these, as they prolifically self-sow. We also have the delicate, black-leaved cow parsley, *Anthriscus sylvestris* 'Ravenswing', as an under storey to tulips as April moves into May. Then come Icelandic poppies (*Oreomecon nudicaulis*), sweet Williams (*Dianthus barbatus*), foxgloves (*Digitalis*) and sweet rocket (*Hesperis matronalis*), which take over as the fillers between not only tulips, but also alliums.

These play the same filler role in the vase. You can pick a handful of tulips and put them in a jug and they'll look lovely, but poke in a base of contrasting coloured wallflowers, or a cloud of white honesty, with a few stems of *Euphorbia amygdaloides* var. *robbiae* or *E. palustris* and you've got flowers fit for a ball.

Some are more cut-and-come-again than others, with Icelandic poppies scoring highest, but even foxgloves go on longer for being picked. Remove the queen flower as the spike starts to extend and you'll spur on lots of princess flowers on smaller stems. You could not call these cut-and-come-again exactly, but by pinching, you are multiplying your harvest.

Don't forget, as well as rich and saturated colour, many biennials have fragrance. The perfume of wallflowers filling a corner of a garden is one of my favourite things, closely followed by the wafting scent of stocks from *Matthiola incana* 'Pillow Talk'. A few stems in a vase will fill any sized room with an old-fashioned, carnation-like scent.

And there's the exotic *Narcissus tazetta*-like fragrance of Icelandic poppies (*Oreomecon nudicaulis* 'Champagne Bubbles' has the strongest perfume) and, of course, sweet Williams and sweet rocket.

Picking and Arranging

Opposite A trug filled with some of the very best May flowers for picking, including *Rosa* 'Duchess of Cornwall' and *R.* 'Gertrude Jekyll', *Cerinthe major* 'Purpurascens', alliums, sweet rocket (*Hesperis matronalis*) and lupins.

We're still picking from bulbs in the cutting garden in May, but this is the month when the flower repertoire moves beyond the tulips and alliums, to include a range of many different plants. Roses are starting to bloom, with one of my early favourites, 'Duchess of Cornwall' (pictured in the trug opposite), and lupins are at their sensational peak.

Picking Alliums

If you love the firework display that alliums give you, it's worth having a succession of good cut-flower varieties that can be picked from the middle of May until August. Within and beyond that period, remember you can harvest the seedheads too, which are equally beautiful. Left in the garden too long, their perfect spheres can be damaged by wind or rain, and by October, a hint of damp will turn them black and mushy, even if they're stored inside.

In mid-May, we pick lots of *Allium hollandicum* 'Purple Sensation' and *A.* 'Purple Rain', and at the end of the month we move on to the spectacular, football-sized *Allium schubertii* and its hybrids, the deeper purple *A.* 'Toabago' (syn. 'Spider') and the white *A. schubertii* 'Arctic Snow'. Then comes one of the best: *A. cristophii*. This is excellent value for money, exceptionally perennial and it gives you huge globes, not quite as big as *A. schubertii*, but nearly.

We garden on heavy clay, so you might think alliums wouldn't thrive, but they do. All the ones mentioned here gradually naturalise. *A. cristophii* is well-behaved, but 'Purple Sensation' and its parent, the paler mauve *Allium hollandicum*, do tend to spread. So much so that their tatty May foliage can become an eyesore. We tend to defoliate our alliums as the flowers emerge from bud, as they look so much nicer, cutting back the foliage to allow the flowers to stand proud. Allium leaves are one of the first things to appear in the garden, often as early as February. That means they've been photosynthesising for many months before the flowers open,

Opposite Picking alliums in the Oast Garden – take care of the sap as you pick. It stains!

Above Foxgloves (*Digitalis purpurea* 'Dalmatian Mixed') are often too tall for our buckets and tip them over if there's a breath of wind, so we load them into a barrow or just pile them on to a shoulder to take inside for conditioning.

so you won't compromise the bulb if you chop the foliage down when it starts to brown at the tip. With the early-flowering alliums, that moment is usually in May.

Alliums – like most bulbs – are super robust and cut stems don't have to be picked and placed straight into water, but it's a good habit to get into. The whopper ones (like 'Beau Regard', 'Lucy Ball' and 'Forelock') will, however, topple a bucket over. So we pick and place those into a wheelbarrow when harvesting, and, as with bearded irises, lay them out with their flowers resting over the front lip of the barrow, so they don't get crushed or bruised.

It's also worth knowing alliums are part of the onion family and their foliage can similarly leave a yellow stain. I've ruined many a white T-shirt and pale-coloured dress with allium juice, as the stain never comes out. Pick with an apron on and take care.

In an arrangement, allium stems tend to age before the flowers, but you can slow this process down by putting a drop of bleach or preferably a good slosh of clear vinegar into the vase water to keep plant bacteria at bay. The acidic vinegar changes the water's pH and stops bacterial build-up. As the stems start to decompose, they become pretty pungent, so this addition to the water has a double role: it keeps the stems going longer and reduces the pong!

Picking Foxgloves (Digitalis)

Like some alliums, foxgloves are too lanky to be picked and placed straight into a normal-sized bucket. If you're picking loads of foxgloves, lay them straight into a wheelbarrow. For a smaller bunch, pick them and immediately take them inside for conditioning, which includes plunging the stem ends into boiling water for 20 seconds.

A Mass of One Plant

Once you've picked your lupins, bearded irises, alliums and foxgloves, how should you arrange them?

I think dramatic flowers like these look best arranged simply on their own. This is obviously very straightforward, because you don't have to think about combinations. But even so, if you're a beginner who likes rules, there are a few things to bear in mind.

Firstly, select stems at different heights. Or cut some stems quite short and leave others as long as you can. You want some stems to be as much as half, or perhaps two thirds, as tall as others. This gives a heart and horizon to your arrangement, and that's key to making a vase look natural and relaxed.

In general, the tallest stem should be between two to three times the height of the vase. Cut the tallest stems any shorter and they can look like they're craning their necks to see out and that you have not given them enough room to impress. If you leave your stems longer, it then makes the vase seem unsteady, top-heavy and like it may topple over.

It's tempting to add handfuls of stems at a time when making an arrangement with just one plant, but don't! Add stem by stem, observing the angles of each stem to create an overall shape that moves out horizontally just as much as vertically. This is even more important with shop-bought flowers, as they tend to be so rigid and regimented. Fan them out, with some stems almost parallel to the surface of the table, with just the tip of their stem in the water. This makes the whole thing look a hundred times lovelier.

Opposite A beautiful mountain of foxgloves, *Digitalis purpurea* 'Sutton's Apricot', 'Pam's Choice' and *Digitalis purpurea* f. *albiflora* in a Nero vase.

Right *Paeonia lactiflora* 'Duchesse de Nemours', 'Sarah Bernhardt' and 'Monsieur Jules Elie'.

Large Urn

This large-scale arrangement brings together the best of May. It's a great opportunity to practise creating balance and form.

When I'm making any large arrangement, I approach the shape as if it is the face of a clock. Imagine 12 o'clock at the top and 6 o'clock at the bottom. To create a good balance, I tend to add most flowers on the right hand side, between 3 o'clock and 6 o'clock, with a lesser collection at 10 and 11, plus a sprig or two at 7 o'clock. This makes the colour feel like it's been dusted across the whole arrangement, quite lightly, but not equally, and that looks natural and elegant.

Foliage, 10 stems each
Guelder rose (*Viburnum opulus* 'Roseum')
Solomon's seal (*Polygonatum × hybridum*)

Bride, 5 stems
Crab apple 'Red Sentinel' (*Malus × robusta*)

Bridesmaid, 5 stems
Hupeh crab apple (*Malus hupehensis*)

Gatecrashers, 10–20 stems each
Tulipa 'Green Wave'
Red campion (*Silene dioica*)

Top left *Viburnum opulus* 'Roseum'
Top right *Polygonatum × hybridum*
Middle left *Tulipa* 'Green Wave'
Middle right *Silene dioica*
Bottom *Malus hupehensis*

225

Step 1

For a large arrangement with heavy-stemmed plants, I use chicken wire for structure, rather than silver birch stems (as I did on p184). You need the extra strength of chicken wire to hold the weight. Ensure you have a bucket that fits neatly into your urn. Loosely fill the body of the bucket with scrunched up chicken wire. Secure with waterproof tape and make sure it is stable and doesn't move about in the bucket.

Step 2

Start to add your foliage. I use the guelder rose first, stripping down most of the leaves as I go. Editing the leaves is key, as it makes the flowers stand out. Add the Solomon's seal for further foliage structure. They are a great duo, as one is quite upright and the other arches beautifully.

Step 3

Add the Bride and Bridesmaid, followed by the Gatecrashers. Use the pink to emphasise the shape I describe in the introduction, focussing your stems at 3 to 6 o'clock.

Step 4

Remember to top up the vessel with water morning and night for the first three days and then reduce this to once a day. Recently cut stems drink more water.

PRACTICAL

May

Opposite Planting out *Cobaea scandens* on robust hazel frames.

May is the month we give the garden a gentle refurb. Spring-flowering bulbs are dying back and the chance of frost will be nil by the end of the month. The polytunnel and cold frames are crammed with plants ready and waiting to be planted out, so as one season comes to an end, the next is bursting to go.

Perch Hill has lots of open days throughout the year, but we tend not to open in May for just this reason: the place feels a bit in between one season and the next. For me and the gardening team, it's a magical time. It's hard work, but I love this moment, full of optimism and creativity, working out or confirming pre-planned designs as we plant, mixing form and colour combinations to make the place sing for at least the next five months.

There are tender perennial climbers to plant, lots of half-hardy annuals and the last few hardy annuals to be planted, plus all of our new dahlias. We plant these between the rows of bulbs, which instantly covers the browning foliage.

Most of our sowing was done earlier in spring, but there's one must-do this month, and that's zinnias. Zinnias hate cold nights and won't do well planted out before the end of May, so they need to be sown in the first week of the month. They don't like root disturbance, so we sow into Jiffy 7s (see p145).

Weeding

Before any planting out, make sure the ground is clear of weeds. It's key for plants to go into clean ground, or the weeds will compete. It's a job that's much easier to do when the beds are relatively empty. Weed first, then plant, and finally mulch to discourage more weeds emerging. That's the order.

Annual weeds

If we've had a wet spring, the warm weather will have brought on lots of annual weeds. It's good to get to know what the common annual weeds look like so you can keep on top of them. Hairy bittercress and groundsel in particular are a pain, because they start to set seed so early. And keep an eye out for chickweed and cleavers.

- Use a double-edged hoe to remove weeds. The double edge cuts in both directions – as you push forward and when you pull back – ensuring the stem is severed from the roots, just below the surface, which means it won't reshoot.
- Do your hoeing during a period of dry weather. You can then leave the weeds in situ and they will die off.
- It's best to hoe little and often. Try to catch any weeds when they are quite young, as they will be easier to remove. It's key to get them before they run to seed. After a day, your weeds should have died and dried up. Either rake them up and put them on your compost heap, or just leave them in situ to rot into the soil. If any have set seed, remove them instead.

PRACTICAL

Below, clockwise from top right Cleavers (*Galium aparine*); ground elder (*Aegopodium podagraria*); sow thistle (*Sonchus arvense*), as an example of a tap-rooted perennial weed; rough horsetail (*Equisetum hyemale*); creeping buttercup (*Ranunculus repens*) as an example of a weed with a running root system; hedge bindweed (*Calystegia sepium*); chickweed (*Stellaria media*); hairy bittercress (*Cardamine hirsuta*), at young seedling stage.

Perennial weeds

Perennials weeds are trickier to control. Our two main problems at Perch Hill are bindweed and ground elder. We had a major battle with couch grass in the past, but it has now virtually gone, and horsetail, which we don't have, can be a similar nightmare. Creeping buttercup is also perennial, but is easier to dig out.

If you're an organic gardener, as I am, the only way to contain these complex, rooting perennials is persistence. We find that we can weaken them – particularly ground elder – by adding the annual *Tagetes minuta* to infested areas as seedling plugs. It releases chemical compounds from its roots called allelochemicals, which inhibit the growth of other plants close by, particularly that of perennial weeds like ground elder, but also bindweed and couch grass.

Then we have to be really consistent with repeat weeding, following the roots and removing them as far back into the soil as we can. If the weed is very stubborn, we might even use cardboard or matting to cover the soil and suppress the weeds. It's safest to burn or bin the roots of these persistent perennials (do not add to the compost heap).

A good way to tackle bindweed is to thickly mulch the area. This encourages the bindweed to root in the top layer, meaning it can then be pulled out really easily, without as many root breakages.

We have also successfully used potatoes in one bed that suffered with lots of bindweed. The potato roots open up the soil structure a good 50cm (20in) down, and make it possible

Below **Planting out**
Cosmos bipinnatus 'Purity'.

to remove the vast majority of the spaghetti-like roots of bindweed. It's this deep, wide and strong root system that makes bindweed so hard to eradicate. That's why you must go back within the month and repeat the whole teasing back process until the ground is clear. It's a pain, but don't give up: you will get on top of it organically in the end.

Planting Out

As soon as we're sure the frosts are over, our wheelbarrows are almost permanently full. All of our cosmos, amaranths, nicotiana, dahlias and scented-leaf pelargoniums are ready to go out at the start of the month and we carry on right until the end with zinnias.

Planting out half-hardy annuals
Tagetes, antirrhinums, cosmos and amaranths should go out early to mid-May, while the zinnias should wait until the end of the month. These are all planted out in the same way (see p194 for instructions). Remember, if your plants look like they are already about to flower, pinch them out or cut them back. This encourages root formation, which makes for a better, stronger plant.

Planting out half-hardy annual climbers
With its large, elegant, bell-shaped flowers and its rigorous nature, *Cobaea scandens* is one of my all-time favourite plants. It can be picked right up until Christmas, which makes it great value for money in any cut-flower garden. By May, our cobaea plants are growing on in

PRACTICAL

Below left **When planting cobaea, try to make sure each plant goes in with its pot frame left intact.**

Below right **Lean the pot frame on to the main frame and tie it in.**

1-litre pots, each with their own mini-pot frame (see p148). Now they need planting out.

I also love the tender perennial climber black-eyed Susan, *Thunbergia alata* 'African Sunset'. Its flowers are a wonderful mix of colours and it is easy to grow from seed, which you can collect from the previous season's plants. It gives beautiful shapes and colours in a vase (pictured on p397) and, like cobaea, it climbs up over an arch or frame, flowers long and late and is an excellent source of forage for all pollinators. It's beautiful interplanted with the grass *Panicum capillare* 'Frosted Explosion', which also provides plentiful food for garden birds. We have trialled training thunbergia up twine to make it easier to pick and it works for creating straighter vines. It's time to plant that out too.

These plants should be planted out in exactly the same way as other half-hardy plants, with the only difference being they need to be tied into a frame (see p150).

The climbers should be in decent-sized pots when they come out of the polytunnel and will already have a climbing frame over which the seedling plants have grown. When you tip them out of the pot, take care not to disrupt this frame. Don't try to separate them from the frame. As you put each plant in the ground, just lean it on to the large, final frame and tie it in. Already up to a good height, with everything left intact, they romp away.

With the very vigorous growers, such as cobaea, plant one plant to every other post of your frame. For thunbergias, plant one to every post of the frame.

Dahlias

May is also dahlia planting time. We don't usually have huge numbers to go out into the Cutting Garden, because all our existing dahlias are left to overwinter in the ground (see p431 in November/December).

We agitate the mulch that was piled on each dahlia crown to gently expose the newly emerging stems. We do this by hand, as using tools might damage the emerging stems. We push the mulch out a little, away from the stems, to form a ring around the plant. In doing this, any slug and snail eggs are exposed for the birds to find. That helps keep mollusc populations well under control.

Our stakes or support frames are usually still in place from the previous year (see p265 in June), so there is very little work to do. But we are often adding new dahlias we are trialling. For those, we plant as follows.

- Dahlias will grow quite substantially once they have been planted out, so you want to leave around 50cm (20in) between plants. By giving them the space they need, you'll get stronger and healthier plants and therefore more flowers.
- Dig a hole twice the width of your potted plant and double the depth of the pot.
- Dahlias thrive in a rich, moist soil, so it's worth upping the organic matter with plenty of well-rotted manure in their planting holes. This will help your plants to retain water.
- Add the plant to the hole and make sure

Below Make sure you dig a decent-sized hole when planting dahlias, so the tuber is covered but not buried deep. Water the area before and after planting.

the tubers are buried, but not really deeply, as this can discourage flowering.
- As you plant, look out for any shoots that are getting leggy, and pinch them back. This promotes axillary bud formation and makes them bushy, giving you more compact plants and more flowers.
- Water and mulch with a 50:50 mix of compost and organic farmyard manure. They really benefit from this extra fertility boost.
- Be on frost alert and cover the plants with fleece if a late frost is forecast.
- Major slug and snail patrol is also important. Dahlias are one of their favourite foods, so put a barrier (oyster shells or seaweed slug repellent) on as you plant. Spread the barrier in a moat around

PRACTICAL

Below *Dahlia* 'Labyrinth' with *Gladiolus* 'Plum Tart' and 'Espresso'. Mulched deeply for winter, these are perennial in our garden.

the plant. And treat nearby box balls, yew and garden hedges as much as you can. That's where slugs in particular hang out in the drier daytime, to come and feast on your dahlias at night.

Interplanting dahlias with gladioli

In May, we plant gladioli throughout our dahlia beds. These add height and interest, as well as good vertical contrast to the dahlia domes (see p301).

The first time we planted gladioli with dahlias, we made an accidental discovery: the mulch we added to the dahlia beds in November additionally protected the gladioli (a tender perennial) from frost. They have since come back every year and don't need replanting each spring.

To plant gladioli, always use a bulb planter, as this causes minimal disruption to the life in the soil (see p390 for instructions).

If you are using a trowel, once you have popped your bulb in the hole, don't cover it over until you have finished digging and placing all the bulbs. This way, you can remember where you have put your bulbs and avoid replanting in the same place.

Plant the bulbs with the pointed end sticking upwards, spaced at around 10–15cm (4–6in) apart.

Watering and Feeding

Our general approach to watering after planting is to water heavily and not too often. Due to climate change, we all need to consider how often we water our gardens, and hosepipe bans are likely to become more prevalent in the future.

May is the most important month to water your plants, as seedlings will have just been planted out, and they will be settling in into early June.

The key to watering is to really drench the soil and plants, so that the water penetrates the soil and draws the plant roots down. If you just lightly sprinkle the soil with water from a can, then the roots of your plants will be drawn upwards in search of the water and this will make them more vulnerable to damage and drying out.

If the water is only sitting on the surface of the soil, it is also more exposed to evaporation, which is wasting this precious resource. By really drenching the soil you will find that you won't have to water as often.

It's important to remember that most of these annual plants – cerinthe, cosmos, orlaya and so on – come from warm and arid regions, and are used to growing in drought conditions.

- We put the sprinkler on for 2 hours after planting out seedlings.
- We wait for 10 days and then put the sprinkler on for another 2 hours.
- This process is repeated, 10 days later in June, when the sprinkler is put on for a final 2 hours if it hasn't rained properly since planting.
- That's it! We don't water again unless there is a prolonged period of drought (2 weeks without rain). By really drenching them, you can then leave them to get on with it.

Feeding

In the wild, you'll find many hardy annuals growing by the side of roads or on brownfield sites. This shows that they do not need rich and nutritious soil to grow well. In fact, if you overfeed them, they will produce more leaves and fewer flowers.

By keeping them a little hungry, the plant is likely to produce more flowers as it will be worried it may die soon and will be forced into producing flowers and therefore seed.

If you've mulched by adding manure or compost into the soil as you plant out, then that is really all the feeding that you need to do for a cut-flower bed for the whole season.

Sweet Pea Maintenance

In May, we attend to our sweet peas, which were planted out in March (see p149).

- As sweet pea plants grow, tie them into the frame, don't leave them to flop around. They'll grow more quickly and make stronger plants tied in regularly, at least once a fortnight by this stage.

- Some gardeners tell you to pinch out all the tendrils, the curly stems they use to cling and climb with. The tendrils do take energy from the flowers and attach themselves to flower stems and bend them, so I try to remove any I see, but it's a lot of work – don't get bogged down.
- To keep them growing strongly, we feed our plants every two weeks. Any tomato food will do. We use comfrey pellets dissolved in water, or you can make your own comfrey feed (see below).
- Water plants properly in a drought. Sweet peas need thorough watering. If you let them dry out, they will get stressed and mildew will soon appear. If no rain is forecast, water each of your plants ensuring the soil is drenched.
- By the end of the month, you need to start to pick the flowers. If you see any seed pods as you're cutting, snip these off as well. You don't want your plants forming seed as that will stop them producing flowers.

Making Homemade Feed

We make our own plant food using potash-rich comfrey (*Symphytum officinale*) and nitrogen-packed nettles (*Urtica dioica*). These two plants provide us with the raw materials to make fertilisers.

Potash is necessary for good root, flower and fruit formation. Nitrogen is the major component of chlorophyll and is necessary for photosynthesis and leaf growth. Various feeds use varying quantities of these, but when making your own fertilisers, you can apply them separately or mix them together for a more broad-spectrum feed.

- Cut the plant (comfrey or nettles) back to the ground. At this time of year, they will grow back quickly for a later harvest. Gather up all the stems and leaves in a trug or wheelbarrow.
- Chop everything up (you can include the flowers) and pile into a bucket or water butt. Ideally, your container will have a tap in the base (such as a water butt), so you can extract the liquid, and a lid is useful as the mixture starts to smell as it breaks down, but any watertight container is fine. Fill up the container with water, add a lid (or secure a bag with a peg) and leave somewhere outside.
- After 3–4 weeks, extract the liquid and store in bottles somewhere cool and dark. Alternatively, just take liquid from the mixture as and when you need it, always topping up a little with more water and plant material.
- To use the fertiliser, dilute with water to a ratio of about 1 part to 10, then apply to the plants.

Below top left and right
Comfrey ready to be harvested and then placed in a bucket, leaves, stems, flowers and all.

Below bottom left and right
Chopping comfrey and speeding up fermentation by covering with water.

Roses
Cerinthe
Poppies
Euphorbia
Salvias
Sweet peas
Foxgloves Late alliums
Orlaya Peonies
Ammi Calendula
Snapdragons

June

As you walk into the Cutting Garden in June, you move in and out of clouds of perfume. Roses one minute, then a pulse of sweet peas and then an intense hit of lily fragrance and the gentle honey smell of an early buddleja, or even sweeter lilac in the hedge. The garden is full of scent and, with it, the house. Every bunch you pick fills a room with delicious perfume.

Among the sweet peas, *Lathyrus odoratus* 'Matucana' has led the way in every one of our fragrance trials over the last 30 years. It is the benchmark by which we measure all other sweet pea perfume. It has the strongest and most divine scent. Other old-fashioned, so-called grandiflora sweet peas are the runners up, including 'Duke of York', 'Lord Nelson', 'King Edward VII' and the ivory 'Mrs Collier'. They are brilliantly scented too, though they do have smaller and fewer flowers per stem than the more recent Spencer types.

In terms of productivity, sweet peas are well known to be stellar. As most of us know, the more you pick, the more they flower. That comes with a word of warning: don't grow too many. If picking time is limited, stick to one frame or arch. That'll give you plenty. And as they grow, keep tying them in as often as you can. Putting the main stem under tension by securing it vertically (we use flexi-tie or twine) increases bud and flower production and stops too many stems bending like a knee.

That's a classic June problem: you don't quite keep up with the tying in, so one whole vine gets blown out and away from the frame. All the flowers on that displaced stem are then lying practically horizontal for a day or two before they turn to the light. That's how the knees form. Then, hoicked up and

Opposite The Annual Cutting Garden with a ton of hardy annuals (*Ammi visnaga*, *Malope trifida* 'Vulcan', *Euphorbia oblongata*, plus *Lathyrus odoratus* 'Judith Wilkinson', 'Emilia Fox', 'Matucana' and 'Winston Churchill'). A few half-hardy annuals are just coming into flower, towards the end of June (here *Cosmos bipinnatus* 'Rubenza', *Phlox drummondii* and zinnias).
Above A brilliant bunch of sweet peas: 'Matucana' and 'Prince Edward of York'.

tied into place, they do the same again, so you end up with stems like corkscrews, not the easiest things to slot into a vase.

With sweet peas, long stems are a boon. Ensuring you achieve this is down to various things. Their growth is helped by generous watering, or a wet spring like we had in 2024. That year, our sweet pea stems reached from my palm to my elbow. You can also improve stem length by cordon training, but that's too time consuming to be worthwhile in my view; regular training and tying in from the get-go works well enough. It's also good to start with varieties that seem to have naturally longer stems. *Lathyrus odoratus* 'Winston Churchill', for example, is a towering giant, and 'Blue Velvet' stands not far behind.

If you've only got room for one or two varieties, then aiming for an extended period of flowering is another valuable goal. We have found *L. o.* 'Anniversary' and 'Blue Velvet' are there to pick for a few more weeks than the others. They just keep going.

Finally, colour is important. I personally look out for the unusual ones, and I love *Lathyrus × hammettii* 'Erewhon' for just this reason: the flowers have an amazing wash of blue as well as purple. And I like the unscented, green, *L. chloranthus* as a brightening contrast to crimson sweet peas. I'm also keen on *L. o.* 'King's Ransom'. Hot off the breeding bench, this new sweet pea is a muted terracotta shade, which you'll either love or hate. I also appreciate *L. o.* 'Nimbus' for its sultry exoticism, its flowers stippled and splashed with the richest purple and crimson.

Next in June's must-have, grow-for-picking list are roses. These are cut-and-come-again, but stem production is much slower compared with annuals, so we tend to slot roses into less intensive areas in the garden. Although we have recently created a six-metre-square bed solely for cut-flower roses, which includes most of the varieties in the picture on p243.

Josie Lewis, Perch Hill's head gardener, has always been crazy about roses, but when she arrived 15 years ago, we were only growing a few. As an organic gardener, I was wary of them, or rather the black spot and mildew that seemed to go hand in hand with the most luscious, scented varieties I loved while living at Sissinghurst.

I wanted *Rosa* 'Madame Grégoire Staechelin' (an early flowerer with stupendous scent), 'Madame Isaac Péreire' and other old-fashioned beauties, but these seemed to defoliate almost completely, stricken by fungal diseases when I first planted them at Perch Hill. They were hopeless.

Opposite Out of a 2024 trial of 65 roses, these are the best for picking, based on longest vase life, most delicious scent and most productive and longest flowering time.
Row 1: 'Hot Chocolate', 'Marjorie Fair', 'Sweet Honey'.
Row 2: 'Champagne Moment', 'Timeless Charisma', 'Queen of Sweden', 'MacMillan Nurse'.
Row 3: 'Julia's Rose', 'Wild Rover', 'Duchess of Cornwall' (three heads from coral to soft pink).
Row 4: 'Timeless Cream', 'Timeless Purple', 'Mocha Rose', 'Tuscany Superb'.
Row 5: 'Cinco de Mayo', 'Goldfinch', 'Summer Song'.
Below Sweet peas growing up a hazel frame covered with jute netting: *Lathyrus odoratus* 'Robert Uvedale', 'Judith Wilkinson', 'Prince of Orange', 'Dark Passion', 'Eclipse' and 'Restormel'.

Then, with Josie's determination to grow more roses, we researched how we could grow healthy plants without a fortnightly dose of fungicide. That's when salvias started to carpet our rose garden. We discovered through experimentation that many salvia stems and leaves contain a percentage of sulphur and, we believe, a volatile oil containing sulphur is released from the leaves of the plant. We think that on a warm day, the oils released are cleansing to plants and kill fungal spores.

We trialled many different salvia forms and concluded that compact varieties are best for the job: they can be tucked in under the skirts of the roses, they won't drown the rose or weaken it through competition and they have a particularly strong, pungent scent. Every *Salvia × jamensis* and *S. greggii* hybrid seems to do well. But the hugely popular *S.* 'Amistad' is too big and it's not very pungent. In my experience, the ones that work are distinctly pineapple-scented (some say blackcurrant), and some almost cat-pee-like and acrid in their intensity. Crush a leaf and you'll know. Both scents are effective!

Below left Rosa 'Champagne Moment', which has an AGM. *Below right* My favourite ever rose: *Rosa × odorata* 'Mutabilis'. *Opposite* A jade glass vase with *Rosa* 'Duchess of Cornwall', *Paeonia* 'Coral Sunset', *Cerinthe major* 'Purpurascens' and peas (*Pisum sativum* 'Blauwschokker'). *Next page* The rose trial bed at dawn with *Rosa* 'Rhapsody in Blue' in the foreground, which looks pinker than its usual purple when backlit. Here, scattered all through our rose picking beds, we have foxgloves and opium poppies (*Digitalis purpurea* 'Sutton's Apricot' and *Papaver somniferum*), and you can't see them here, but there's an underplanting of salvias to keep our organically grown roses fungus-free.

Our ultimate test to really prove the salvia–rose companion planting theory worked was to plant problematic roses with a carpet of salvias below. Even roses like 'Rhapsody in Blue', famously prone to fungal disease, are now thriving here.

Once we'd cracked growing healthy roses, we then moved on to trialling for scent and extended vase lives. The picture on p243 shows our current favourites across a broad colour spectrum, but of course it changes every few years as we discover new varieties. That's the magnificence of roses – the range is so vast and ever expanding.

If I had to select just three or four roses to provide cut flowers over a long season, with good vase lives, delicious perfume and beauty, it would be 'Duchess of Cornwall', 'Champagne Moment' and *Rosa × odorata* 'Bengal Crimson' or, even better, *R. × o.* 'Mutabilis'.

'Duchess of Cornwall' opens pink and turns coral, has three or four flushes of flowers through the year, boasts a great vase life of around five days, and magnificent, crumpled-handkerchief flowers with heavenly scent.

'Champagne Moment' has all the attributes of 'Duchess of Cornwall', but with wondrous cream flowers, which have a

beautiful butterscotch hue when they first open. This flowers prolifically for *ages*.

The two China roses, *Rosa × odorata* 'Bengal Crimson' and 'Mutabilis', flower gently from May to November, have a soft scent and a pristine, super-healthy habit. There's a 'Mutabilis' shrub that my father planted by a wall in my parent's garden 60 years ago and it's still thriving. They're beautiful in a vase, one of my favourite flowers to have as a companion on my desk. With stem ends seared, they only last three days, but are perfect. The flower is like a butterfly crossed with a handkerchief, in the most wonderful series of colours from apricot (when they first open) to deep and then soft pink as the flowers develop, hence the Latin name meaning 'changing'.

Along with roses, many people would insist on peonies being part of a good-sized cutting garden, but after growing them for 30 years, I disagree.

Jonathan Buckley, the photographer I work with (and to whom this book is dedicated), has been coming here with his camera for at least 30 years. He arrives fortnightly, from the middle of March until the middle of October. Yet despite Perch Hill having a three-metre row of peonies for picking

Opposite A row of peonies in the Perennial Cutting Garden, including three excellent cutting varieties *Paeonia lactiflora* 'Duchesse de Nemours', 'Sarah Bernhardt' and 'Monsieur Jules Elie'.

Above Roses and foxgloves in the Herb Garden, including the briefly flowering but beautiful roses 'Sissinghurst Castle' and 'Saint Swithun'.

(including the deliciously scented *Paeonia lactiflora* 'Duchesse de Nemours' and long-lasting 'Sarah Bernhardt'), he's only managed to coincide with their peak flowering time three or four times in nearly three decades. That's no use!

With their complex, many-petalled flowers, they're exceptionally vulnerable to wind and rain, and are truly only at their best for a few days. Miss that moment and you've got to wait another year. I'd encourage anyone who loves cut peonies to buy them rather than giving up precious space to this beautiful but fairly meagre cut-flower crop.

Roses and sweet peas are the top cut flowers for June, but they have a good back-up crew and these should not be forgotten. You'll hardly see a view of Perch Hill at this time of year without glades of hardy annuals (see July for more on those) and spires of foxgloves. These thrive in sun, or even better, dappled shade. And that's valuable. We all have a rather dowdy patch of shade that could do with a sprinkle of foxglove glamour.

The foxglove spire is a beautiful thing. Twisting gently this way and that, each one giving great shape and drama, and they look splendid packed into a large vase on their own and just as beautiful piercing through flowers with a more fluffy

Opposite A border at the edge of our Perennial Cutting Garden filled with *Euphorbia characias* subsp. *wulfenii* 'John Tomlinson' (this starts to dull in June), with *Digitalis purpurea* 'Pam's Choice', *Cirsium rivulare* 'Atropurpureum' and *Allium macleanii* 'His Excellency'.
Above Carrying a whopper bunch of *Allium cristophii* to enjoy in the house and then to dry for winter.

or horizontal habit, such as cow parsley or ammi. Both of these flower at just the same time as foxgloves, from May to June.

Finally, for drama, I'd recommend June-flowering alliums. It's almost a cliché, but these truly are your summer garden fireworks. For side tables, dinner parties, bedrooms and bathrooms, vases of roses and sweet peas are ideal, but for simple, wowzah showstopper vases, alliums are just the thing.

Try just one stem of *Allium schubertii* in a narrow-necked vase and it'll draw all sorts of attention. Or get a massive bucket, urn or even bin and fill it with *A. cristophii*, then leave the stems sitting there for a couple of months until they brown and dry. That gives you a double bounty: simple, stylish flowers for now, and sparkler seedheads to return to in winter. Practical, beautiful and sustainable. See p219 for more on picking alliums.

Picking and Arranging

Opposite Carrying a mixed bucket of June cut flowers, including foxgloves, roses, clematis, geraniums and the later-flowering *Allium schubertii* 'Magic'.

In June, it can be hot and bright in the middle of the day, so it's more essential than ever to pick early in the morning or late in the afternoon, and to place stems straight into water in the shade.

If I'm in a hurry, I do occasionally pick and arrange a small bunch straight into my hand (see tips for this on p289). I condition them as a bunch, all the stems plunged into boiling water together, the moment I'm back indoors. But as a general rule, this is not ideal. Instead, follow the advice from p78: cut, strip most of the leaves into one bucket, and plop the stems into a second bucket of cool water.

Store your flower-filled buckets somewhere shady and cool. In our trials, we've found the shock between life on the mother plant and as a solitary cut stem is eased, in all flowers, by at least a few hours rest in the cool and dark. This is particularly important if the flowers are destined for somewhere warm, like a marquee.

Shop-bought roses can look and smell like classroom rulers: straight, rigid and plastic. So much so, I'd rather not have them. With our homegrown roses, the problem is a little different. We find that the stronger the perfume, the shorter the rose tends to last in a vase. And, with heavy flower heads, some roses can be tricky to arrange.

This means I use our cut garden roses in one of two ways: either as mini bunches for putting by a bed or bath tub; or as table centrepieces, arranged in bowls with the roses supported by a grid. Both are quick and easy to do and will last three to four days.

Bedside Table Roses

Obviously, this couldn't be easier. To extend the vase life of your roses, the key is to sear the stem ends in boiling water for 20 seconds. And to save your hands as you arrange, remove the thorns first, at least at the stem ends.

You can pick a handful of roses and place them in a vase. Done. But if you want to go slightly bigger, use a pin holder (known also as a florist's frog) attached to the base of the vase with waterproof floral clay.

You can also bend and feed a handful of pliable twigs into the belly of the vase (see p184). Both of these methods will give you structure and the ability to separate and arrange your stems.

Below left A highly scented arrangement of *Rosa* 'Gertrude Jekyll' with *Lonicera periclymenum* 'Serotina'.
Below right One stem each of five roses: 'Cinco de Mayo, 'Hot Chocolate', 'Tuscany Superb', 'De Resht' and 'Wild Edric'.

Opposite A muted arrangement of roses that almost matches the Sanderson wallpaper. The roses here are 'Koko Loco', 'Julia's Rose', *Rosa × odorata* 'Mutabilis' and the showy, very fragrant one in the middle, 'Calendar Girl'.

Centrepiece Roses

You can extend the life of your roses by a day or two by reducing the length of the stem. The best way to do this is to arrange roses on very short stems into a bowl over a grid. See p107 for instructions on making a reusable and collapsible grid with materials you can find in the garden and shed.

For arrangements, I usually opt for a mass of just one rose or stick pretty rigidly to one of my palettes (see p56), and use the Bride, Bridesmaid, Gatecrasher rule (see p47). That makes it simple.

Above *Rosa* 'Hot Chocolate' (Bride) and *R.* 'Munstead Wood' (Gatecrasher), arranged in a grid with *Antirrhinum majus* 'Chantilly Purple' (Gatecrasher) and *A. m.* 'Chantilly Bronze' (Bridesmaid). Plus foliage from *Alchemilla mollis* and *Eryngium giganteum*.

Opposite top A rich mix of peonies and roses, again supported on a grid with the crimson *Paeonia* 'Command Performance' (Bride), *P.* 'Coral Sunset' (Bridesmaid), with *Rosa* 'James Mason' (Gatecrasher) and *Clematis* 'Nubia' Boulevard Series (Gatecrasher).

Opposite bottom Here, it is more about matching soft pinks, with *Rosa* 'Sweet Juliet' and 'Aphrodite' like fluffy marshmallows, with the dark, central, crimson blotches of the pretty, single rose, 'For Your Eyes Only' providing the all-important contrast.

Sweet Peas

It's a terrible thing to say, but picking sweet peas can almost become a chore. Anyone who has grown them will know it's hard to keep up with your harvest. I tend to pick them in bunches and carry elastic bands on my wrist: pick, gather a bunch, elastic band, plop into water. It's super quick and prevents breaking and damaging stems, as can happen if you add them to water one by one.

Searing stem ends makes no difference to the vase life of sweet peas. But a little squirt of sugar syrup (essentially a teaspoon of sugar melted in a tablespoon of boiling water) prolongs their cut life by a day or two.

One thing to note when picking sweet peas is that they often have pollen beetles at the nose of the flower where the stigmas are situated. These insects do no harm; they're just feeding away on the pollen. If there are lots, place your cut sweet peas near an open window overnight. As the sun comes up, the beetles can fly off towards the light. A little shake should help to get rid of any hangers on.

When it comes to extending your sweet pea season, be mindful of seedheads. These form all too quickly and impact the crop, so remove them as you see them. The flower stems get shorter and shorter as the season goes on, too – they end up fit only for a small vase or jam jar. Because of this, particularly towards the end of their season, I stop picking individual stems and instead cut the top section of a whole vine, complete with several flowers and side stems. By picking roughly the top fifth of a vine, you end up with about 45cm (18in) of stem, which can be used in a larger vase and will hold its own, cascading and frothing this way and that (pictured on p263).

We also find that by removing the top section of stem, even in July as sweet pea season nears its end, plants seem to get a new lease of life, producing axillary buds and extending the picking season by a few weeks. Encourage this by feeding them with comfrey (see p236 and p297), and giving them a good watering after harvesting.

Even with sweet peas, I have a few tried-and-tested ideas to guide me when arranging. These help to elevate sweet peas from the slightly fussy and cutesy English cottage garden image they can sometimes be tarnished with. I've outlined these ideas on the following pages.

Opposite Picking sweet pea – *Lathyrus odoratus* 'Mollie Rilstone' – with elastic bands on my wrist to bunch them quickly before putting them in a bucket of water. This variety has long stems and large flowers and sits well in either of the pastel palettes, Cashmere Jersey or Champs-Élysées.

Idea 1 Firstly, and in my view importantly, don't mix all the colours up willy-nilly when you're picking and arranging sweet peas. At the start of the season, a colour jamboree can be jolly, with sweet peas stuffed into a jug on the kitchen table to celebrate summer's arrival. But it's more stylish to stick to a defined palette or just one colour or variety.

Above
Cashmere Jersey (soft and warm)
Picking for a Cashmere Jersey sweet pea vase, including 'Apricot Sprite', 'Princess Elizabeth', 'Anniversary' and 'Mollie Rilstone'.

Right
Venetian Velvet (dark and rich)
A vase in our bathroom with sweet peas 'Lord Nelson', 'Black Knight', 'Blue Velvet', 'Beaujolais', 'Almost Black', 'Winston Churchill' and 'Emilia Fox'.

Left

Champs-Élyées (soft and cool)
A simple mix of two cool-coloured sweet peas – 'Erewhon' and 'Almost Black' – and a few stems of the unscented green pea, *Lathyrus chloranthus* threaded through.

Below

Boiled Sweet (bright and brilliant)
A scented and joyful table arrangement of flowers, including sweet peas 'Prince of Orange', 'Winston Churchill, 'Judith Wilkinson' and 'Emilia Fox'.

Left An entire table filled with *Lathyrus odoratus* 'Prince Edward of York'. I've kept the variety (and so flower colour) the same. It's the shapes and colours of the vases that change. However, all are luminous and made of glass, so they feel like they're part of a family.

Opposite The top quarter of seven sweet pea vines arranged together. Here, again, it's the highly scented 'Prince Edward of York' welcoming people in on our hall table.

Idea 2 Rather than having one large, central vase, you can group together a number of vases for real impact. Keep the flowers the same, but change the shape, size and colour of the containers. Once you have filled your contrasting vases, position them on a windowsill or sideboard, ideally backlit. That makes for a more luminous group. An alternative option is to use multiple flower colours, but keep the vase style, shape and colour consistent.

Idea 3 This won't be suitable for every sweet pea vase you arrange, but if you've picked the whole top of a vine (see p259), you're bound to have a clutch of tendrils – and so much the better. You get plenty of movement and more interesting and natural shapes with more vine and tendrils (so there's both a practical and aesthetic reason for this mode of harvest). Increasingly, this wayward way of arranging sweet peas is my favourite; it reminds me of their wild cousins, scrambling up over a roadside bank in Sicily or the south of Spain.

PRACTICAL

June

Opposite Harvesting *Allium* 'Purple Rain' seedheads for winter.

This is the time of year when one's focus turns to keeping things in good heart in the cutting garden, rather than new planting or making radical design changes. So it's mainly about picking, watering, weeding and maintenance, all little and often.

There are, however, two major jobs still to be done. The first is staking and supporting plants and the second is sowing biennials and completing the second sowing of half-hardy annuals, which will prolong your harvest until November or even up until Christmas in a mild winter.

If not already done in May, harvest early-flowering allium heads (such as 'Purple Sensation') before they become dry and get blown away. We store them until we need them for decoration in the winter. We tidy up their browning, messy foliage at the same time to make room for the emergence of late-season perennials like echinacea, as well as for planting the final batch of half-hardy annuals.

Staking and Support

You may have made climbing frames and support structures for certain plants such as cobaea, but early June is the time to turn your attention to the rest of the cutting patch.

As the weather warms up there will come a point when all your plants take off at once. Hardy annuals, from their mid-spring sowing, are rocketing now and need proper frames. And the half-hardy plants – such as cosmos and dahlias – are usually well-established and tall enough to need support.

Annuals in particular grow so quickly that they don't have time to develop much lignin in their cell walls; lignin is a plant polymer that creates rigidity. It's crucial to the development of tree bark and wood, but because of their fast growth, annuals hardly form any lignin, making them much softer and more flexible. That's why cutting-patch plants in particular need careful staking.

It's really important not to miss this moment, as if you do not stake plants in time you'll end up with curved stems. That happens as a result of plants flopping over and then righting themselves naturally. The growth tip and all the axillary buds turn to the light when they're flopped over, which, if you then hurriedly stake them upright, turn again to the light, so you end up with stems like corkscrews. This not only stunts the growth, but also makes them tricky to slot into a vase.

At Perch Hill, we use a few main systems for staking.

Gates

Positioning gates alongside beds is the quickest system of staking. We slot these ready-made supports beside floppy plants to hold them up and off a path and encourage them to grow upright. Our gates are 40cm (16in) tall, and this suits shorter, stockier plants such as *Euphorbia oblongata*, which can be left without support, but then ends up taking up more room than it needs when it collapses and sprawls. To maximise every inch of space, supporting them up and off the ground allows for more paths or planting. Simply push the gates in, or if your ground is solid, hammer in

PRACTICAL

Below left **Chestnut gates holding up** *Euphorbia oblongata* **and encouraging straighter stem growth.**

Below right *Cosmos bipinnatus* 'Double Click Cranberries' and *Scabiosa atropurpurea* growing up through jute netting stretched tight between kiln-dried willow stakes.

posts and attach your gates to those. The only downsides to this system are that it doesn't work for taller plants and the gates can be expensive.

Twine, willow, silver birch and hazel

With light-stemmed plants, a simple support is often enough. We place stakes around the edge of the plants and then criss-cross lengths of twine between them. For chunkier and taller plants, we create stronger frameworks constructed out of hazel (as the main posts), willow and jute netting.

- Knock the hazel posts into all four corners of the bed with a hammer.
- Add willow stakes all the way round the edge of the line of plants, keeping within the bed. We use kiln dried willow so that the stakes don't root in the soil. Space them about 1.2m (4ft) apart along the sides of the bed.
- Over the top, add a network of support using jute netting or a zigzag of twine. We used to use plastic pea netting, but we are now committed to using natural materials. Place the jute netting over the hazel corner posts to a height of about 30cm (12in) off the ground and get it as taut as you can. Continue down the line, putting the jute netting over all of the willow stakes.
- The stems of your plants will then grow through the netting and be supported, which will help them to grow straight. If any plants are at the right height, thread them through the netting to get them started.
- For taller plants, such as cosmos and cornflowers, you can add a second layer of

Below top **A clove hitch knot is the ideal support for heavy-stemmed plants such as sunflowers, staked here.**

Below bottom **The four stages of making a clove hitch. A forward loop, and then another, which you tuck (do not rotate) one behind two. Loop that over a stake and, once tightened, it will never slip.**

netting. You can do this after a month or so of growing. This should be at about half the height of the plants and will then provide enough support for the rest of the growing season.

If you don't have these materials to hand, you can improvise. We often sandwich a line of flowers between hazel, willow or birch posts, woven with birch and linked with hop twine, which is about twice the thickness of standard twine and very strong, but still gentle on plants as they grow. We cross the twine at regular intervals to give the flowers something to grow up through.

Individual posts

One of our main methods of staking during the summer months is to use a single stake with a clove hitch knot. This is the best system for chunkier stems and anything that is top heavy, such as sunflowers and towering giants such as tithonia, which may be too strong for jute netting. We don't use bamboo canes here because they aren't strong enough, and harvesting our own wood is much more sustainable. We sometimes use kiln-dried willow stakes, as these won't root.

- Knock your wooden stake into the ground with a mallet.
- Create a clove hitch knot using twine and secure your plant to the stake.
- Tie your plant loosely so that it still has movement, but won't blow over.
- As your plant grows, add on another clove hitch knot, and another, if required.

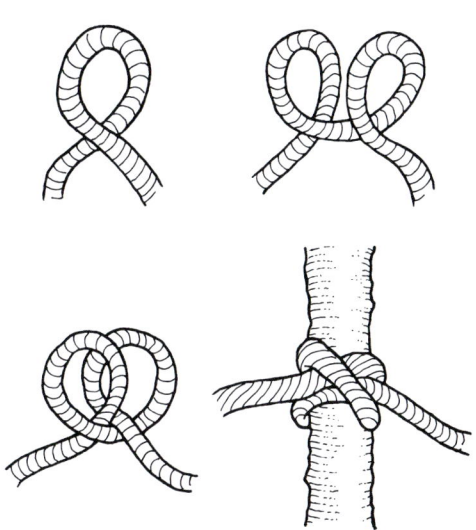

PRACTICAL

Below top A cat's cradle of hop twine over chestnut and willow stakes, supporting dahlias.

Below bottom This system should last a few years with some mending each spring, before the dahlias get too tall.

Dahlia Staking

Once dahlias have reached about 60cm (24in), they need to be staked. We use two systems.

Canes and twine

If the dahlias are on their own or in a small group in a mixed bed, we support them by encircling them with willow or hazel canes. You can do this in a triangle formation for small clumps, or in a circular formation for larger clumps.

Once the canes are around the edge of the dahlias, use hop twine to complete the circle or triangle, to create a 360-degree support. Start off with a clove hitch knot and then, in a sort of zigzag or star formation, take the twine from cane to cane across the clump, to keep the stems enclosed and supported as they grow.

Another reusable and simple option is to use decorative iron frames, though these can be pricey. Or use simple iron hoops, as these will give enough support, but you need one hoop for every dahlia plant.

Chestnut posts and hop twine

This is the staking system we use in our permanent dahlia beds, where the frames stay up all year, and we repair or replace sections as and when it is needed. Large chestnut posts are installed along the edges of every path, with smaller hazel stakes in between. And hop twine is then woven from stake to stake. I love the cat's cradle effect this gives these beds in the Perennial Cutting Garden through winter – as well as the crucial role they play for summer and autumn.

Sowing

We do two lots of sowing in June. The top priority is sowing biennials. They can be sown anytime between mid-May and mid-July, and we like to do it in June. We also do a second sowing of some annuals. See p143 for advice on sowing.

Biennials

Most biennials sown now (bar the earlier-flowering wallflowers and honesty) will be flowering in May and June the following year. With just a bit of planning, your spring and early summer garden will be fuller, more scented and more colourful.

Sweet William (*Dianthus*)
We're fans of the black sweet William, *Dianthus barbatus* (Nigrescens Group) 'Sooty'. It's the crimson stems and black-crimson wash over the green leaves, as well as its black velvet flowers, which makes it so exceptional. And for extraordinary vigour and a vase life of three weeks, we grow 'Electron Mix'. 'Sooty' is best sown under cover in seed trays, but we have sown 'Electron Mix' successfully both direct into a seed bed in June, as well as inside.

Foxglove (*Digitalis*)
We all know and love the creamy white foxglove, but for me, *Digitalis purpurea*

PRACTICAL

Below Sowing foxgloves, which have tiny seed, so sow in large trays from a height to achieve a wide and even seed distribution.

Wallflower (*Erysimum*)

You can hang on until early autumn and buy bare-root wallflower plants or grow your own from seed to give you more choice. My long-standing favourites are the delicious, rich crimson *Erysimum cheiri* 'Blood Red' and burnt orange 'Fire King'. Though the new Sunset varieties, 'Sunset Apricot' and 'Sunset Dark Purple', are stealing the show. They're stronger growers and suffer less from flea beetle. Wallflowers are super sturdy and easy to sow direct.

Clear a small seed bed in the garden, get rid of any weeds, and rake to create a fine soil tilth. Then sow your seeds, placing each individually, a good 10cm (4in) apart so you won't need to thin out. As the seeds germinate, you will need to cover with fleece to protect against flea beetle. This is also the case for brassicas, such as honesty.

'Sutton's Apricot' reigns supreme. Its dusky apricot pink is a key colour in my warm palette, so I grow lots of this. The vertical spires are irregular, each one with a slight twist, which gives them an ease in a vase.

With tiny seeds, these are best sown into large, deep plastic or polystyrene crates, three or four times the size of a usual seed tray, filled with compost. You should be able to get good containers from a greengrocer or fishmonger. Scatter the seeds as far apart as you can. Sown widely, you won't need to prick out. With a good depth of compost and seedlings well-spaced, you can skip the pricking out stage and take the whole tray out into the garden and transplant straight from there about 6 weeks after sowing.

Sweet rocket (*Hesperis*)

Lovely for clouds of white and mauve in May and June, sweet rocket is easy to sow direct. Follow the instructions for wallflowers.

Honesty (*Lunaria*)

I love purple honesty and, even though it pops up in my hedges, I sow lots of this, as well as the white, *Lunaria annua* var. *albiflora* and the dark-leaved 'Chedglow'. These are as valuable for their spring flowers as they are for their apple-green seed pods in summer, which can be dried for winter decoration. Sow into gutters to minimise root disturbance when it's time to plant out.

Icelandic poppy (*Oreomecon nudicaulis*)
Like many in the poppy family, these don't like root disturbance and struggle with being sown direct. So we tend to sow these into Jiffy 7s or gutter pipes and give them protection inside. Icelandic poppies need a bit more TLC than most things we grow and, even with it, we lose about 50 per cent. I recommend sowing twice the number of seeds so you end up with the right amount of plants.

Annuals
We also do a second sowing of a few half-hardy and hardy annuals, which seem to better withstand the cold and wet late autumn and early winter compared to the ones sown in March.

Snapdragon (*Antirrhinum*)
We find this does well from sowing in February (see p120), but we also try to sow it now in June to give us a harvest almost up until Christmas.

Honeywort (*Cerinthe major* 'Purpurascens')
If sown now, cerinthe will supply lovely foliage for the vase until Christmas (if no hard frost comes). The garden is usually so chock-a-block at this time of year, sowing into a gutter is the easiest option.

Below Sowing Icelandic poppies in a gutter to avoid the need for too much handling and root disturbance. These are transplanted straight into the greenhouse for an early spring crop, or into the garden under a cloche until they've settled in.

Blue-flowered painted sage
(*Salvia viridis* blue-flowered)
This salvia is invaluable as a filler-foliage and Bridesmaid in many of our arrangements. From a spring sowing (or self-sowing from the previous season) it is going over by September. We sow in June to ensure we have this until the first hard frost (usually by Christmas). It's most efficient to sow this in a gutter.

Sweet scabious (*Scabiosa atropurpurea*)
This keeps flowering well as light levels fall.

July

July is paradise for cut-flower-garden lovers, as production is at an all-time peak. Beautiful nigella, cornflowers, ammi, larkspur, corn poppies and sweet peas are major players at the start of the month. And two or three weeks later, they're joined by cosmos, snapdragons, ageratum and phlox. By the middle of July, some hardy annuals are starting to fade, but half-hardies are there to step into their shoes. The harvest from one group declines as the other increases, so your vases are never empty. It's good to be aware of this midsummer flower glut when you plan what to grow – don't cultivate too much, or it may overwhelm you.

Annuals are the definition of cut-and-come-again. By picking the top flower, just above a pair of leaves, you promote the development of axillary buds, which develop into flowers the following week. In July, you'll see this plant physiology working hard on your behalf, ensuring a constant harvest, even from a small patch or window box.

The key is to keep on picking. If you don't pick flowers or deadhead them, annuals run to seed. If left on the stem, seed formation takes precedence over new flower production. Even flowers with a short vase life, such as poppies, should be picked: they may only last a day or two (searing the stem ends helps prolong their vase life), but the fact that you've picked the flowers or newly formed seedheads – and will go on doing so – can double their garden life and your enjoyment of them.

If you are planning on going away during July, invite friends and family to come and pick your flowers to their heart's content – just remember to show them where on the stem to cut and how to condition them – and you'll return to

Opposite My cutting patch in 2023 with sweet peas, including *Lathyrus odoratus* 'King Edward VII', 'Almost Black' (in foreground) and 'Judith Wilkinson', 'Emilia Fox', 'Matucana' and 'Winston Churchill' (on the frame at the back). Also *Euphorbia oblongata* and *Ammi majus* for foliage, plus the bloomy-blooms of *Cosmos bipinnatus* 'Rubenza' and *Malope trifida* 'Vulcan' – the former just coming out as the latter becomes less prolific.

Below The gymkhana-like rosettes of *Echinacea purpurea* 'Summer Salsa', *Echinacea* 'Eccentric' and 'Marmalade' with *Cosmos bipinnatus* 'Rubenza' and *Dahlia* 'Magenta Star'.

Next page Solar lights strung up for a party in the Perennial Cutting Garden.

a full, flowery garden. The old saying, the generous gardener has the most flowers, is never truer than now.

As well as a huge array of annuals, dahlias are also coming on stream. It's no secret that I love dahlias, and we have a patch dedicated to them, interplanted with narcissi, alliums and hyacinths (see p391). I recommend creating a bed that includes exactly these plants and to make it as large as you can to generate a really generous harvest. Dahlias dominate in September (see p333), but your vases will start to include them by the middle of July, or even earlier if you grow the single and semi-double-flowered forms.

The Bishop, Honka and the Anemone-flowered varieties start to bloom from late June onwards, with *Dahlia* 'Totally Tangerine' usually the first. They are absolute stalwarts from this moment on.

With simple planning, abundance in July is a given, so this is a good time to focus on flower form and, with that, each plant's unique role in the vase. Make sure you grow a good range of shapes, habits and forms – of flowers *and* foliage – in the right quantities, so you always have the material to create incredible vases. See p47 for more on form and foliage.

Above The beautiful poppy, *Papaver rhoeas* 'Amazing Grey', which lasts two to three days in a vase with stem ends seared. Opposite A jumble of hardy annuals with edible flowers (*Calendula officinalis* 'Neon', 'Indian Prince' and 'Sunset Buff', with *Centaurea cyanus* 'Black Ball') picked to decorate salads in Perch Hill's school kitchen – but then deemed too nice to decapitate.

Sometimes you may just want a bunch of bloomy-blooms, with saucer shapes, spires or pompoms (the three classic flower forms), arranged in jugs and vases on their own, a simple mass of one beautiful thing. Or you might want to pair a saucer-shaped flower, such as cosmos, with a different form, say, a pompom or a spire.

For early summer and midsummer, English marigolds are the perfect example of a saucer or 'face' flower, and they are one of the simplest cut flowers you can grow. I've had the crimson-backed *Calendula officinalis* 'Indian Prince' in the Cutting Garden every year for over 30 years and I'd be bereft without it looking splendid in vases, jugs and jam jars on its own. And I often pick it to mix with the black-button-like cornflower, *Centaurea cyanus* 'Black Ball', which flowers at the same time. Both, incidentally, are edible flowers that we use a lot; we scatter their petals over salads and puddings. I also love the subtle tones of *C. o.* 'Sunset Buff', which has soft apricot petal fronts and crimson backs. This is a pivotal flower for the soft and warm Cashmere Jersey palette (see p62) and we pick it by the bucket-load.

Opposite top left A posy I picked as I walked round the garden, including *Cosmos bipinnatus* 'Double Click Cranberries' with the flowers and buds (as the upper storey) of *Scabiosa atropurpurea* 'Black Cat'.

Opposite top right A pure-white arrangement of hardy annuals in our Nero vase to light a dark corner of our sitting room. I've picked *Ammi majus*, *Malope trifida* 'Alba', *Centaurea cyanus* 'White' and *Clarkia pulchella* 'Snowflake'.

Opposite bottom left One of my favourite ways of quickly and easily filling a table with flowers is to top a pewter tray with mini vases. Here, *Cosmos bipinnatus* 'Fizzy Rose Picotee' and *Petunia* 'Tidal Wave Silver', together with two foliage plants, *Ammi visnaga* and *Plectranthus argentatus* 'Silver Shield'. This takes just a few minutes to pick, condition and arrange.

Opposite bottom right A Bristol blue, bedside table vase with the rich-coloured *Cosmos bipinnatus* 'Rubenza' and 'Dazzler'.

Wonderful at this time of year are malopes, both the rich magenta *Malope trifida* 'Vulcan', with its vivid green eye, and the pretty, pure white, 'Alba'. These have magnificent, saucer-shaped flowers. Make the most of them right now. They flower for most of summer and then have elegant seedheads. I love these arranged on their own, but they're even better mixed with *Scabiosa atropurpurea* 'Black Cat'. That makes one of my favourite summer combinations, both grown together and picked for a vase. When the malope has gone over, a rich-coloured cosmos makes the perfect replacement, such as *Cosmos bipinnatus* 'Double Click Cranberries' or 'Rubenza'.

The spires of snapdragons are at their peak now too, and they come in pretty much any colour these days, bar blue. Rich velvet textures are the name of the game here, with metre-high flower stems and a vase life of ten days. They are instantly and easily spectacular. If you prefer pastel colours, go for *Antirrhinum majus* 'White Giant' and 'Appleblossom', the latter is a snapdragon variety that has the bonus of a cinnamon scent. These are great in a tall vase, just on their own, or fluffed out with ammi and combined with a matching cosmos. This gives you spires and saucers, which is always a good flower shape combination (pictured on p282).

I love to pick poppies for vases in July, as transient as they are. To get as many on show at the same time, I often sit and gently peel back the calyx enclosing their flowers so that they all emerge to give major brouhaha.

As the weeks go by, the cosmos becomes a mainstay and remains so until the middle of autumn. Cosmos flowers are perfect for smaller arrangements and hand-tied bunches, or as fillers for whopper vases, backed by, say, a dahlia or sunflower, which has a bit more heft.

Cosmos bipinnatus 'Purity' is the pure white, classic cut flower and border filler, which gives a bigger harvest per square metre than any plant we've ever grown (see p22). The newly bred 'Apricotta' is subtle and beautiful, ideal for the soft, warm Cashmere Jersey palette. That's become a favourite of mine, as is the rich, velvety, top class 'Rubenza'. Or select one of the smaller, container compatible forms, such as 'Sonata White' or 'Sonata Carmine', for pots and window boxes. All are great arranged on their own or with echinacea, zinnias or dahlias in harmonious or contrasting shades.

All of these flowers will give you simple vases, which are often enough just as they are, but sometimes one wants more.

Opposite My favourite jade glass vase with *Ammi majus* as a simple cloud foliage base and a classic July/August mix of harmonious *Antirrhinum majus* 'Costa Silver' and 'Appleblossom' in soft pink with just the lightest contrast from the pink and apricot *Cosmos bipinnatus* 'Apricot Lemonade'. Below One of the best forms of oregano from our trials, *Origanum laevigatum* 'Herrenhausen'.

That's where having varied, interesting, beautiful foliage is a boon, and in July, there's an abundance of possibilities for these background flowers and leaves. They may not be bloomy-blooms, but these fillers and more architectural stems look good in silhouette, emerging out the top of a bunch or vase. See p49 for a breakdown of the different foliage types.

Euphorbia oblongata is looking good from a spring or autumn sowing. If you keep picking it, it will remain zingy and bright, or you may want the colour to mellow a little. To achieve this, don't harvest it all, rather let some stems mature. And *Ammi majus* and *A. visnaga* are at their peak right now, too. June and July are their main months for harvest.

At this time of year, I also pick an array of herbs as foliage. With stem ends seared, many have a long vase life, reaching a couple of weeks in the case of mint. Oregano, lemon balm, hyssop, scented-leaf pelargoniums and even flat-leaved parsley are excellent to use as foliage, and are all at peak production. Some will even be flowering now, including oregano and the agastache crew. Of these, the most vigorous and quick-growing are giant hyssop 'Rose Mint' (*Agastache pallidiflora* var. *neomexicana* 'Rose Mint'). Perennial herbs keep on looking

Below left Variegated pineapple mint (*Mentha suaveolens* 'Variegata').
Below right Bowles's mint (*Mentha × villosa* var. *alopecuroides*).
Opposite French tarragon (*Artemisia dracunculus* French) and giant hyssop 'Rose Mint' (*Agastache pallidiflora* var. *neomexicana* 'Rose Mint').

good and taste stronger if you cut them down to the ground, water and then let them regrow. So picking them is an all-round good plan rather than leaving them to run up to flower and set seed.

Mint adds both scent and strong structural stems to an arrangement. For a pastel combination, I tend to pick the variegated pineapple mint (*Mentha suaveolens* 'Variegata'). And I find the felted, silvery Bowles's mint (*Mentha × villosa* var. *alopecuroides*) goes well with every palette, even the dark. Its velvety texture helps it fit in, even though it's a strong contrast.

The other posse of invaluable foliage providers in July are hardy annuals as they begin to run to seed. Nigella pods, like green footballs, make excellent primary foliage if you pick whole stems. They act as structural sieves into which you can drop other ingredients, holding them in a sort of loose, lacy net. Used as single stems, they also work as filler foliage, nestled in between the stems of a primary foliage, such as euphorbia. And they are perfect hovering as mini balloons right out the top as an upper storey.

Opium poppy seedheads serve a similar purpose; we harvest lots while they're still silvery and fresh. And finally, this is the moment for using biennial honesty (*Lunaria annua*) seed pods, before they turn papery and dry. We harvest as much as we can when it is at the green stage. Again, tucked in as a filler or sitting proud above a vase or bunch, it creates a hovering silhouette and is top class.

The great thing about July is that you're spoilt for choice when it comes to flower and foliage forms. It's just a question of deciding which ones to grow and pick.

Picking and Arranging

Opposite Cut flowers picked to decorate Perch Hill's school and greenhouse dining room for one of our July open days. *Lathyrus odoratus* 'King's Ransom', *L.* × *hammettii* 'Erewhon' and *Malope trifida* among the phlox, ammi, sunflowers, scabious and nasturtiums.
Right This is the Annual Cutting Garden on the day I harvested some of the flowers for the bunch pictured on p289. There's *Nicotiana* 'Whisper Mixed', *Ammi majus*, *Echium vulgare* 'Blue Bedder' and *Antirrhinum majus* 'Appleblossom' and 'White Giant'.

July is a massively rewarding moment in the cutting patch, but with heat and light levels often at their peak, conditioning anything you pick is key to maximising the impact of the harvest. See the Vase Life chapter on p78 for tips. The picture on p90 shows our flower room: it's cool and shaded, and the kettle is constantly on the boil as we sear almost every stem as quickly as possible.

Simple Hand-tied Bunches

I love to create light, ethereal, hand-tied bunches as I walk round the July garden. It breaks the rules, of course, picking into one's hand, rather than following the advice I have stressed about picking and plonking stems into a bucket of water. But, if done on a cool day, this is a quick and easy way to bring flowers into the house. It should take less than five minutes to get a decent-sized arrangement in hand, so you can fill the house with several bunches in 30 minutes.

The key thing when creating a bunch on the go is to keep it simple. I am still following my rules around foliage (see p49), colour palettes (see p57) and my classic recipe starring the Bride (see p47). But it's all pared back to a minimum.

I recommend three or four ingredients: one or two foliage plants, these are often umbellifers for small bunches; and two flowers (such as the Bride and Gatecrasher). This selection can be all in one palette, or even a dominant colour, with just one Gatecrasher for contrast.

Primary foliage *Ammi majus*, 7 stems
Secondary foliage *Orlaya grandiflora*, 7 stems
Bride *Nicotiana* 'Whisper Mixed', 11 stems
Gatecrasher *Papaver rhoeas* 'Amazing Grey', 7 flower stems and 7 bud stems

Opposite A July hand-tied bunch made as I walked round the garden. There are flowers only here, with the Bride acting as the foliage to create the structural sieve into which everything else is threaded. I seared the stem ends of the whole bunch for five seconds.

Foliage / Bride
Trachymene coerulea, 10 stems

Bridesmaid
Lathyrus odoratus 'Albutt Blue', 7 stems

Bridesmaid
Phlox drummondii '21st Century Blue Star', 7 stems

Gatecrasher
Phlox drummondii 'Crème Brûlée', 7 stems

Step 1

Go for an open, airy flower first, ideally with a plateau shape, to create a structural base. I've used *Ammi majus* here, ensuring the selected stems are straight (quite often the heads curve at the stem's apex). Almost any umbellifer works in the same way, particularly the ones with decent saucer-sized flowers.

Step 2

I've chosen a whiter-than-white umbel – *Orlaya grandiflora* – as my next ingredient to add freshness to this bunch while filling out the structure. With your arrangement in one hand, poke the stems in from the top, dotting it throughout the ammi.

Step 3

For my Bride, I've chosen something that will create an upper storey – something that bounces and sways above the rest of the arrangement and gives an interesting horizon (a sense of height and width). I've chosen *Nicotiana* 'Whisper Mixed', which brings a splash of pink in contrast to the whites. Thread this in from the top, using the ammi and orlaya as a sort of sieve that catches the stems and holds them in place.

Step 4

For glamour, I've used short-lived poppies. *Papaver rhoeas* 'Amazing Grey' is a classic saucer flower with beautiful buds, like crumpled silk. Seek out equal numbers of buds as open flowers to give the arrangement greater longevity. Once cut, if fully unravelled, these poppies only hold their petals for a couple of days, but they are worth it. Dot the poppies through, some at the plateau level of the bunch, others standing proud. Again, poke these in from the top.

Step 5

Trim the stem ends at the bottom so they are all the same length. Tie the bunch using a simple knot. Take a length of twine and double it over. Wrap it around the bunch and feed the two loose ends of twine through the loop on the other side. Pull one end around the bunch to the left and the other end around the bunch to the right. Tie and cut off the excess twine.

Step 6

Plunge the stem ends into boiling water for roughly five seconds. Immediately place the bunch into its final vase of cold water to cool the stems. Once in the vase, cut the string and settle the whole bunch so it relaxes. If you don't need them immediately, keep the flowers somewhere cool and darkish, so they can acclimatise to life indoors.

Edible Arrangements

I've always loved vegetables in arrangements as it so instantly suggests homegrown and of the earth. That, for me, is a good thing. And there's an excellent tradition of it. Constance Spry – a pioneering florist of the mid-twentieth century – used kale and leeks in her arrangements. Shane Connolly, one of the greatest British florists of our time, has taken on the mantle. I remember him demonstrating an arrangement using courgette leaves whitened by mildew, mixing them with twirling clematis vines and soft-coloured roses. The beautiful, marbled courgette leaves instantly dispelled any twee sweetness – just three leaves transformed the vase.

I have a few favourite edibles I use in the summer. For scale and boldness, you can't go wrong with a chunky kale or brussels sprout leaf. And for delicacy, I love peas, broad beans, and yellow or crimson runner and French beans, plus figs and the Texan cherry tomato, *Solanum lycopersicum* 'Micro Cherry'. At just the right size and scale, all of these edibles fit well with flowers, their fruits or pods hanging on their stems in an elegant way.

And if you grow pea and bean varieties that also have rich-coloured flowers, you've got double the bounty. We grow the broad bean *Vicia faba* 'Crimson Flowered' for its edible

Top I love filling our kitchen table with ornamental, edible crops. Here, alongside the purple-podded pea, *Pisum sativum* 'Blauwschokker', I've picked kale leaves, crimson-flowered broad beans and tomato axillary buds that were pinched out.

flowers more than for the beans themselves. I'm also mad about the climbing French bean *Phaseolus vulgaris* 'Monte Gusto', which has yellow beans, and the scarlet-flowered, black-podded runner bean, *Phaseolus coccineus* 'Black Knight'. For peas, we grow *Pisum sativum* 'Blauwschokker'. I like to split open the pods using the tip of a small, sharp kitchen knife: score the line where the two sides of the pod join. Always choose pods that are not quite ripe as they give the loveliest, freshest colour and the peas are small and tightly held so they won't fall out (as they do when ripe). Once in the vase, place them where they will be backlit and they will glow like an intricate piece of Murano glass.

Right *Pisum sativum* 'Blauwschokker' with *Lathyrus odoratus* 'Lord Nelson'.
Below left Carefully score the pea with the point of a sharp knife at the join.
Below right Open out the pea pod so you get the contrast of the purple pod and green peas.

PRACTICAL

July

Opposite **Harvesting hardy annual seedheads** – poppies and nigella – to dry for winter arrangements.

Things are really calming down in the Cutting Garden now and there is time to sit out and relax. I often forget to stop in this way, but you learn so much by sitting and looking.

There is one experience that stands out as one that changed me as a gardener. It was a rare few days when I was on my own, and I had a book deadline. I was late to deliver and needed to put the hours in. To make the whole process more enjoyable, I decided to move a table and chair out to the Perennial Cutting Garden. The weather was perfect and, in the end, I spent most of the day just looking at, and being in, the garden. It was early summer and the lupins were at their most splendid, but we had a bad case of lupin aphid, along with a heavy infestation of less specialist aphids, coating and devouring an increasing number of stems.

The evening before, I had used a hose to jet the aphids off the flower spires – that's a good way to get rid of them – but it only works if they haven't already got hold in great numbers. I was pretty sure I'd left it too late. That would be that for my beloved lupins.

But, sitting about ten metres away that morning, I noticed a clutch of just-fledged blue tits, still pretty rough with their new punk-rocker plumage, moving in a continual circuit between the hedgerow and the lupins. Once there, they were hopping round at ground level for a moment and then, one by one, proceeding up the flower spires.

Soon a pair of blackbirds came to join them and then three robins down at ground level. After an hour, I went to see what was going on. Throughout the whole line of lupins, 30 plants at least, there was not a single aphid.

This was my eureka moment: look after the garden birds and they'll help keep pests under control (see more on p201 and p343). But there was more to it than that. I wouldn't have realised this if I hadn't been sitting out in the garden, for a good long time, watching how it was working as an ecosystem. Just sitting can make you a better gardener. So, as I often say to myself, don't always be in a rush!

Luckily, there are very few jobs to do at this moment. As we harvest, we deadhead the flowers. It slows us down a bit, but gets two jobs done in one go. If we have not picked for a few days, some hardy annual stems are bound to be running to seed, and it's off with their heads! Unripe, spent heads go in one bucket (for the compost heap), fresh flowers, fit for drying, in bucket that had some water in.

There are two other things we harvest at this time: hardy annual seedheads for drying and also seeds. As we harvest the hardy annual seedheads – poppies, nigella and cornflowers – to use for winter arrangements, the flowers are bunched and hung upside down. For drying, cornflowers are picked either in bud or in full flower, not when they're going over, because their garden and vase life is very short. Hung upside down, they keep their colour and dry well. Their seed is also very easy and rewarding to harvest (each seed looks like a tiny paintbrush). To save the seed, go for the flower heads that are going over and dry them in the same way before collecting the seed.

Biennials sown last month also need sorting in July. If sown under cover in seed

PRACTICAL

Below Mulching with our own compost around second planting of scabious.

trays, they'll need pricking out. If sown direct into the garden, they will need thinning out. And there's usually a small amount of planting to do now – perhaps a few biennials that are ready early, such as wallflowers, and half-hardy and hardy annual seedlings that were sown late. For example, if you did a May sowing of snapdragons and a June sowing of rudbeckia, *Salvia viridis* blue-flowered and cerinthe, these can all go out. They are all hardy enough to take a few cold nights so will be invaluable for an autumn to winter harvest.

And finally, one of the most commonly asked questions at this time of year is about watering and feeding our cut flower patches, particularly our dahlias. As a basic rule of thumb, we hardly ever water, even in the hotter, often dry months of June and July. And we don't feed at this time of year either. We rely on organic matter added to the soil in spring and autumn (and/or on planting out) to give our plants health and strength.

Watering

We have a farmer's attitude to watering our cut flower areas: it's done infrequently or not at all; and when we do water, we give things a thorough soaking. Light watering does not penetrate, it will simply evaporate and won't do the plant roots much good. Thorough watering, very occasionally, is a much better practice (see p235). That way, the water penetrates deep, down to the micro water roots, sustaining the plant, but also reaching levels where it can be stored rather than evaporate.

If you have plenty of organic matter added to your soil, it helps hugely. We plant sweet peas with lots of organic matter at the roots, but with most other plants, we water and then top mulch when we plant out.

We mulch deeply, spreading a carpet of organic matter on top of the soil in autumn, when we put our dahlias to bed, and again in the spring, as we're planting out. All this means our soil holds on to plenty of water.

On free-draining chalk or sand, watering fortnightly may be required. How do you know? Look at your plants and they'll tell you. They start to wilt if they're badly water deprived. The softer, lusher flowers – particularly spires – usually show the signs first, so keep an eye on lupins, foxgloves and snapdragons for an early warning.

Below **Watering comfrey feed at the base of sweet pea plants.**

Feeding

The only thing we feed in the Cutting garden at this time of year are sweet peas. We make comfrey feed (see p236) and water the plants at their roots. Comfrey feed is rich in potash, which is necessary for good root, flower and fruit formation, and it is an important tonic for sweet peas. We have found in our trials that using it every ten days or so, particularly towards the end of the season, significantly prolongs flowering and helps keep mildew at bay.

To use the comfrey feed, dilute with water to a ratio of about 1 part to 10 parts in a watering can and then water plants liberally.

We also use comfrey feed to reactivate our compost heap. You can just spread the comfrey leaves straight on to the compost in layers. Or, for a supercharged effect, water the heap well with water and then sprinkle on the comfrey feed in its concentrated form.

PRACTICAL

Below, clockwise from top right Harvesting the seed of wild carrot (*Daucus carota*); seedheads of *Papaver somniferum* 'Dark Plum'; harvesting seed of yellow rattle (*Rhinanthus minor*); and, collecting seed from *Cerinthe major* 'Purpurascens'.

Harvesting Seed

By July, some hardy annuals will have started to go over. It's important to keep an eye on them so you know what to remove and when. In most cases, we want to avoid the annuals scattering tons of seed everywhere, as we find this gets a bit overwhelming. It's best to get the plants out before the seed is 100 per cent ripe and harvest it instead.

For long-season flowerers, such as scabious and *Salvia viridis*, cut the plant back by around a third. Prune the whole line or block of plants to the same level with hedging shears; you don't need to do this delicately. With these plants, we find cutting them back spurs them into producing axillary buds and new flowers about two weeks later, and they'll continue until September, the scabious even longer. Collect the trimmed stems and dry them according to the instructions that follow.

Most of the other plants – such as nigella, ammi, malope, cornflowers, annual poppies, cerinthe and calendula – don't reflower when cut back, so just uproot these as the seedheads turn brown. Spread the plants out on a tarpaulin or sheet. Use scissors to cut off the seedheads before putting the rest of the plant on the compost heap. Nigella cross breeds, as do opium poppies, so they are unlikely to come true from seed, but they're still lovely.

1. Whichever way you harvest, bunch the seedheads together in small bunches and hang them somewhere dry.
2. Envelop the bottom of each bunch with a brown paper bag or cotton or hessian bag or even a pillowcase. Ensure there is plenty of space for each bunch in its bag as you need good air circulation below.
3. Attach the bag to the bunch with an elastic band. The rubber shrinks back as the stems dry and holds them firm.
4. The seeds will drop to the bottom of the bag in a few weeks.
5. Once the seed has dropped, sort the seed from the husk and clumps of grit or dry soil. You can use a fine mesh sieve for this. Store in paper bags, which can then go into a clip-lock box, ideally with a silica sachet inside to keep everything dry. Place in the fridge.

August

August is another carnival month in the garden – it's full to bursting with floral fireworks, bold colours and a brilliant sense of energy. There are still a few soft, cloud-forming flowers, with pale and white cosmos at their peak, but it's the more robust, fiesta flowers that take centre stage.

Overall the colour palette is strong. Rockets of gladioli are shooting up through the Catherine wheel dahlias and we usually have our second flush of lupins, with their vertical plumes standing proud. There are zinnias in every shade; velvet rudbeckias and amaranths; double echinaceas; and heleniums, sunflowers and snapdragons all producing buckets of flowers to fill our vases. We're also harvesting nasturtiums along with Mexican marigolds – these look great, and their flowers are edible too, so we use them to top our salads and puddings throughout August.

Let's start with the gladiolus, which as a bulb (technically a corm) is not cut-and-come-again, but we grow it in such a way that it is perennial. Planted through our dahlias, with a top-up of new trial varieties each spring, the gladioli get mulched with the dahlias in the autumn. Sitting under 15cm (6in) of compost during the cold, wet months, they overwinter in the ground well. They're now coming back with us reliably year on year, reaching their peak in August, so they provide great value and have become an ideal partner to our dahlias.

When selecting new varieties to plant in May, we go for gladioli that will either offer maximum contrast, or as near a colour match as possible to the dahlias. I love the lime-green *Gladiolus* 'Green Star', which lifts the rich textures and colours of nearly black dahlias, such as *Dahlia* 'Rip City' or

Opposite A harvest from the Cutting Garden, including a plethora of dahlias, a few gladioli and a range of perennials such as asters and persicaria, with the velvet tassels of *Amaranthus* 'Red Army' for invaluable foliage.

Below Our dahlia and gladioli trial beds with a couple of stellar grasses in the foreground, *Chasmanthium latifolium* to the right and *Panicum capillare* 'Sparkling Fountain' to the left. We pick in good quantities now and on through the autumn.

'Sam Hopkins'. Equally strong is the contrast between an orange dahlia, such as the hugely productive 'Blitzer' (grown widely in the Netherlands as a cut flower), and one of the almost black gladioli, like *Gladiolus* 'Espresso', 'Belle de Nuit' or 'Black Surprise'.

For harmony, *Dahlia* 'Perch Hill' perfectly matches *Gladiolus* 'Chocolate'. Varieties of gladioli (or maybe just their names) seem to come and go, but there are always plenty of unusual colours to choose from to layer in between your dahlias, thereby upping the square-metre productivity in the easiest of ways.

Sticking with bulbs, lilies are luxurious to pick, in fact almost too much so for me to harvest more than the odd stem. They're one of those flowers, like peonies, that I'd rather buy, not grow as cut flowers. That doesn't mean we don't have them in the garden in dappled shade, where I adore their exotic, towering stems that reappear, taller and more flowery every year.

My two favourites are *Lilium henryi* and *L. speciosum* var. *rubrum*, which both flower in August. I usually allow myself to pick a few stems. They last two weeks if kept cool, and I relish their architectural elegance. When picking lilies, if you want them to come back well the following year, leave one third

Opposite top I love the architectural elegance of *Lilium henryi* and *Lilium* 'Black Beauty', which both last ten days or more in a vase.

Opposite bottom A bedside arrangement of *Zinnia elegans* 'Queen Lime Red' and *Phlox drummondii* 'Cherry Caramel', with just a few stems of *Calendula officinalis* 'Sunset Buff'.

of each stem and the foliage that goes with it. That enables sufficient photosynthesis to continue, feeding the bulb to support perenniality.

Another queen of the August cutting garden is the zinnia. Zinnias are being bred in more and more amazing shapes and colours and have become hugely popular with flower farmers in the UK. Bred mainly in the hotter, sunnier USA, zinnias used to be temperamental flowers that struggled and sulked in dreary, wet, British summers. I would lose at least 50 per cent of *Zinnia elegans* 'Envy' to botrytis every year, but this hardly seems to infect newly bred forms, and particularly when we have a good season. Zinnias now form hedges nearly one metre high by late summer.

I love green flowers and a long-standing favourite zinnia is 'Benary's Giant Lime'. I'd been growing 'Envy' for years and loved it (in fact it features on the first page of *The Cutting Garden*, the book I wrote some 30 years ago), but it was prone to fungal diseases. The Benary's Giant series is hugely improved, strong and healthy. I also adore the faded colours in the Queen series, particularly *Z. elegans* 'Queen Lime Red'. Erin Benzakein and her team at Floret (a popular USA flower farm and cut-flower seed producer) is also breeding some interesting soft-coloured mixes, which we've been trialling for the last couple of years.

To grow zinnias, sow into Jiffy 7s or gutter pipes. Or direct sow into pots or a border (at the front), ensuring seeds are well-spaced; thin the subsequent seedlings in situ. No zinnia likes root disturbance. And they hate cold nights, so wait until late April/early May to sow and the end of May for planting out.

Sunflowers are also at their best now. We plant them alongside our paths to create avenues and love to pick them. They are fantastic for pollinators (particularly bees), as well as birds, of course. We have droves of garden birds that flutter through our sunflower jungle, feasting on the seeds as they ripen. It can feel like a natural aviary. As well as plenty of great tits and blue tits, we've got a pair of marsh tits that visit every afternoon. They go for the sunflower hearts and strip them one by one, then hide the seeds in the top of our chestnut posts or cracks in the walls of the shed.

Sunflowers never fail to be impressive in a vase. We grow the odd yellow sunflower, but increasingly prefer the clarets and the café au lait varieties, mixed with a crimson such as *Helianthus annuus* 'ProCut Plum' or 'Ruby Eclipse'. I've grown the smaller-flowered *Helianthus debilis* 'Vanilla Ice' now for three decades, and I still love it. It has a shorter, bushier form

Right Flower heads of the excellent, new, vigorous and disease-resistant *Zinnia elegans* Queen series floating in a bowl.
Opposite top My pride and joy late last summer and into autumn was the tastiest ever climbing French bean, *Phaseolus vulgaris* 'Monte Gusto', paired with *Helianthus annuus* 'ProCut Plum'. Not only beautiful in a jungly way, but also edible.
Opposite bottom left A sweet pea frame clad with sunflowers (*Helianthus annuus* 'Claret') in early autumn, providing a perch for blue tits to feed on its seedheads.
Opposite bottom right A vase of the beautiful, muted sunflower, *Helianthus annuus* 'Ruby Eclipse' in our hall.
Next page The Perennial Cutting Garden at its frothy, August peak with heleniums, eryngiums, dahlias, gaillardia, *Setaria viridis* and tagetes. And the lupins are giving us a light third flowering.

compared with the *H. annuus* varieties, and even without pinching produces a much greater number of smaller flowers that easily fit in the palm of a hand. That makes it ideal for hand-tied bunches.

A good bridge between the saturated colours and the soft pastel flowers is the superb annual *Phlox drummondii*. Annual phlox cuts brilliantly, and with stem ends seared, lasts a week in water. We use the deep red and velvety '21st Century Crimson' in lots of our containers, and we grow good, wide lines of 'Crème Brûlée' and 'Cherry Caramel'. Both have flimsy stems (particularly 'Crème Brûlée'), but grown with jute netting to support them (see p265), they're one of my go-to August flowers.

Grasses provide another bridge between the different August colours, combining equally well with all four colour palettes. You name it, we grow it, from stipa and setaria to panicum and wangenheimia (along with briza and lagurus, though both are mainly over by this time of year) – and we are always on the lookout for more. One word of warning: some of the grains and grasses, setaria in particular, self-sow prolifically, so pick them hard to keep them under control.

Below *Echium vulgare* 'Blue Bedder' and *Cosmos bipinnatus* 'Xsenia' are great together in a border and picked for a vase.
Opposite top left A mix of *Cosmos bipinnatus* 'Apricot Lemonade', 'Xanthos', 'Apricotta', 'Candy Stripe' and 'Fizzy Rose Picotee'.
Opposite top right I love this mix of *Cosmos bipinnatus* 'Apricotta', *Coreopsis* 'Redshift', *Dahlia* 'Kelsey Annie Joy' and *Bidens ferulifolia* 'Hot and Spicy'.
Opposite bottom left *Cosmos bipinnatus* 'Apricot Lemonade'.
Opposite bottom right A pastel sweet mix of *Cosmos bipinnatus* 'Purity', 'Xanthos', 'Fizzy Rose Picotee' and 'Versailles Tetra'.

But don't let that put you off: all of them create ripples of movement and airiness in the garden, as well as many of our vases, throughout summer and into autumn, when their colours soften and fade. Many are also great for drying (see p323).

If you love soft, gentle and romantic, cosmos are at their cloud-forming peak right now. Pink and yellow were never to be seen together ten years ago, but are currently all the rage. Snapdragons can give you that colour pairing (see the Snapdragon Love Heart arrangement on p317), as can cosmos. Look to the newly bred *Cosmos bipinnatus* 'Xanthos' and pick with any of the soft pinks, such as 'Sonata Pink' or 'Versailles Tetra'. And with 'Apricot Lemonade', a new and already popular form, you've got the yellow-pink pairing in one flower.

I love this moment in the garden, but mourn it a little too as one's attention starts to turn to planning and planting for next year. The mid-twentieth-century writer and gardener Vita Sackville-West referred to summer as a garden's middle age, compared with the adolescence of spring, and that's what August in particular feels like.

Picking and Arranging

Opposite A bucket of dahlias, zinnias, hydrangeas and sunflowers on a bench in the cutting garden at Chatsworth House, picked by Becky Crowley who was then the cut-flower grower there.

With so many showstoppers in the garden, now is the perfect time to make two classic cut-flower-garden arrangements: a large vase brimming with different flower ingredients and a hand-tied bunch. I think of both as the florist's store-cupboard essentials, the skill of making them is well worth mastering.

Whether it be for a vase or hand-tied bunch, when picking for a mid-sized, mixed arrangement I select six plants I want to arrange with: three foliage plants and three flowering ones. I sometimes pick seven, by adding a fourth foliage plant (such as a trailing vine), to add in as a finishing touch. For an overview of the foliage I recommend and its purpose, see p49. For the flowers, I always pick in odd numbers: five stems, seven, nine and so on. The irregularity makes an arrangement feel more natural. For an overview of the recipe I use, see Form from p46.

And I recommend always cutting to scale to suit the size of the arrangement. I want my arrangement to have a few stems that are very tall – at least three times the height of the vase – to give it airiness. And I want some stems splaying out, so the overall breadth of the arrangement is about four or five times the width of the vase diameter. This makes for a glamorous and relaxed look. So don't pick stems too short, but not too long either, because that's a waste – you lose all the flower buds on the unused length of stem. With perennials and shrubs, it's especially important to pick sensitively; look at the plant to see how you could improve, or at least not impair, its shape. Don't pick your stems all in one place – take one here, one there, so that you're thinning out, not mowing flowers.

As well as picking fresh flowers, we're keeping our eyes peeled now for good seedheads and flowers that dry well and keep their colour and texture to be used in vases, wreaths and swags through the latter part of autumn and winter, including Christmas. So I've added a list of plants that are ideal for dry arrangements.

Nero Vase

There is a shape of vase – I call it the Nero – that is perfect for arranging. The key benefits of the shape are listed on p182, but it essentially makes arranging flowers a breeze and looks good with a mixed bunch or a mass of one thing. In my house, the Nero rarely gets put away.

Primary foliage, 5 branched stems
Aloysia citrodora (lemon verbena)

Secondary foliage, 7 stems
Hydrangea paniculata 'Limelight'

Spiller foliage, 9 vines
Jasminum officinale (jasmine)

Bride, 7 stems
Dahlia 'Otto's Thrill'

Bridesmaid, 9 stems
Dahlia 'Sweet Sanne'

Gatecrasher, 7 stems
Dahlia 'Break Out'

Flowers for small vases
A few stems of the same ingredients, plus *Dahlia* 'Polka' and some sprigs of rosehips

Fill the vase with water and add flower food (you can buy this or use a drop of bleach or a slosh of clear vinegar to stop bacterial build-up). Lay out your conditioned flowers and foliage so you have everything to hand before you start arranging.

Foliage First create a structure using the primary foliage, slotting the stems right down into the base of the vase. Move on through the foliage ingredients, adding them one by one. Use stems of different lengths, to make sure your vase has a heart (the centre and main structure) and a horizon (its height and width). It's a common mistake just to shove the stems in as you have picked or bought them, at completely regular heights. The arrangement then looks boring and two dimensional. Trim some short and leave others long.

Flowers Now add the flowers all the way through the vase. Even though this vase is sitting by a window and you won't see the back, I concentrate on creating an arrangement that looks good in the round – this makes it seem less formal. Slot the stems in from the top. And – as suggested above – cut your stems to different lengths, ensuring some stems emerge from the vase at an almost horizontal angle.

Quantities Don't stuff too much in. It's good to see some air in an arrangement, as you can here, just above the neck of the vase.

Aftercare Top up the vase with water every day. Every second or third day, place the vase in the sink and leave the water running into the vase to flush out and freshen the water. Ideally, add flower food after doing this.

Snapdragon Love Heart

Foliage *Thlaspi arvense* 'Green Bells', 9 stems
Bride *Antirrhinum majus* 'Costa Silver', 9 stems
Bridesmaid *Galega officinalis* – I've picked the mauvy-pink flowers, 9 stems
Gatecrasher *Antirrhinum majus* 'Costa Apricot', 9 stems

This is a very simple arrangement, made with just one fantastic foliage that holds all the flowers in place on its own. Thlaspi has an airy and interesting silhouette, so needs nothing with it. And it allows the snapdragons, in shades reminiscent to pastel sweets, to shine.

Powder Puff Pink

Foliage *Pyrus salicifolia* 'Pendula' (pendulous willow-leaved pear), 9 stems
Bride *Lavatera trimestris* 'Dwarf Pink Blush', 7 stems
Bridesmaid *Linaria purpurea* 'Canon Went', 5 stems
Gatecrasher *Ammi majus*, 11 stems

Again, I've gone for simplicity here, in terms of ingredients: there's only one foliage and three flowers. Having the smaller vases in support elevates it to a showstopper.

Summer Hand-tied Bunch

I think few would dispute that there's nothing better than arriving to dinner with friends with a bunch of flowers – an easy, portable way of gifting them a slice of your garden.

When picking for a hand-tied bunch, you'll usually harvest less than you would for a vase, particularly a Nero vase. You need about five or six ingredients: two or three foliage types and three flowers. You might even manage with just four ingredients: one foliage and three flowers. I pick an average of seven stems of each, depending on the plant's branching characteristics and its overall size. You can also manage with shorter stems for a hand-tied bunch. Around 30cm (12in) is ideal, as it makes it easier to handle the arrangement.

A very neat, spiral hand-tied method is often recommended and practised by florists. But, in my experience, that is tricky to master if you have small hands or you're a beginner. With my alternative system, everything is held together from an early stage using the primary foliage, so you don't have to keep hold of each and every stem as you spiral it into the bunch. It makes the process easier and, in the end, creates a more natural-looking arrangement.

Before you start arranging, clear the decks. As with cooking, you need things tidy and close to hand, especially when one hand is busy holding the bunch. Lay out your conditioned flowers and foliage in the order you will use them. Cut a length of string or ribbon, 1m (3ft) long, double it over and put it to one side.

Primary foliage, 5 stems
Amaranthus 'Red Army'

Secondary foliage, 5 stems
Amaranthus cruentus 'Hot Biscuits'

Bride, 9 stems
Phlox drummondii 'Crème Brûlée'

Bridesmaid, 7 stems
Calendula officinalis 'Sunset Buff'

Gatecrasher, 7 stems
Rudbeckia hirta 'Sahara'

Step 1
Start with your primary foliage to get the scaffolding right first. Holding the bunch in your left hand (if right-handed), use your right hand to add the crimson amaranth stems, one by one – the idea is to form a circular sieve shape. This is the sieve into which everything else will be threaded through. Make sure it is rounded in shape – look down on it, it should not be rectangular or long and thin. Get this bit absolutely right before you move on.

Step 2
Continuing with the bunch in your left hand, add the secondary foliage, one stem at a time, threading it into the stems of the primary foliage from the top, until each is supported on the structure. Then draw each stem in from the bottom with your right hand, until it sits where you want it in terms of place and plain (up high or pulled lower into the heart of the arrangement). Pull, don't push the stems. You'll break them if you push them down into place.

Check you're happy with the foliage before moving onto the flowers. There's no upper storey foliage (such as a grass) in this bunch, because amaranths form such a good silhouette on their own.

Step 3
Go for your Bride next, spacing the stems evenly through the foliage base, again threading through from the top, then pulling the stem from the bottom.

Step 4
From now on, you don't need to thread each stem through from the top, as your hands will get too full to hold everything. When you add the Bridesmaid and Gatecrasher, poke a few in from the top, but also add stems around the edge, ensuring each stem is caught by the foliage structure to hold it in place. With flowers around the edge, as well as the centre, and at different levels, the bunch will have a heart and horizon and lots of points of interest.

Step 5
When you've added all the flowers, pick up your folded ribbon and wrap it around the bunch. Thread the two cut ends through the loop. Then take one end one way around the bunch, and the other end in the opposite direction. This allows you to tighten the ribbon and then twist the ends round the stems again another couple of times to make sure everything is secure.

Step 6
Cut the stem ends to the same length so they retain your design when slotted into a vase. Try not to cut off all the ends you have seared. If you have to, and you have delicate plants like poppies in the bunch, sear the whole bunch again. I always say, searing never does any harm and it does many cut flowers a lot of good.

Sunflowers and Zinnias

Foliage *Ammi majus*, 9 stems
Bride *Helianthus annuus* 'ProCut Plum',
7 stems
Bridesmaids *Phlox drummondii* 'Cherry Caramel' and *Zinnia elegans* 'Cresto Cream',
7 stems of each
Gatecrasher *Rudbeckia hirta* 'Cherry Brandy',
7 stems

This hand-tied bunch is very simple, using only one foliage, one Bride and two tonally linked Bridesmaids. It's constructed in the same way as the Summer Hand-tied Bunch, with the ammi forming the sieve through which you thread everything else.

Velvet Zinnias

Foliage *Nicotiana* 'Lime Green', 7 stems
Bride *Zinnia elegans* 'Benary's Giant Deep Red', 7 stems
Bridesmaid *Rudbeckia hirta* 'Cherry Brandy',
7 stems
Gatecrasher *Zinnia elegans* 'Benary's Giant Lime', 7 stems

For this one, the foliage base is *Nicotiana* 'Lime Green', which forms a great, branched structure into which everything is laced. This bunch is all about the velvet texture of the petals, as well as their colours, and the nicotiana complements this perfectly.

Rich Dahlias

Foliage *Amaranthus* 'Red Army', 5 stems
Bride *Dahlia* 'Nicholas', 7 stems
Bridesmaid *Dahlia* 'Zundert Mystery Fox', 7 stems
Gatecrasher *Dahlia* 'Karma Naomi', 7 stems

This one is simpler still, using one foliage and three flowers. In this case, the amaranth forms the structural sieve.

Everlasting Flowers and Seedheads

This is the month we really start to concentrate on everlastings – dried flowers – which we'll use to decorate Perch Hill through the winter. We've done a lot of trialling and testing of flowers for drying in the last five years, and we've been building up a good range of bunches in our mini drying room. This process begins each April, with tulips hanging, well-spaced, from the ceiling, but August is the month we add more and more, week by week, until the cold and damp set in.

I, like many people of my generation, used to be prejudiced against everlasting flowers. Anything dried, even lavender, carried the whiff of a maiden aunt for me. But that's no longer the case. The first thing that changed my mind was a walk I took a few years ago across the island of Sifnos in Greece. It was May, and the olive groves and hillsides were already brown and burnt to a crisp, all except the wild *Limonium sinuatum* (or statice, as it's commonly known). This had flowered the previous year, but was still pristine, greeting us like a purple flag beside the stony path. Against all the odds, every spire retained its brilliant colour.

I have also been educated recently by several creative floral designers (such as Bex Partridge, Kitten Grayson, Milli Proust and Graeme Corbett), who all use plenty of dried flowers and seedheads in their arrangements, for anything from a Christmas bauble to huge, natural installations for a hotel foyer or gallery. Whole worlds can be created with dried flowers and seedheads, and it's fantastic for extending the life of your cut flowers in the most sustainable and economical way.

Picking and drying practicalities

- Getting stems inside, out of the rain and high levels of humidity in the atmosphere, is key. We've made the mistake in the past of collecting allium seedheads and honesty seedheads and placing them in the polytunnel, but they turn black and start to rot by autumn. Storing them somewhere truly dry is crucial.
- Hanging them upside down, well-spaced, helps the drying process along. With some stems – two examples of many include bells of Ireland (*Moluccella laevis*) and straw flower (*Xerochrysum bracteatum* syn. *Helichrysum*) – it's essential. If you don't hang straw flowers upside down, the stems don't set firm, and bells of Ireland retain their colour better upside down and with good air circulation between the stems as they dry.
- Storing the dried stems carefully, without them touching each other, is also essential. When all our stems are properly dried, we take them down from their hanging hooks and store them flat, wrapped gently in tissue paper or brown paper, ensuring each seedhead is as separate from the next as possible. Chucked in together, they get tangled up, and because they are so fragile – and some as sticky as Velcro – the whole lot will disintegrate when you try to pull them apart.

Opposite Flowers hanging to dry, including zinnias and straw flowers (*Xerochrysum*), along with seedheads of smyrnium, honesty (*Lunaria*) and alliums.

Flowers for Drying

These are the plants we grow each year that can be transformed into beautiful dried flowers and then used in arrangements.

Key
A = Annual
B = Biennial
P = Perennial
Bu = Bulb/Tuber
S = Shrub

- *Acanthus mollis* **'Rue Ledan' (bear's breeches)** A favourite that thrives in shade, flowers prolifically and has much better mildew resistance than the sun-loving *Acanthus mollis*. (P)
- *Achillea* **(yarrow)** Big, flat, saucer flowers. The golden varieties in particular keep their colour well. (P)
- *Acroclinium* **(everlasting)** Mini, papery flowers with starry shapes that last well. (A)
- *Amaranthus* The spires and tassels keep their colour more than their leaves; we grow the crimsons such as 'Red Army' and the caramel-coloured 'Hot Biscuits'. (A)
- *Centaurea* **(cornflower)** The dark cornflower 'Black Ball' keeps its colour better than the blue. (A)
- *Consolida* **(larkspur)** The pink and blue retain their colour best. (A)
- *Cynara* **(artichoke/cardoon)** Place in a vase with just a little water. The stems will absorb a little at a time until the water runs dry and the flowers gradually dry. The dazzling purple lasts for months. (P)
- *Dahlia* The large-flowered varieties age with elegance, especially the crimsons and those with saturated, strong colours. The whites, such as 'Café au Lait', morph into gentle sepia shades. It's a question of preference. Flower size matters as most shrink by about two thirds once fully dried, so small-flowered varieties almost disappear and turn to dust by winter. The same applies to zinnias. Hang individually. (Bu)
- *Gypsophila* **(baby's breath)** The double-flowered forms ('Jolien', for example) last best. (A and P)
- *Helichrysum* **(straw flower)** See *Xerochrysum*.
- *Hydrangea* Almost all are superb and the odd one, like 'Wedding Gown', keeps its crimson colour for years. (S)
- *Limonium* **(statice)** With modern breeding, there are now lovely apricot tones as well as the very bright purple and yellow shades. I love the pink spires of *Limonium suworowii* (syn. *Psylliostachys suworowii*). (A)
- *Moluccella laevis* **(bells of Ireland)** A great apple-green colour. (A)
- *Sanguisorba* **(burnet)** The small, drumstick flowers in clutches dry brilliantly, like crimson caterpillars on the stem. (P)
- *Tulipa* **(tulip)** Doubles, particularly in dark colours, dry best. Hang the stems individually rather than in bunches. (Bu)
- *Xerochrysum*, syn. *Helichrysum* **(straw flower)** Similar to *Acrolinium*, this provides paper stars that last well. Pick when only the first couple of rows of petals have opened and the centre is still closed. They open as they dry and keep their colour. (A)
- *Zinnia* The intense, saturated pinks and reds seem to keep their colour best. Much like dahlias, these get smaller as they dry. (A)

Opposite A towering vase of globe artichokes (*Cynara cardunculus* Scolymus Group) with almost luminous purple flowers. This colour fades in time, but is spectacular into autumn.

Grasses and Grains for Drying

Grasses are utterly invaluable for everlasting vases, adding, even when dried, airiness, movement and an elegant silhouette.

- *Briza maxima* **(greater quaking grass)** Like raindrops on a stem. Pick and store these from May to July. (A and P)
- *Chasmanthium latifolium* **(North American wild oats)** A supremely elegant grass that grows wild in the USA. I love it picked green from August on, and it dries perfectly, like a sheaf of corn, but flat. (P)
- *Hordeum jubatum* **(foxtail barley)** An ornamental grass with great feathery whiskers. (A and P)
- *Lagurus ovatus* **(hare's tail grass)** This has little, white, fluffy pompoms. It's another early hardy annual grass, best picked and stored from May to July. (A)
- *Panicum capillare* **'Frosted Explosion' (witch grass)** One of our all-time favourites, as it's the only grain/grass I've come across that is cut-and-come-again – you can harvest the leader to reveal more buds below. It's also elegant and delicate, like a fibre optic wand in soft brown and green. (A)
- *Panicum miliaceum* **'Violaceum' (millet)** The curving heads tinged with crimson gradually brown. This is also one of the best seed-bearers for garden birds. (A and P)
- *Stipa gigantea* **(golden oats)** We use this grass all the time, both fresh and dried, to add a sparkler effect to arrangements. (P)
- *Wangenheimia lima* **(fishbone grass)** One of my newfound favourites. It looks like a fish skeleton from an old cartoon. (A)

Right *Chasmanthium latifolium*, *Briza maxima* and *Panicum capillare* 'Sparkling Fountain' with metallic-sprayed pumpkin 'Jill be Little' and *Nicandra physalodes*.

Opposite *Allium cristophii* seedheads (with one *A. schubertii*, behind right) and straw flowers drying in our Chelsea shed.

Seedheads for Drying

- *Allium* Dried allium seedheads are everlasting queens. With their sparkler, starry look, we use them a lot at Christmas. (Bu)
- *Angelica* The great, architectural, umbellifer heads last for years. (B)
- *Crocosmia* (**montbretia**) The arching stems create elegant curves. (P)
- *Dipsacus* (**teasel**) Classic, egg-shaped seedheads that last for years. (B)
- *Lunaria* (**honesty**) Coin-like, luminous seedheads that need to be peeled on both sides to be enjoyed at their best. (A and B)
- *Nicandra* (**shoo fly plant**) This has green, Chinese-lantern style seed pods with black markings late in the year. (A)
- *Nigella* (**love-in-a-mist**) The crimson and green seed pods keep their colour best. (A)
- *Papaver* (**poppy**) The pepper pot seedheads of opium poppies (*Papaver somniferum*) are the ones you want. (A)
- *Physalis* (**Chinese lantern**) If dried properly (upside down) they keep their brilliant orange colour for months. (P)
- *Scabiosa stellata* (**starflower scabious**) Papery, spherical seedheads with starry eyes. (A)
- *Selinum wallichianum* An elegant umbellifer that is a bit more robust than cow parsley and so dries and lasts better. (P)
- *Smyrnium perfoliatum* or *S. rotundifolium* These are elegant and long-lasting standing in the garden or picked for a vase. They have a silvery sheen and are one of my all-time favourites when dried. (B)

PRACTICAL

August

Opposite Planting out hardy annual poppies while they're still small, as they don't like being transplanted when large. Below Deadheading dahlias. New buds have a round shape, whereas deadheads are pointed.

With many gardeners juggling the school holidays at this time of year, August is the month people are often away. Conveniently, it's not a busy time in the cutting garden. If you're not picking, make sure you are deadheading every so often. Or better still, why not offer your garden as a free flower source to family or friends in return for watering the odd pot or two while you're away. We don't feed or water our cutting garden in August (see more on that on p235 and p296), so they won't be tasked with a mammoth job.

There are a few bits and bobs to do, such as harvesting seedheads for winter arranging (see p323). And it's often this month we take our sweet peas out. Even though we feed them with comfrey feed (see p236 and p297), they are fading now and starting to look ropey. We cut the vine down to the ground, but leave their nitrogen-fixing roots in the soil.

It's also the time to prune Mediterranean flowering shrubs, such as lavender and rosemary. We rarely prune our rosemary (any that get leggy are replaced with new cuttings), but we do tidy our lavenders. The June flowerers, such as the English lavender, *Lavandula angustifolia* 'Hidcote', will have gone over and can be cut back into neat domes. But leave the French lavenders well alone. They have flowering potential for another good month or so. To prune these, we cut all the dead flowers off and prune above new shoots, never cutting back into old wood. We then end up with a compact, rounded plant that will put on some new growth before winter. We prune again in early spring if necessary.

One of our big preoccupations at this time of year is taking cuttings of our stalwart tender perennials. And our final big job is planting out biennials sown in the last couple of months. We find if we plant these in their final flowering position during August, we're guaranteed whopper plants before the late autumn cold sets in. Their roots develop quickly at this time of year, with the soil warm, but increasingly moist at night. We want to use this naturally perfect growing environment to our advantage for as long as we can. The same rules and system apply for biennials as it does for annuals (see p194 for planting instructions).

PRACTICAL

Opposite Taking cuttings of tender perennial *Heliotrope arborescens* 'Reva', which has a delicious and powerful scent, so is lovely picked for bedrooms and bathrooms right through summer and autumn.

Taking Tender Perennial Cuttings

We find that it's in late summer into autumn that we have the highest success rate with rooting tender perennial plants, including salvias, heliotropes and pelargoniums. Many of these originate in the southern hemisphere, so it's now that their ancestry and genetics tell them it's spring. We can root pelargoniums pretty well in spring too, but salvias definitely give us better results if propagated now. They all play an important role in our arrangements towards the end of the year.

We also propagate rosemary and some lavenders in August and use some of our prunings as cuttings.

- Cut a short piece of stem from the main plant ensuring it is from the current year's growth. Ideally choose a non-flowering stem that has a soft tip but has hardened at the bottom.
- Trim to just below a leaf node (joint), so the cutting is 5–6cm (2in) long. Short cuttings root better than long ones. Just below a leaf node is where there is the highest concentration of natural rooting hormone. We don't use rooting hormone powder as we find a high percentage of our cuttings root consistently and quickly without it.
- Strip off all leaves except the top few.
- Pinch out the stem tip. It's at the top that the growth hormone concentrates, so by pinching it out, apical dominance is removed to encourage root formation.
- Fill a series of small pots with a mix of one-part sand to two-parts compost.
- Insert the cuttings round the edge of the pot, spaced about 4–5cm (1–2in) apart so their leaves don't touch. By placing them round the edge, not in the centre, you encourage quicker root formation, as the new roots hit the side of the pot, then break and branch into more lateral rootlets.
- Water the compost well.
- Place the pot in a polytunnel or greenhouse with shading if it gets too hot.
- Only water when the compost is dry. Avoid water touching the leaves if you can.
- Cuttings often root in 3 to 4 weeks. Check for roots showing in the drainage holes and once formed, pot each cutting on individually.
- If any of the cuttings show the slightest signs of botrytis (browning of the cutting or visible mould), take them out as this will quickly spread to the others.
- Store them under cover through the winter, for planting out next spring.

September

This time of year is all about dahlias. They are the most productive, low maintenance cut-flower crop you can grow. As climate change leads to shorter, milder winters, dahlias can increasingly be treated as perennials, and in all but the coldest, most elevated locations, they can be left in the garden throughout winter. All you need do is cut them back and mulch them deeply in late autumn. They need no more looking after than, say, a peony.

I know peonies aren't in flower in September, but they are many people's favourite cut flower, so the comparison to dahlias is worthwhile. Peonies are glamorous and beautiful, but looked at objectively, they are hopeless flower producers, best left to farmers with plenty of space. Us gardeners should go for dahlias: they are prolifically cut-and-come-again, pumping out more than 30 times the flowers per square metre compared with peonies. I've done exactly that experiment, counting stem by stem, and was flabbergasted by the difference.

And dahlias do this almost immediately, starting to produce flowers within six to eight weeks of their May planting (unlike peonies, which take three years to reach peak production). Several of the Single-flowered, Collarette and Anemone-flowered dahlia forms bloom from mid-June until November, even longer than the stalwart half-hardy annual cosmos. And then, like peonies, they continue on and on for decades, left right where they are.

And with recent breeding, there is a dahlia to suit every taste. No one can truly claim they don't like *any* dahlia. There are bold and brassy ones, crazy spidery ones, delicate and

Opposite Dawn over the dahlia trial beds with *Dahlia* 'Orange Girl' (central), 'Tartan' (stripy tall one), 'American Sunset' (central), 'Copperboy' (at the back) and lots of others scattered through, including 'Manoa', 'Nuit d'Été', 'Cryfield Harmony' and 'Engelhardts Matador'. Plus the annuals *Amaranthus* 'Red Army' and *Nicotiana knightiana*.

Below Buckets of cut flowers being conditioned for the Covid-impacted Chelsea Flower Show in 2021, which unusually took place in September. These include *Cobaea scandens*, *Gladiolus* 'Evergreen', *Cosmos bipinnatus* 'Dazzler', *Helianthus annuus* 'Ruby Eclipse', *Panicum capillare* 'Frosted Explosion' and several dahlias.

sweet ones as pretty as a rose, and some with beautiful, curvy petals and soft colours… just like a peony.

There are also varieties perfect for pollinators at the very moment when forage is becoming sparse. There's still quite a lot in flower across the garden in September, but by late October and November, dahlias are a key source of nectar and pollen before pollinator hibernation.

As cut flowers, they are increasingly stellar. In the old days, you'd be lucky to get five days from a dahlia stem in water, but with recent breeding, this has been improved and there are now dahlias with a vase life of over a week.

The Ball and Pompon forms like 'Vino' and 'Copperboy', together with the matt-petalled 'Night Silence' (a Decorative form), all last six or seven days. And there are three other standout varieties that last a good ten days in a vase if kept cool – 'Perch Hill', 'Molly Raven' and 'Sissinghurst'.

I had a hand in selecting these three in the last few years. 'Sissinghurst' we discovered in a huge trial field in the Netherlands in the summer of 2023. I picked a bunch, dumped it into a bucket in the back of the car and drove home two days later. Even after all that, it went on for a week on our

Above Three of my favourite dahlias, including 'Sissinghurst', 'Waltzing Mathilda' and 'Bishop of Auckland'.
Opposite *Cobaea scandens* and *Thunbergia alata* 'Sunny Susy Brownie' cladding the arches down the central path in the Perennial Cutting Garden.
Next page Dahlia borders leading to what we call our Chelsea shed, including dahlias 'Blue Bayou', 'Labyrinth', 'Gardenetta', 'Bright Eyes', 'Adam's Choice', 'Night Silence', 'Dalaya Aruna' and 'Dreamy Hot Chocolate', with *Antirrhinum majus* 'Costa Apricot' on the right and *Cobaea scandens* growing up the frames.

kitchen table. That's remarkable, and to me, was the final string to the bow of this perfect cut flower. At this time of year in any cutting patch or garden, it should be dahlias all the way!

I think dahlias look best planted with other things in a border. Planted in lines, they can look a little plastic and stiff. You easily get rid of this formality if you grow them with half-hardy climbers, which twist their way through a dahlia gathering, or with gladioli erupting like rockets from their domes (see p301 and p234), or with robust, tall-growing, late-season annuals such as amaranths and the castor oil plant (*Ricinus communis*), which bring different shapes and textures.

We grow *Thunbergia alata* and *Ipomoea lobata* trained up frames and arches all through our dahlia beds, and we also plant them without frames. These climbers happily find their own way up and out into the sun using dahlia stems as their support. You do have to pick and choose which main dahlia stems to harvest, so as not to destroy the climber's frame, but it's worth this extra fiddle for the looseness they provide. And they do just the same in a vase, creating great twists and turns and a sense of movement. We also have *Cobaea scandens* on arches romping up beside our dahlias all summer and autumn.

Below Our main dahlia trial bed at dawn, featuring dahlias 'Perch Hill' and 'Bishop of Auckland' with lots of self-sown dill.
Opposite A perfect colour match of a 'volunteer', self-sown *Persicaria orientalis* with *Dahlia* 'Nashville'.

Dahlia 'Blue Bayou' and cobaea make one of the best-ever pairings. As the autumn weeks progress we pick cobaea's cups and saucers more and more for vases.

Our dahlia beds also feature some fantastic self-sowers that return year after year. Not least because their seeds end up in our homemade compost, which we use as mulch for the dahlias in autumn. So these plants are self-perpetuating, either self-sowing in place or else spreading through the compost mulch. Among them, we have opium poppies (*Papaver somniferum*) growing throughout our dahlia beds. These are over by September, replaced by dill (*Anethum graveolens*), which gives way to *Nicandra physalodes* (shoo fly plant) and the tall *Nicotiana knightiana* and *Persicaria orientalis*. All are what are often referred to as 'volunteers', spreading themselves liberally through our dahlia beds. We're grateful for these as they reach full height right now alongside the dahlias, and we encourage them to make themselves at home. However, we do restrict their numbers by thinning them out at the seedling stage, reducing them by about two thirds. Left to their own devices, they would grow in great numbers and choke the dahlias as their shoots emerge in April and May.

Opposite top A great tit foraging for *Helianthus annuus* 'Claret' seeds.
Opposite bottom *Amaranthus* 'Red Army', *A. cruentus* 'Hot Biscuits' and *Dahlia* 'Bishop's Children' with Swiss chard on the vegetable bank at Perch Hill.

To complement these, we actively plant a few statuesque annuals such as a range of amaranths (*Amaranthus* 'Red Army' and *A. cruentus* 'Hot Biscuits'), as well as sunflowers and the seed-dense *Panicum miliaceum* 'Violaceum' and *P. capillare* 'Frosted Explosion'. The birds love the seeds of these plants so much, they're stripped bare, leaving nothing left to self-sow. We propagate them each year and plant out as many seedlings as we can squeeze in.

They're a great addition to the garden and as cut flowers, but vitally they attract more of the right sort of birds into the patch to feed. With hedges, or vigorous climbers on your fences, and nesting boxes placed in sheltered spots, you can easily give birds a winter hiding place. All these small efforts will encourage them to make a permanent home with you. And when they nest and bring up their young in sight of your dahlia patch, you will have exactly the help you need to keep on top of slug, snail, caterpillar and aphid numbers. At the very moment when the dahlias are vulnerable and sprouting in April and May, many garden bird fledglings are crying out for protein, and we know where we want them to find it! In April, we also push away the mounds of mulch that were protecting the dahlia crowns – as we do, we sometimes find slug or snail eggs. Exposed, they are speedily found and devoured by birds.

With all this in mind, it's worth noting that hedges or densely covered boundary fences are important to a dahlia success story. They help hugely with biodiversity. They also help with the overall aesthetic of the garden, by dividing the space into squares and rectangles to give a bit of visual rigour and crispness to the dahlia chaos. For just this reason, we keep our hawthorn hedges clipped smart and tight when the dahlias are at their peak. Our hedges are shaped to echo the ups and downs of the hills beyond, with a crab apple, *Malus* × *robusta* 'Red Sentinel', planted in every undulation.

The crab apples are just starting to ripen in September, but it's next month that we pick branches for large arrangements, and that's when we notice the birds having a major feast. If the birds are happy, on the whole, so are we – and so are our dahlias!

Opposite top left *Dahlia* 'Burlesca' being conditioned in a bucket.
Opposite top right Arrangement of dahlias 'Peaches', 'Copperboy', 'Josudi Mercury', 'Mats' and 'Apricot Desire'.
Opposite bottom left *Dahlia* 'Rancho' being conditioned in a bucket of water.
Opposite bottom right A hand-tied bunch of pale dahlias, including the elegant fimbriated *Dahlia* 'Tsuki-yori-no-shisha', along with oyster-pink 'Shiloh Noelle' and 'Café au Lait'.

Dahlia Groups

There are 15 dahlia groups, but this selection focuses on the ones that make particularly good cut flowers.

Ball and Pompon

Ball and Pompon dahlias have a drumstick formality and were once deemed uptight, but they are increasingly popular with florists, in large part because of their good vase life. Often referred to as 'buttonholes', for obvious reasons, they are an ideal contrast to the showy dahlia blooms that are so fashionable right now. I came across 'Burlesca' in a Dutch trial field ten years ago and have grown and loved it ever since. Newfound favourites include 'Brown Sugar' and 'Copperboy' in similar rich bronze shades, as well as the trendy neutrals 'Nathalie G', 'Linda's Baby' and the more raspberry toned 'Catlin's Joy'.

Waterlily

These are very neat dahlias shaped like waterlilies, with just a few broad and rounded petals and flat flowerheads. They make good cut flowers with a better than average vase life, and I like 'Rancho' very much.

Cactus, Semi-Cactus and Fimbriated

The classic, spiky flowered Cactus dahlias have the strongest architectural presence as a cut flower, with needle-like petals pointing this way and that. I love them. They are excellent as single stems in individual vases (see p354). And you can't go wrong with the Cactus forms as floating flowers (see p352). Either thread them through a grid to hold their petals out of water and to improve their vase life, or simply plonk them in. I've long loved 'Chat Noir' and 'Nuit d'Été' (which are similar crimson shades), as both pick well. A newer discovery is 'Preference' in a soft pink – it's a cracker, very floriferous with a reasonable vase life. In the Semi-Cactus group, 'Rip City' is the dahlia I have grown and loved for longest.

Fimbriated dahlias have a fringed effect, with highly cut petals. There is often call for a white dahlia, and the most spectacular is 'Tsuki-yori-no-shisha', which has an almost frizzy petal edge.

Opposite top A massive armful of large-flowered dahlias, the main one here is the whopper 'Emory Paul', along with 'Fairway Spur', 'Islander', 'Belle of Barmera' and 'Penhill Dark Monarch'.

Opposite bottom left What we call the Raven Clan Collection – all the dahlia varieties we've been involved in breeding, including 'Rosie Raven', 'Sarah Raven', 'Molly Raven' and 'Perch Hill'.

Opposite bottom right A red admiral butterfly stopping on the brilliant, Anemone-flowered *Dahlia* 'Blue Bayou'.

Decorative

These tend to be the ones with the largest flowers with lots of petals that are often broad but pointed at the tip. They have been popular for years with competitive growers and are now equally popular with cut-flower growers.

Decorative dahlias are subdivided by their size and the very large dinner plate varieties are particularly fashionable. Until a few years ago, everyone slammed these bonkers whoppers, but now they're filling every flower farmer's plot, both here and in the USA, because three heads make a bridal bouquet or fill a vase.

Their scale tends to curtail their vase life, but these are valuable drama queens. At the smaller end, I like 'Nicholas' very much, and also 'Labyrinth'. This lot also includes the famous whopper, 'Café au Lait' in that soft, gentle mix of ivory, white and milky coffee. And I love the crazy, huge and dazzling 'Emory Paul': just one floating in a bowl or arranged in a narrow-neck bottle will have everyone ogling!

Best for vase life are 'Molly Raven' and 'Perch Hill', which we selected after noticing in a trial that they had excellent longevity, as does 'After Dusk' (sometimes classified as a Waterlily), which is a deep crimson, and 'Dark Butterfly'. These all have a vase life of at least seven days.

Anemone-flowered

These are the ones that look like they have a flower within a flower. They're good for pollinators and are very glamorous, but they don't tend to have a good vase life. The ones we've bred are called 'Rosie Raven' and 'Adam's Choice', and they break the mould and last well. For all open-flowered dahlias, pick before much yellow pollen is showing to improve their vase life.

Below left Bees love the Single dahlias like 'Honka Fragile'.
Below right One of my very favourite dahlias 'Verrone's Obsidian', though sadly it only lasts a couple of days once cut.
Opposite *Dahlia* 'Lou Farman' growing in the dahlia trial beds at sunset.

Single-flowered

These are simple, single flowers with either rounded petals (such as those in the Happy series), or pointed and architectural petals, such as the Honka series, which look like Catherine wheels. 'Honka Fragile' is not fragile at all and makes a surprisingly long-lasting cut flower. We also pick 'Lou Farman' a lot, which has long, elegant stems. Named after my friend and the co-founder of my plant nursery, Lou Farman, it is a variety we have bred that (along with 'Blue Bayou') is the absolute favourite of butterflies.

A famous group of dahlias within the Single-flowered classification was developed from the historical variety 'Bishop of Llandaff'. They are all excellent for pollinators and have chocolate-coloured foliage. This gives them presence, but they don't have great vase lives. The single-flowered, seed grown 'Bishop's Children' is lovely grown and arranged with *Verbena rigida*.

Miscellaneous

This is a bit of an I-don't-know-where-to-put-you group, but includes one of our winners for picking, the supremely elegant 'Waltzing Mathilda'. It only lasts four to five days in a vase, but is beautiful, and can hold its own in a single-stem vase.

Picking and Arranging

Opposite A collection of dahlias picked at Perch Hill and arranged by my gardening friend and colleague, the florist Arthur Parkinson. The dahlias here are 'Molly Raven', 'Lou Farman', 'Waltzing Mathilda', 'Rhubarb and Custard', 'Polka' and 'Bishop of Auckland'.
Right Gladioli are too top heavy for buckets, so we pile them into a wheelbarrow or just carry them inside and place in dustbins full of water.

Picking reaches its peak in September, both in terms of volume and the range of flower colour and form. We've got spikes and spires from gladioli and snapdragons, which are still going strong. There are pompoms from the black scabious. There are airy and delicate saucers from cosmos and spring-sown Icelandic poppies. And there are swags and flower curtains from clematis and the tender perennial climbers, which are reaching their full potential this month. Alongside all of these are dahlias in every shape and colour.

In terms of practicalities, some of the heavy-headed dahlias and most of the gladioli are difficult to balance in a bucket, so I usually lay them flat in a basket. Or if I'm picking loads, I hold them over my shoulder or place in a barrow to avoid damaging the stems.

Cutting and Conditioning Dahlias

Dahlias are cut-and-come-again plants, so don't cut flower stems right to the ground. Instead, cut above a pair of leaves. This way, axillary buds quickly develop between the leaves and the main stem to form another flower in days or weeks.

The lower you pick in the plant, the longer it takes to produce another flower, so try to cut with the vase or arrangement you are creating in mind. If you cut a stem one metre long and then cut 50cm (20in) off the end when you put it in the vase, you'll have wasted all the buds on that lower section of stem.

Pick dahlias in the cool of the evening or morning (particularly important if we're having a hot and late summer, which seem increasingly common) when the flowers are fully open, but the petals at the back of each bloom still look fresh. On average, dahlias picked at this stage should give you a vase life of four to five days. If you only need them to last a day or two, you can also pick flowers that are more mature and then strip off any ageing petals.

I sometimes remove all the petals to leave just a green boss (the calyx), which provides an additional shape and colour to the flower arrangement. And I sometimes pick green, round buds for the same reason. Most of these won't open once harvested, although we've found in our trials that if the stems are kept cool, some buds do develop and open.

Opposite A collection of dahlias from the Cashmere Jersey palette (see p62) floating among the waterlilies in our water feature at Perch Hill. Outside, floating in water, the flowers last three or four days. The amazing *Dahlia* 'Sissinghurst' can last five days!

Floating Flowers

I remember walking into a fancy hotel in Morocco in the late 1990s to find a swimming pool full of floating flowers – mainly roses and dahlias – and candles floating on tinfoil saucers. It remains a memorable and beautiful sight, and I still try to recreate it, albeit more simply, in an old trough water feature in the garden.

You can also apply the same principles on a much smaller scale. You can use single dahlias in a small bowl to place on a bedside table, or create a table centrepiece with flowers filling the biggest bowl you can find. I sometimes pack my watertight metal trug with dahlias to greet people as they come into the house.

Arranging flowers this way is very easy, with few rules involved. I do recommend focussing on a particular palette. Add just one key colour, or a mix of two or three harmonious colours, for the most stylish effect. Go for dahlias with interesting shapes and a large surface area to ensure the flowers are good to look down on. The dinner plate forms from the Decorative group or the spidery shapes of the Cactus group, as well as Single-flowered dahlias in the Honka series, have strong impact. Consider adding leaves – such as scented-leaf pelargoniums – for contrast.

Cut the flower stems very short. You don't need a grid to hold the heads out of water, because dahlias are so prolific, you can pick flowers to your heart's content, but also if the bowl is placed somewhere cool, they will last as long as those in a vase. Before you add the flowers to the bowl, place it where you want to showcase the arrangement and, using a jug, fill it to the brim with water. If you fill the container first and then carry it, it will splosh all over the place.

In the evening, you can float tealights among the flowers (leave the candles in the metal containers, or they will sink). The arrangement should last two or three days inside, up to four if they are somewhere cool like the garden.

A Table Full of Flowers

There is no better time of year for an abundant display of flowers and no better flower to achieve that with than the dahlia. Single stems placed in a series of bottles are spot on, and really you need nothing more.

As you're picking and arranging, think about the contrast – or harmony – of the vases and the dahlias to go into them. Not only in terms of colour, but also the shapes and silhouettes. Pick some stems quite short, so the flowers almost nestle in the neck of the vase to create the heart of the whole arrangement, and leave others longer so they stand proud and give an interesting horizon. That's important – the variety makes the whole thing multi-dimensional.

You can gather the vases together and contain them on a tray, but for me, more is more. I often literally fill the whole table with flowers. If you need to eat at the same table, make space at the centre and cram in as many vases as you can, leaving just enough room for the place settings. Serve the food from somewhere on the side; it's worth it.

If it's a daytime display, position the table so that it's backlit, if you can. It adds so much atmosphere and accentuates the different shapes of each flower. If it's for the evening, scatter candles to give vertical lines and height to the whole scene. I usually use a mix of candle colours that echo the flowers.

Above Our kitchen/dining room table with just enough room for plates. That's how I like it when our dahlias are super-abundant in September. I've added coloured candles that pick up on the flower colours scattered between.

Left Vases, with spiky dahlias, including the crazy 'Hollyhill Spiderwoman', 'Honka Fragile' and 'Verrone's Obsidian'.

Above My desk full of dahlias including 'Verrone's Obsidian', 'Radegast', 'Tartan', 'Santa Claus', 'Moor Place', 'Thomas A. Edison' and 'Samourai', with the foliage of *Pelargonium tomentosum*.

PRACTICAL

September

Opposite Deadheaded dahlias filling a wheelbarrow after a wet few days in September at Perch Hill.

Many of the half-hardy annuals and dahlias will need a good clean up now, so it's time to get into the garden to do some thorough deadheading, particularly if you've been away in August and no one has been picking over your patch. Deadheading early in the month will ensure a good crop for another six to eight weeks, at least.

As you deadhead dahlias, particularly after rain, remove fallen petals from the leaves too. Flat petals sitting on flat, wet leaves easily become a source of the fungal disease botrytis. Also remove lower leaves from all your dahlia plants at this stage in the year to increase air flow, which will help to keep mildew in check.

September is also the time to do some early autumn sowing. There are several hardy annuals that survive winter in the garden and are transformed by sowing and planting out now, rather than in spring. The biennials you sowed in June also urgently need planting out now, before the soil loses its warmth and nights start to get properly cold.

If you didn't get around to it last month, it's time to propagate any tender perennials you love to pick. It's full steam ahead on scented-leaf pelargoniums (we propagate lots of 'Attar of Roses' now), and the deliciously perfumed *Heliotropium arborescens* 'Reva' – just a single sprig can fill a room with scent. We also take cuttings of several of the salvias we use for fungal control for our roses (see p241).

Chrysanthemums are just opening and coming into their own. They're key for flower succession into autumn. They usually go on flowering until the first proper frost (often not until late November here), but they

can easily get trashed by the weather before that (see p373 for how to protect them).

Hopefully you've ordered bulbs ready for October planting, and if not, this is a reminder. Other than that, I think September is one of the loveliest months to sit back and enjoy what you've created before it all disappears for another year!

Above Damage to dahlia foliage caused by wet petals sitting on the leaves. Always clear fallen petals as you deadhead dahalis.

PRACTICAL

Below Finding 'volunteer', self-sown hardy annuals – here, *Cerinthe major* 'Purpurascens' – for transplanting.

Forcing Amaryllis

Now is the time to plan ahead for flowers at Christmas and into the new year. I force a few narcissi (see p406), as well as amaryllis (*Hippeastrum*) to use as cut flowers and potted plants indoors. Forcing simply means to bring the plants into flower earlier than they would flower naturally.

To force amaryllis, you need to hydrate the desiccated roots of the bulb by soaking them in tepid tap water overnight. The easiest way to do this is to rest the base of the bulb on the rim of a jam jar so that all the roots (but not the bulb), can sit in the water below. Plant into a tight-fitting pot with about 2.5cm (1in) between the bulb and the side of the pot.

Amaryllis has a tendency to rot, so drainage is vital. Put a handful of crocks in the bottom of the pot to help with this. It's important that the shoulder of the bulb (about one third) sits above the surface of the compost. It's the apex of the bulb (where the leaves emerge) that is most vulnerable to rot and where water can seep in and decay the heart, so this must not sit wet on watering.

They will need some support, so tap in a cane and tie in the stem as it gets to a decent height. Place it in a light and well-ventilated spot, free from draughts, somewhere that's about 20°C (68°F). Keep the compost moist until a shoot appears and then water more frequently, about twice a week. Water from the top, and once the water has drained through into the saucer, tip it away.

Autumn Sowing

Annuals can be hardy (these can handle some frost) or half-hardy, which can't and won't survive the wet and cold of winter. It's the hardiest of the hardies that should be autumn sown, and they will transform your cutting garden and ensure early flowers.

At Perch Hill, without autumn-sown hardy annuals, the garden in mid-May would be pretty colourless and dull. Plants such as *Allium hollandicum* 'Purple Sensation', a few aquilegias and the early poppy, *Papaver* 'May Queen', do their best, but that's about it. If we sow hardy annuals now, this May colour gap is plugged.

Below top Sowing *Viola* 'Sorbet Antique Shade' in a half-size seed tray.

Below bottom Sowing hardy annuals in guttering. I'm individually placing *Cerinthe major* 'Purpurascens'.

The earlier you sow, the bigger and better the resulting plant. If a seed germinates in September, it forms a small plant, growing several centimetres before going into semi-hibernation as winter sets in. Light intensity, hours of daylight and temperature all decrease, and the growth above soil level stops, but root growth below ground continues. Over the winter, a large root ball develops, supporting a small amount of leaf. As light intensity, daylight and temperatures increase again in early spring, the plant can romp away and you'll get a stupendous and long-flowering colour giant.

A seed sown in the spring doesn't have that head start: in March and April, conditions are perfect for top and root growth, so it will do fine, but will never become a flower factory like its autumn-sown siblings. It's hugely worthwhile to get going early.

Find volunteers

Before you start to sow, have a hunt in the garden for self-sown seedlings of hardy annuals such as cerinthe and euphorbia. You'll probably find volunteers. Water before you move them to help the soil bind together so the seedlings retain good root balls. Transplant them into a row, spaced at 30cm (12in) apart, in a sunny patch.

Sow under cover

We get better results starting our seeds under cover compared with sowing direct into the garden, largely because of our heavy clay soil. At this time of year we often use half-size seed trays or short gutter pipes to restrict numbers.

Sowing inside, as opposed to direct into the garden, speeds up germination, which means you can get these seedlings out while the soil is still warm and moist. That helps promote vigorous root growth and gives them a better chance of surviving the winter.

We sow small seeds into trays (see p144) and the larger seeds into a gutter pipe (see p145) and keep them somewhere light and warm.

Plant them out in four to six weeks. But do note: anything sown inside needs to be planted out by the middle of October at the latest in Sussex; if you're in the north, bring that forward by two or three weeks. See p194 for planting out instructions.

PRACTICAL

- *Ammi majus* and *A. visnaga*
  I'd be bereft without the magnificent, light, airy umbellifer that these ammis provide. They're both fantastic in big drifts and lovely as background to more substantial flowers. Sow in gutter pipes.
- *Cerinthe major* 'Purpurascens'
  Don't miss out on the beautiful, nectar-rich honeywort. It survives the winter with us as seedling stage, growing outside, but only in a sheltered spot. Sow in gutter pipes.
- *Orlaya grandiflora*
  These usually survive winter just fine and seem better able to resist viral diseases when sown in autumn. Sow in a seed tray.
- *Salvia viridis* blue-flowered
  You can sow this in gutter pipes or direct outside.
- *Scabiosa atropurpurea* 'Tall Double Mix'
  Sown in September, this wonderful annual scabious will flower for almost twice as long as its spring-sown counterparts – up until Christmas, if you keep picking or deadheading it. Sow in a seed tray.
- *Viola*
  We sow and grow lots of violas for winter pot toppers, and we pick from them too. Sow in a seed tray. It's getting late for these now, but it's worth doing if you didn't get around to it in August.

Sow direct
Start sowing the tougher hardy annuals at the beginning of the month. You want to get them sown and growing before the soil cools and everything goes into its dormant winter phase. In early September, good germination should be quick, but if you've left it too late, you're better off waiting until early spring.

Get going with cornflowers, poppies and nigella. Cornflowers are the hardiest of the lot and will survive even the harshest winter. Sown in autumn, these have been known to grow into a 2-metre tall hedge at Perch Hill.

If you don't have space to sow outside, sow into gutter pipes and keep under cover until ready to plant out. Poppies and nigella don't like root disturbance, so it's best to direct sow.

1. Rake over the soil to create a fine tilth the texture of apple crumble topping.
2. Sow in parallel lines or a noughts-and-crosses grid, with the lines about 30cm (12in) apart.
3. Don't pour the seed straight from the packet or the palm of your hand. This creates a clump of seeds in one place, with too many tiny plants competing for light, food and water, followed by a bare patch. Instead, sow sparingly, one seed every 2.5cm (1in) or so. These will be easy to thin and there'll be no waste.
4. For tiny seeds like poppies, where individually placed seed is impossible, take a small pinch from the palm of your hand and sow swiftly in a swoop. This will give you a thinner distribution of seed than if you're meticulous and slow.

Below top Sowing *Centaurea cyanus* direct outdoors. I'm individually placing the seeds, which gives seedlings more space and decreases the chance of needing to thin them out hard later.

Below bottom Covering the seed with soil.

5. Mark in the soil where you get to so you don't miss a bit or go back over the same soil again. I make a line with my finger across the drill.
6. Most seeds start to germinate after a couple of weeks and small seedlings will appear. When the seedlings are about 2.5cm(1in) tall, be brutal. Thin them out, checking the back of the seed packet for the exact thinning distance.

October

As someone who thrives when colour and flowers are in abundance, I find the winter tricky. In October, flower production is tailing off, but there are still so many other sources of natural colour that I don't feel the garden is lacking – and with a well-planted cutting patch, you shouldn't either.

As autumn progresses, the arrangements start to become more minimal and skeletal, with colour from leaves, hips, berries, fruits and haws still on the branch (see the next chapter for ideas for using fallen leaves and bare branches), as much as from flowers. We are busy harvesting and storing flowers to dry at this time, too, and you can turn to a whole section on everlasting flowers and seedheads in August on p323. In this chapter, I begin with berries and foliage.

One after another, leaves start to turn this month, with intense scarlets and oranges as well as soft and subtle colours emerging. If we have a succession of cold nights, this colour change can happen quite quickly across a few days. For a speedy and simple arrangement, there's nothing nicer than showcasing the mix of colours you so often find in October, using turning leaves and the architectural seedheads of flowers such as crocosmia, Japanese anemones and agapanthus.

It's the maple trees that often kick off the autumn-leaf show. We don't grow whopper maples here, but I can still pick sprigs to bring indoors. Their colours are the making of a simple vase once you add in a few dahlias or chrysanthemums in soft, warm shades or even rich crimsons. The blush-coloured, autumn foliage of peonies is ideal too, together with flowers in soft, cool colours. I love having small arrangements like these in as many places around the house as possible.

Opposite The Perennial Cutting Garden at Perch Hill in October, still full of colour and stems to pick. The main dahlia trial beds are lined with *Salvia microphylla* 'Cerro Potosí'. Late-performing, good-for-picking perennials such as heleniums, rudbeckias and caryopteris are all flowering in other beds.

Below left *Acer palmatum* 'Sango-kaku' is a great tree for a small garden. It looks delicate and airy from spring to autumn, when we pick sprigs for smaller vases and go on doing so until the last leaves drop.

Below right *Acer palmatum* 'Sango-kaku' arranged with *Dahlia* 'Rhubarb and Custard' and 'Strawberry Bob Bon'.

I also love a large vase of just one variety of turning leaves. The mix of fiery shades you find naturally together on the smoke bush (*Cotinus coggyria*), is a winner for me. The colour range is as dramatic as the best autumn or winter sunrise.

If you have a larger garden, a katsura tree (*Cercidiphyllum japonicum*) gives you not just an incredible flare of colour in amber and ochre, but also a unique fragrance. It fills the place with a rich, crème brûlée aroma, which once smelt is never forgotten. If you can climb a ladder to cut a branch or two, they will last, with branch ends seared, two weeks indoors before dropping their leaves. A vase of these heart-shaped leaves was an annual tradition when I was a child, and it would fill our hall with that delicious scent. Having just planted one here, I can't wait to do the same at Perch Hill.

We have plenty of wild spindle (*Euonymus europaeus*) growing in the hedgerows. It's been invisible for ten months, but in October it suddenly looks like a coral reef. For two or three weeks, the leaves are zingy and brilliant, and when they drop, you're left with the neon seedheads with orange berries at their heart, bare on the branch, standing out like sweets on the tree. I divert my walks on purpose to take in places where

Clockwise from top right
The berries of *Euonymus europaeus*, one of my favourite things to pick this month and next. *Cotinus* 'Grace' in autumn colour. The lovely cluster of rosehips you get with *Rosa* 'Francis E. Lester', which are green all summer and flame-orange all autumn. *Viburnum opulus* 'Compactum' has great redcurrant berries and, in October, its leaves turn scarlet. Another spindle (*Euonymus alatus* var. *apterus*), often selected for gardens because it makes a neater bush than *E. europaeus*. This has red (not pink) outer seed pod shells.

I know it grows, in order to pick a sprig or branch.

Another berried shrub that is well worth growing for picking is the guelder rose, *Viburnum opulus* 'Compactum'. This is different than *V. o.* 'Roseum', which is so lovely for picking in late April into May (see p153). 'Compactum' was hugely popular as a cut flower when I started out 30 years ago, though you rarely see it in florist shops now. It's a shame, because it's one of the best shrubs to use as primary foliage. Gather three or five stems together and you've got the perfect structure: robust and upstanding, but airy, with plenty of gaps into which you can slot other stems. It has redcurrant-like berries (not poisonous, but not edible either) from the end of August. In October, its leaves turn various shades of red to complement the fruit. It needs to be left unclipped in a hedge if you want the berries from one year to the next.

This is also a great month for rosehips. These jewels will last firm and smooth-skinned for up to three weeks if picked now. I love the hips on branches of dog rose (*Rosa canina*) from the hedgerows, any of the *R. rugosa* (the hips are big and fat) and the elegant, *R. glauca* and *R. moyseii* 'Geranium'. It's also worth having one of the vigorous ramblers, such as 'Francis E. Lester', for trusses of smaller, bead-like hips. In summer, I use *R. glauca* in large vases for its silver-leaved, arching stems, and I harvest it again now. If you pick any of these now, bear in mind that you will prune in a month or so. Follow the pruning rules as you pick (see p426), and you won't do the bush any harm by picking even quite statuesque, arching boughs.

Stems from crab apples survive longer than roses in a vase, so we pick them towards the end of the month and continue to do so until December. The first to bring colour here is *Malus hupehensis* – a beautiful crab apple tree for garden and vase, both in May and October. And we take the loppers to branches of *M. × robusta* 'Red Sentinel', which grows in the hedge line around our dahlias (pictured on p368). The fruit of the former are miniature, each one no bigger than a fingernail, whereas the fruit of 'Red Sentinel' is the size of a cherry, packed on each branch in showy clusters – they look like they're made from china or glass.

Now on to the best October cut flowers. Dahlias are still out there and we can harvest stems by the bucket (see September). Keep picking – or deadheading – and if it's not too wet, they'll continue for another four to six weeks. Just be aware that their colours can fade as the weeks go by,

Below View of the dahlia trial beds from under our lovely avenue of *Malus* × *robusta* 'Red Sentinel'.

Opposite top A table full of dahlias in our kitchen, including 'Autumn Orange', 'Black Jack', 'Downham Royal' and 'Chat Noir', with holly and *Cobaea scandens*.

Opposite bottom left A chance combination of *Chrysanthemum* 'Avignon Pink' with self-sown *Nicandra physalodes*.

Opposite bottom right *Chrysanthemum* 'Pandion Bronze' flowers for ages, has a vase life of over two weeks and has – I think – great colour and form.

Next page A vase of chrysanthemums (including 'Pip Sunny', 'Rossano Elizabeth', 'Spider Bronze' and 'Tula Improved') picked at Perch Hill and arranged by Arthur Parkinson, with oak leaves and *Euonymus europaeus*.

particularly with the softer-toned varieties such as *Dahlia* 'Fairway Pilot' and 'Labyrinth'.

As dahlias recede, chrysanthemums become our key plants for flower drama. I love them, but you need to make careful choices. Chrysanthemums can easily look old-fashioned and stiff, verging on those plastic flowers you see in graveyards, but there are also magnificent varieties. I find that the more wayward and crazy the flowers, the better they look. That said, a few of the needle-petalled, starry ones such as 'Flyaway' and 'Pink Splendour', have thin flower stems and their showy heads aren't always properly supported. Discovering these details is one of the reasons we do so many flower trials.

Reliable chrysanthemums I recommend include 'Avignon Pink', 'Astro Bronze' and 'Pandion Bronze'. They are huge flower producers and early to flower, sometimes from September, making them ideal if you don't have anywhere under cover to bring them in. Look also to the Tula series (including 'Tula Carmella', 'Tula Green', 'Tula Improved' and 'Tula Sharletta'), mixed in with 'Spider Bronze', and a dash of something bright via 'Pip Sunny'. The latter and 'Avignon Pink' flower the longest.

Opposite top We lift some of our chrysanthemums from the garden in October and bring them into the glasshouse at Perch Hill.
Opposite bottom It feels luxurious to be able to pick armfuls of flowers in October – and that's why we grow chrysanthemums that come into their own at this time of year. Here, 'Tarantula Red', 'Avignon Pink' and 'Pandion Bronze'.
Right A bowl of floating chrysanthemums from the spiky, spiny-petalled Tula series, which I think are some of the best for shape and colour.

If you have a greenhouse or polytunnel or even a sheltered, sunny porch, here's a good tip for chrysanthemum growing from October onwards. Lift your chrysanthemums, pot them up in very large (7- or 10-litre) pots and move them inside. We dig up the whole plant, place them in a wheelbarrow and transplant them to the greenhouse growing beds (to replace the tomatoes), where they will be protected. With their shaggy, complicated flowers out of the wind and rain, we can then harvest flowers almost until Christmas.

Less is more when it comes to arranging. Much like alliums, chrysanthemum flowers are wasted crammed in tight together. And they have some of the longest vase lives of any flower you can grow – up to three weeks if you regularly cut off the stem ends and refresh the vase water. Like dahlias, they look magnificent – and with their large surface area, work really well – arranged as floating flowers (see p352 and p138). Alternatively, you can create mini bunches or add just single stems to vases to place on a mantelpiece or bedside table.

Our October flowers also include *Nerine bowdenii*, which gives bold splashes of colour into November. With strong shapes, all twizzles and turns, and a vase life of nearly two

Below left *Chrysanthemum* 'Avignon Pink' is a perfect match for *Nerine bowdenii* 'Ostara', which happens to flower at the same time.
Below right A tray of autumn flowers, including the great *Hydrangea macrophylla* 'Madame Emile Mouillère', *Dahlia merckii*, *Tulbaghia violacea* and *Nerine bowdenii* 'Ostara'.
Opposite top Our south-facing, narrow border of *Nerine bowdenii*, including 'Favourite', 'Isabel', 'Ostara', 'Amandi' and 'Like a Virgin'. We have bearded irises in this border, available to pick in May and June.
Opposite bottom All the varieties listed above arranged together in a firework mix along with *Nerine* 'Zeal Giant' and *Euonymus europaeus*.

weeks, nerines can make a small, colourful arrangement and even a single stem in a vase is lovely.

When I first started growing cut flowers, it was really only the species, *Nerine bowdenii*, that was hardy enough to grow outside, but with recent breeding and milder winters, there's now a great range to choose from. *Nerine* 'Zeal Giant' is quite something, with bumper-sized flowers in the richest pink, while *N. b.* 'Like A Virgin' gives you the palest pink down to white in just one flower. In the old days, the standard *Nerine bowdenii* would take three or four years to settle in and start flowering well, but again, recent breeding of a new group called × *Amarine* (hybrids between *Amaryllis* and *Nerine*) has reduced that time.

All nerines and their hybrids like a thin soil over a stony, rubble layer that gets a good baking from the sun. We grow them in a narrow, south-facing bed, alternating them with bearded irises, which thrive in the same conditions. Both are ideal for a tricky, parched corner. Plant in spring so they have time to settle in before any hard frosts in autumn and winter. Once in a vase, keep their water clean by changing every three days. Cut the stem ends again when you do this and add a slosh of clear vinegar to keep bacteria at bay.

Opposite The scent of *Heliotropium arborescens* 'Reva' is fantastic, and it's the strongest grower of all we've trialled; we grow enough to pick plenty in October. Here I've arranged it with the scented *Gladiolus murielae* (syn. Acidanthera).
Below *Rudbeckia hirta* 'Sahara' with the foliage spires of *Dysphania botrys*.

October can also be a great month for *Gladiolus murielae* (syn. *Acidanthera*), depending on when you plant them. Add corms into pots or a cutting patch once the frosts are over in mid-May and you'll have flowers from late summer and stems to pick up to October. Planted in late April in a sheltered spot, you might have them as early as mid-August. The flowers have a soft scent that reminds me of the huge *Magnolia grandiflora*. We grow this spiking up through a mass of the most fragrant of all heliotropes, *Heliotropium arborescens* 'Reva'. This is a relatively quick-growing, tall heliotrope that is not only a good container plant, but (with stem ends seared) lasts well as a cut flower.

There are a few other late-season bulbs worth growing for their rich, stained-glass colours, all the more precious now, late in the year. I love toad lily (*Tricyrtis formosana*), which you can tuck into a dark corner in a north-facing bed. And the South African native, *Hesperantha coccinea* (syn. *Schizostylis coccinea*). This thrives if you have a sunny, damp corner (they were originally found on the bank of a stream in full sun in South Africa). All three of these can be slotted in (in the right place) and then ignored. They'll reappear for decades, at just the time of year we need them most.

Below left The October flowers of *Hesperantha coccinea* 'Major', *Petunia × atkinsiana* 'Tidal Wave Red Velour', *Tricyrtis formosana* and *Papaver rupifragum*, which only lasts a day in a vase, but gives a great splash of orange.
Below right The autumn-flowering *Hesperantha coccinea* 'Major'.
Opposite A Nero vase filled with late-season dahlias, including 'Blue Bayou', 'Autumn Orange', 'Iced Tea', 'Comet', 'Zippity Do Da', 'French Cancan' and 'Zundert Mystery Fox'. The foliage is *Hydrangea paniculata* 'Limelight' and the aster, *Symphyotrichum* 'Vasterival'.

There are also a few long-performing annuals still going strong, and the very best are cut-and-come-again. Good old *Euphorbia oblongata* is still out there for the picking and has been since spring. And, depending on the season, so are the snapdragons (*Antirrhinum*) that were sown in May or June, as well as rudbeckias. If we have a very cold or soggy winter, they'll be beginning to look tired by the middle of this month, but when the summer is long and late, they just keep going. Both of these have a great vase life, lasting ten days if kept cool.

Annual and short-lived perennial forms of scabious are miraculous for how long they bloom. We're still picking *Scabiosa* 'Kudo Blue', as well as the pink 'Magic' (aptly named for its length of flowering). I love picking these for simple bathroom and bedroom vases and they last ten days or more.

In terms of perennials, my favourite for October is one particular aster, *Symphyotrichum* 'Vasterival'. This has lovely, towering ebony stems and well-spaced flowers. We tend to use it more as a foliage base for a vase, rather than as a Bride flower. That said, it also looks great in a large vase on its own or dotted through with Japanese anemones.

Opposite An arrangement created following a trial of long-flowering roses, including 'Hot Chocolate', 'Julia's Rose', 'Aphrodite', 'For Your Eyes Only', 'Louise Odier', 'Pumpkin Patch', 'William Shakespeare' and 'Cinco de Mayo'.

Last, but definitely not least, are the late roses (for more on summer roses, see p241). At this point in the year, we record which roses are still flowering. We are always on the lookout for prolific flowerers and varieties that bloom from late May until October. From our trials, I can't say we've found one that will be in flower every week throughout those months, but there are a few that come and go, and they are invaluable.

From these, we identify the healthy, strong growers with reasonable vase lives. *Rosa* 'Calendar Girl', considered a bit bold and brassy for some, comes up trumps (pictured on p255). The flowers have magnificent scent, even late in the year. We are also crazy about two similar-toned roses, 'Hot Chocolate' and 'Cinco de Mayo', both the colour of burnished copper. Their scent is faint, and some people don't like the redness of tone, but they are stupendous flower producers.

For classic pink roses, 'Aphrodite' is still going strong. We have nicknamed it the marshmallow rose for its huge, open-structured blooms. It has a slight scent and a vase life of three to four days, but it almost never stops flowering.

For deeper colour, the pink to purple *Rosa* 'Timeless Purple' is a cracker. For us, it's taken over from 'Gertrude Jekyll' for late picking. And there's the splendid 'Duchess of Cornwall', one of my personal favourite picking roses. This opens coral turning pink as the flowers develop. It cuts fantastically, has strong perfume and flowers on and off from May to November.

The final pair of colours you may want are an ivory and a turmeric yellow. For the cream, flowering hard, long and late, it's *Rosa* 'Champagne Moment', and for yellow into gold, top picks would be 'Graham Thomas' or 'Pumpkin Patch'.

When I had to support myself through medical school forty years ago, I got a job arranging flowers for a beautiful house in the Cotswolds with a well-stocked cutting garden. I remember, with freezing fingers, picking 'Graham Thomas' one morning. Despite the time of year and the weather, the flowers were still pristine, and went on to last five days in water. That's hard to beat. 'Pumpkin Patch' is a new sort of yellow rose, which morphs from coral to gold and even to mustard. I love that mix of colours on one plant, and its scent is strong enough to throw itself across the garden, even on a misty autumn morning.

What with rosehips, crab apples, turning leaves and late-season flowers, October is the last abundant month of the year, before the garden is cut down by frosts, gales and rain. So when it comes to planning, I'd say keep it simple, but go for it.

Picking and Arranging

Opposite As the flowers in the garden fade, we turn to decorative squash and sweetcorn placed in trays and large bowls. They usually last until after Christmas.

Our garden harvesting extends beyond flowers and foliage this month, as I love bringing in pockets full of conkers and shiny chestnuts, some still in their brilliant green, spiky football cases, along with elegant, serrated leaves. I scatter these over the table or collect into trays or bowls as centrepieces. I also use pumpkins and squash (small varieties, such as pumpkin 'Jack be Little', which is the size of a tennis ball), and the crazy, twisty stems of squash 'Tromboncino'. Ornamental corns are also beautiful used in the same way, and they last months or even years, looking as colourful and shiny as the day they were picked. And recently I've started to pick kale for the vase, as well as end-of-season courgette leaves, all the more glamorous for their dappling of mildew, which softens their colour.

As temperatures cool, I move to picking into baskets rather than buckets, and by this stage in the year, I only condition a few things. Stems have been growing and ripening for months now and so they have had time to lay down plenty of lignin. Even on a sunny day, they will stand well after harvest.

I sear the stem ends of seedheads, particularly if the leaves are part of the show (spindle, for example), as it can delay the shedding of leaves by a couple of days. And I float some branches and stems in cool water overnight (or for a minimum of four hours) in a bath or sink. I always do this with hydrangeas and with plants that have a large leaf surface area, such as cotinus, as well as stems I'm planning to use out of water, such as ivy in a wreath. This helps to make them look fresh for longer.

A Galaxy of Mini Bottles

This is one of my favourite ways of having everyday flowers at home and I turn to it more regularly when the pickings start to get leaner, which is from this time of year right the way through to the middle of March and the emergence of spring.

I go out into the garden on a Saturday morning and pick small bunches of this and that – anything that draws my eye, but as always with me, I soon have a colour theme in mind. For this collection, it was *Cobaea scandens* that was my inspiration and my Bride.

I pick each mini bunch and bind them separately with elastic bands before placing them in a basket and swiftly taking them inside to sear the stem ends for five seconds. I put them in a bucket of water somewhere cool and dark to sit for a few hours before arranging them.

Bride, 7 stems
Cobaea scandens

Bridesmaid, 5 stems
African blue basil (*Ocimum* 'African Blue')

Gatecrasher, 7 stems
Petunia 'Tidal Wave Silver'

Foliage
Kale 'Spigarello', 3 stems
Indian borage (*Plectranthus ciliatus*), 5 stems
Cobaea scandens, 3 vines with seedheads

Step 1
I've used a mix of vase shapes, but all in clear glass to unify them. This also makes the containers seem quiet and almost invisible, allowing the flowers to dominate and shine. Arrange your vases first and then your flowers.

Step 2
Think of this arrangement as one in reverse: instead of starting with the foliage, place your Bride flowers in first. But only place them in the vases on one side of the display.

Step 3
Add the Bridesmaid to all the vases: left, right and centre. At the opposite end to the Bride, add the Gatecrasher, so they echo each other.

Step 4

Add the foliage to create an interesting silhouette, shape and a sense of movement. Leave some stems long, so they stand proud, up to three times the height of the vase they are in. Cut others short, so they only just peep out of the neck of the vase – not more than double the vase height. It's important to have this variety in height to create the most interesting arrangement.

Then use the cobaea vines to link the display from one vase to the next, horizontally, which will make the arrangement feel whole.

PRACTICAL

October

Opposite Heading to the compost heap with a wheelbarrow of cleared annuals. We only remove things if they look really terrible and aim to leave as much intact as possible for wildlife habitat and food.

I'm a bit of a fair-weather gardener and October is the month I transition from being in the garden most of the time (enjoying it and of course picking flowers), to withdrawing inside to write and plan. I still have forays to the garden to do important jobs, but it is the start of a retreat indoors that continues until next February or March, when I emerge again.

The key jobs that there's no avoiding include carrying on with the deadheading, at least until the rain gets too much. And we also spend a good deal of time tidying the garden.

The areas filled with annuals are starting to look tired, with fewer and fewer flowers. Out come rows of cosmos, zinnias and snapdragons to make space for the bulbs, but we leave plenty standing too – leaving some in place is good for overwintering wildlife. Rich seed-bearers (such as verbenas and nicandra) stay for longer, until they're stripped bare of any forage by our garden birds. The sunflowers have their heads cut off (if they're still holding on to seed) and we tuck these in and around the fences to create a natural bird café.

And early on in the month, the final bit of sowing and planting for the year needs to be done before it gets too cold. It's now mass bulb-planting time for us. That's our biggest October job and it continues well into next month. We always have plenty of new narcissus to trial. And it's now time for alliums, hyacinths and pretty much every bulb but tulips to be planted – tulips can wait a bit.

Deadheading

Continue to deadhead dahlias, particularly if the weather has been, and continues to be, mostly dry. This becomes more and more of a chore if it's a wet and windy month, as the buds stop developing and turn to mush, and it starts to feel like you're pushing against the tide. See deadheading tips on p357, and remember to take care to remove dropped petals from the foliage as you go.

PRACTICAL

Below left The hardy annual *Cerinthe major* 'Purpurascens' sown in guttering is ready for planting out now. We find it usually survives the winter outside. It might look quite ropey by March, but the large root ball then creates strong and productive plants.

Below right Plant out, one by one, seedling by seedling 30cm (12in) apart. Push them into a premade hole.

Sowing

There are two final bits of sowing: schizanthus and the third and final sowing of snapdragon (*Antirrhinum*) seeds. You need some undercover growing space to store the seedlings – a greenhouse, polytunnel or cold frame.

Both are sown into half-size seed trays (see instructions on p144). They'll need pricking out in six weeks (see p148). Prick out into 9cm (3½in) or 1-litre pots to grow on through the winter. Their rootballs then develop slowly to fill the pot space and give you strong, sturdy plants. If it's growing in a greenhouse, schizanthus will be in flower from April. We pot them into terracotta so they look great as they grow. The snapdragons can go out into the garden in a mild spell in April to be in flower a month or so later. These steal the show, arriving six to eight weeks earlier than those sown in February.

Planting Hardy Annual Seedlings

Top of our list of priorities is planting out any hardy annual seedlings that have not yet made it into the garden. All the seeds we sowed last month – cerinthe, ammi, scabious, cornflowers and so on (see p358) – need to go out before the soil starts to cool and light levels plummet. Planted out now, you will have flowers to harvest late next spring. See p194 for instructions on how to plant out from a gutter, and p195 for a seed tray.

Below top **Digging up and removing half-hardy plants – here cosmos – ready for composting.**

Below bottom **Chopping up stems and leaves for the compost heap.**

Composting Annuals

To clear a clump or line of annuals, cut the plants to the ground with hedging shears and then pull out the roots, shaking off as much soil as you can. If the stems are hollow, use them to create habitat for solitary bees. Tie a few together in short sections and place somewhere quiet in the garden.

At the compost heap, chop the plants into short sections with hedging shears (if they are woody plants, put the stems through a shredder or snip them into chips). It makes a significant difference to the speed at which they will compost – the smaller the better. It's best not to just dump them.

PRACTICAL

Below Planting allium bulbs using a long-handled bulb planter.

Planting Bulbs

From around mid-October, bulb planting becomes our priority. We start with hyacinths, muscari, anemones, alliums and narcissus. Why these first? It's because their foliage emerges early in the year – by February at the latest – while tulip and camassia foliage generally doesn't appear until March. Those early to emerge benefit from being in the ground while it's still warm, so their root growth becomes well established before the demands of their natural growing season. Tulips and camassias are able to go in during November or even December, and a frost or two before that will also help kill any fungal spores hanging around from any previous tulip blight.

We have two systems of bulb planting here, using a bulb planter/trowel or as a bulb lasagne.

Planting with a bulb planter or trowel
Drop your bulbs on the ground or cast them out in swathes, as this will help them look natural when they grow. We plant them alongside all the paths of the cutting garden. Dig a hole for each using a bulb planter, which is a tool with a shaft-like spade that acts like a corer, removing a cylinder of soil. Planted like this you minimise disturbance of mycorrhizal fungi and invertebrates in the soil.

Dig a hole, ensuring it is at least twice the depth of the bulb. Drop in a little spent compost or grit in the base (if on heavy soil). Plop in the bulb. Before you cover it up, cut the next hole with the bulb planter, this will

Below Planting a bulb lasagne, one section at a time.

create a cylinder of soil that plops out, which you can then use to fill the previous hole. Plop that in over the first bulb, and on you go.

Cut flower bulb lasagne

We've used a layered planting technique for bulbs in pots for decades and have evolved a similar system for highly intensive bulb beds for picking. Narcissi, along with hyacinths, alliums and Dutch irises are all planted in a lasagne, with soil as the pasta in between, and dahlias at the top. Due to our increasingly wet winters, we are experimenting with adding the dahlias in spring, to avoid losing them to wet weather in their dormant season.

- In your chosen bed, dig down to approximately 30cm (12in). Pile the soil to one side. If you have a very large bed or raised planting area, you can divide the bed into sections and do one block at a time.
- On heavy soil, scatter a 3–4cm (1½in) of grit in the base to aid drainage.
- The bottom layer is narcissus. Place the bulbs (pointy end up) in the bed. Space the bulbs evenly over the grit at 15cm (6in). This spacing is a little wider than usual to ensure the foliage is not too dense; the wide spacing also enables the planting to last for a decade, with no need to lift and divide congested plants. The bulbs should fill most of the surface of this base layer, but leave a border at the edge.
- Place allium and hyacinth bulbs in an alternating pattern at the edges. These bulbs are part of the bottom layer, at the same level as the narcissi. They both have robust and prolific foliage that tends to choke other things. Placed at the edge, most of their leaves flop over the path, so do less damage.
- Backfill half of the dug out soil over this bulb layer, adding more grit if the soil is heavy and claggy.
- Next, add a layer of Dutch irises to the central section of the bed, over the narcissi. They don't compete well with the allium foliage if placed at the outer edges. Backfill the remainder of the soil and label the bed.
- Now plant dahlias. We take these from elsewhere in the garden, either from pots or borders. Plant them spaced about 45cm (18in) apart (depending on variety). Mulch with compost over each crown to a depth of 15cm (6in) and a diameter of 30cm (12in) (so they look like a field of molehills). Label.

November & December

Early winter weather can vary hugely. The first frost usually hits us in November or December, and every two or three years we get a proper snow fall, so what is out in the garden and available for picking is unpredictable. Still, it's important to plan for a few key players that are reliable performers.

A strong contender for my favourite flower for picking now is *Cobaea scandens*, the cup and saucer vine. The purple, green-budded species is the easiest to germinate and we always have curtains of that for harvesting in these last two months of the year. We also grow the hardy perennial *Cobaea pringlei*, which is white and is doing well in our trials so far.

We sow all cobaeas in January or February (the earliness is important, see p120) and grow them under cover until the frosts are over, before planting out alongside frames over which they climb and flower from July until the first hard frost – they are pretty much the last things standing.

Cobaea is a vigorous, self-clinging climber. I love the picture of it literally climbing up the steps (see p397), proving why one of its common names is staircase plant. With stem ends seared, it picks brilliantly for a vase. The bells drop off the green calyx on day three or four, but cobaea still looks good without them. I love picking a good handful of tendrils to enhance an arrangement's silhouette. In small bowls, a simple glass or large vase, they can't fail to look good.

It's worth remembering the importance of flowers – not just for us pickers – but for the late pollinators that need food and water in the garden before they hibernate. Cobaea is stacked full of both pollen and nectar and is often busy with honey, bumble and solitary bees when there's less around to forage.

Previous page The Perennial Cutting Garden from above during the cold snap we had in December 2022.
Below *Salvia involucrata* 'Hadspen'. Cut quite short and with stem ends seared, this impressive flower lasts well in a vase.
Opposite top A shallow bowl with *Cobaea scandens*, *Thunbergia alata* 'African Sunset' and *Clematis orientalis* 'Bill MacKenzie'.
Opposite bottom left *Cobaea scandens* growing up the steps in the Oast Garden.
Opposite bottom right *Cobaea scandens* picked as a bunch, with almost as many stem ends (with tendrils) as flowers. I love the shape and silhouette they create.

Talking of which, I passionately recommend an ever-increasing clan of salvias for the late-season cutting garden. They are big favourites with pollinators and very jolly for a vase. I suspect a plant's aromatic fragrance gives us a hint about its importance to pollinators, as I'm sure it draws them in. If you sit and watch the comings and goings of butterflies and bees this late in the year, a fragrant clump of salvias is likely where you'll see them heading. It seems to be the blue, pink and mauve colours that attract them most, and salvias are rich in these. And let's not forget salvias are great seed bearers, so you'll find them visited by birds towards the end of the year, when we allow flower spikes to run to seed.

We often plant salvias with roses as fungal protection (see p241) and I also love pairing them with dahlias to extend their mutually handsome, flowery season – their forms (rockets and Catherine wheels) go well together. Depending on how wet the autumn turns out to be, dahlias can look pretty soggy by now, but salvias keep going, fresh as the day they came out until temperatures become near freezing. So between them, they make an excellent pair to pick for four to five months.

Opposite top A great, late-autumn mix of *Salvia* 'Pink Amistad' with *Dahlia* 'Hans Auinger'.
Opposite bottom left From what we call the Jewel Salvia Collection, which features nine varieties, still flowering in November. *Salvia* × *jamensis* 'Royal Bumble', *S. microphylla* 'Cerro Potosí', *S.* 'Amante', *S. guaranitica* 'Black and Blue', *S.* 'Amistad', *S.* 'Rockin' Blue Suede Shoes', *S. involucrata* 'Hadspen', *S.* 'Rockin' Fuchsia' and *S. microphylla* 'Wendy's Surprise'.
Opposite bottom right A simple trumpet vase filled with *Nerine* 'Zeal Giant' and *Salvia involucrata* 'Hadspen'.
Below An autumn wreath made from *Hydrangea macrophylla* 'Madame Emile Mouillère', *H. paniculata* 'Little Lime' and 'Wim's Red', *Panicum capillare* 'Sparkling Fountain' and *Malus* × *robusta* 'Red Sentinel'.

For vases, they all need their stem ends seared (even late in the year). And I advise cutting stems under 30cm (12in) to help them last longer. Some don't do well on longer stems (such as *Salvia* 'Amistad'). Their large leaves tend to shrivel, but you can remove some or all the foliage before arranging.

The showiest we grow to pick now is *Salvia involucrata* 'Hadspen'. That's my favourite. But for arranging en masse, you can't go wrong with lots of jewel-like colours mixed together in a jug, or in a tall, elegant vase.

Hydrangeas are our next port of call for a bumper flower harvest. It's not that we haven't been picking these from mid-summer, but it's now that they become invaluable, with so little around. We use them in vases and for making swags and wreaths. Hanging outdoors, these last for ages, as they're kept cool, and the ones we hang indoors dry well, too (pictured on p400 and p405).

There's no doubt that the showiest we grow is the huge-headed *Hydrangea arborescens* 'Incrediball' (syn. 'Strong Annabelle'). This is a hybrid of 'Annabelle', with its soft green flowers, bred for larger heads, and crucially, stronger stems. The trouble with the lovely 'Annabelle' is that its heads

Above *Hydrangea arborescens* 'Incrediball' and *H. macrophylla* 'Merveille Sanguine' on our marble mantelpiece.
Opposite An everlasting indoor wreath, using *Hydrangea arborescens* 'Incrediball' and willow as the base, and decorated with physalis, *Chasmanthium latifolium*, bracken, nigella and astrantia seedheads, globe artichokes and *Xerochrysum bracteatum* 'Dragon Fire'.

sag after a bit of rain, often the extra weight of the water brings its branches almost on the ground. 'Incrediball', by comparison, remains pretty perky and keeps its purity of colour longer, the browning stage delayed by several weeks. The vast pompom heads are what we want when making a huge wreath, as they cover the base so quickly and easily.

My favourite for picking is usually *H. paniculata* 'Limelight'. I love its pyramidal flower shape and its colours as it progresses from June to November. It emerges from bud the freshest green, gradually whitening through the early summer, then flushing pink, which deepens in its tone by October, until it eventually browns in November and December. Picked at that stage and dried, it lasts for yonks. I use them dried to make the simplest swags to run along the centre of a table or a mantelpiece at Christmas. Once dried, you can store them from one year to the next.

If you have a small cutting garden, go for *H. paniculata* 'Little Lime', which is bred for containers and is a brilliant small-scale substitute for 'Limelight'. *H. p.* 'Wim's Red' is also elegant, with stems that start claret and become slate-coloured. I have a good drift of three plants right by the back

Opposite A wreath constructed from the vines of *Hydrangea petiolaris* and decorated with *H. macrophylla* 'Madame Emile Mouillère', *Eryngium giganteum*, silver birch (*Betula pendula*) bark stars and a string of fairy lights.
Below What we call 'hydrangea alley' round the shady, north side of our house. Here, still standing in December, are *Hydrangea arborescens* 'Incrediball' and *H. paniculata* 'Limelight'.

door and I cut single stems to make an elegant vase. We also have a good line of *H. macrophylla* 'Madame Emile Mouillère', which is famously the hydrangea that puts up with the worst conditions. It will grow in deep shade if its roots are moist or in a drier position if it has a tad more light, making it the ultimate picking plant to fill the most unpromising of corners. We have just such a dingy corner – dry and shady – at the back of our kitchen, and it's filled with 'Madame Emile Mouillère' and the climbing *H. petiolaris,* and both are as happy as can be.

The skeletal flower heads of *H. petiolaris* are beautiful picked during the winter – they are almost always still intact in December. If you – or a friend – have one of these growing in the garden, beg, steal or borrow some heads. Every three or four years we give our plant a hard prune and find the vines also make a good base for a wreath – I still have a giant wreath made with the vines (pictured opposite) hanging ten years on.

In more open positions, we also grow more exotic forms, such as *H. macrophylla* 'Merveille Sanguine', which needs more light to do well. It has the richest crimson flowers. We use its fresh flowers in summer and dry the heads in winter to scatter

Below One of the most reliable hellebores for winter picking, *Helleborus niger* 'Christmas Carol'.
Opposite A wreath made from *Hydrangea macrophylla* 'Madame Emile Mouillère' and sprigs of silver birch (*Betula pendula*).

over our Christmas table and even our tree. I like the generous crimson clouds dotted over the evergreen pine, and once dried, they also last from one year to the next.

'Merveille Sanguine' keeps its colour well, as do another couple of favourites, *H. paniculata* 'Magical Starlight' and *H. macrophylla* 'Wedding Gown', both equally fabulous for drying. I have three stems of 'Wedding Gown' in my bathroom in a narrow-necked vase and I love their rich wine-red presence, even several years on. I dunk them in the bath every so often to keep them dust-free!

In the shade, we've got hellebores. Most of the ones we grow for picking come into flower after Christmas (see p102), but there are a few blooming now. The first is *Helleborus niger*, the so-called Christmas rose, with beautiful, white, saucer flowers, and the second is *H. × sahinii* 'Winterbells'. Originally bred as a winter window box perennial and fine as a houseplant, 'Winterbells' is reliable as a cut flower, too.

We often have the Corsican hellebore (*H. argutifolius*) just starting to flower, with its clear green flowers in impressive collections at the top of each stem, as well as the native *H. foetidus*. But my favourite for this time of year is

Opposite top left *Helleborus* × *sahinii* 'Winterbells'. This has an excellent vase life and flowers from late autumn to spring.
Opposite top right A single stem of the beautiful, green, amaryllis, *Hippeastrum* 'Green Valley'.
Opposite bottom left A grid arrangement of orange-berried *Ilex verticillata* and white amaryllis. If I arrange a low table centrepiece bowl like this a few days before Christmas, it still looks good for New Year's Eve.
Opposite bottom right Paperwhite narcissi, lovely and fragrant in the corner of a room. Keep them cool or they go over quite quickly.

H. × *ballardiae* 'Maestro'. Its slate-crimson, matte-textured flowers are glamorous and, if you follow the conditioning instructions on p106, it lasts well in a vase.

To bring spring and the flowery optimism that goes with it forwards to this side of Christmas, I force a few narcissi and amaryllis (*Hippeastrum*) to use as cut flowers as well as potted plants to cheer up a dark corner.

We grow quite a few amaryllis, storing bulbs from one year to the next. There are some lovely rich and crimson reds; 'Mandela' is a favourite for this time of year. I also love the pure whites and almost any with a hint of green (such as *Hippeastrum papilio* and *H.* 'Lemon Lime'), and best of all the crazy, spidery ones. These look exotic and delicate and are just as easy to grow, but they don't last as long in a vase.

One amaryllis stem gives such visual punch, you don't need more than that on a side table or, at most, three for a table centrepiece – and they last well over two weeks. They are an ideal flower to take you through from Christmas celebrations to beyond new year, as long as they are conditioned correctly (see p414). To force amaryllis, you need to plant them at the end of September so they can be in flower in eight to ten weeks (see p358 for instructions).

The main, reliably early narcissus are paperwhites (we grow the large-flowered variety 'Inbal'), and we supplement these with 'Avalanche' – lovely for its primrose-yellow perianth – and the orange-hearted 'Cragford'. All three are excellent for picking, have good scent and usually start flowering through December if grown inside (see bulbs for early picking on p159).

Forcing these in pots is very simple. The bulbs begin to grow as soon as they are planted, with flowers appearing in seven to eight weeks. Plant them in October (they thrive in a moist, fertile potting mix) and leave the pot somewhere cool and dry – they need a cold spell (under 10°C/50°F) to flower well. Keep the compost moist. Once they really start to shoot, with leaves up to 20–25cm (8–10in), bring them indoors, somewhere warm. If you want to keep them flowering in pots, pick one flower in every three or four for small vases to dot around the house and you'll barely notice they're missing.

Beyond fresh flowers, there are certain notable plants still hanging on to their fruit and berries later than others and they're well worth growing. We make a note of the peak moment of fruitiness of each so we can ensure a good succession for picking and for our garden birds.

Below left A juvenile ring ouzel feeding on the berries of *Malus hupehensis*.
Below right A wreath made from herbs and decorated with lights.
Opposite Some of my favourite branches last a lifetime as Christmas decorations. Here, silver birch (*Betula pendula*), angelica and honesty (*Lunaria*) seedheads lit up with lights.

Malus hupehensis is stripped bare by the blackbirds by now, but the fruit of *M.* × *robusta* 'Red Sentinel' and 'Evereste' usually remain into December. *M.* × *zumi* 'Golden Hornet' and *M. transitoria* provide crab apples even later.

I also love picking the odd sprig from our compact strawberry tree (*Arbutus unedo*) and from bushes of myrtle (*Myrtus communis*) – very on theme for Christmas as one of the gifts of the three kings – which is busy with birds feasting on the black, juniper-like berries well into March. We pick this fragrant evergreen a lot in the winter; crush a leaf and it fills the room with delicious fragrance. It's fantastic for vases and wreaths.
It needs a sheltered spot, out of the way of cold winds.

Also in a sheltered spot, we grow lemon verbena (*Aloysia citrodora*) and a range of scented-leaf pelargoniums. Together with the most perfumed, 'Attar of Roses', we grow *Pelargonium quercifolium*, *P. tomentosum* and 'Chocolate Peppermint', as they are all brilliant for winter foliage. We pick 'Attar of Roses' and lemon verbena before they get frosted or drop their leaves and tie them up in big bunches to hang upside down, or sometimes combine them with mint to make a drying wreath for teas – hung on the wall, they're available for anyone to

then take a sprig or two to make tisanes throughout winter. We also grow plenty of rosemary and bay and harvest them often to make great aromatic bunches that we use regularly for indoor and outdoor wreaths, as they last well out of water.

A few good seedheads are always important for late in the year as they're ideal for making skeletal arrangements as flowers become minimal. Honesty (*Lunaria*), along with alliums (picked in summer and stored, see p219) are my two favourites. We pick honesty seed pods for fresh arrangements in June, harvest some for drying in August and forage stems that are still standing in the garden now. These are ten times more light-catching and glamorous with the two outer shells peeled off the coin-shaped seedhead, as it reveals the opalescent wafer in the centre. And don't chuck the peelings. They combine to give lovely colours – straw to milky coffee, with flashes of purple or pink and a few soft greens – and you can use them to create a decorative chain to run down a table, over a mantelpiece or cascade down your Christmas tree. Simply thread them together, using a length of silk thread and a needle, to create a garland. They're brittle and you'll lose a few, but it's worth doing.

Opposite Decorated silver birch (*Betula pendula*) branches make one of the best and most sustainable Christmas trees.

There are a few plants that serve the dual role of being excellent both fresh and dry. Hydrangeas, for example, are fantastic cut flowers in summer, and also excellent dried heads. Similarly, there are several clematis we grow for flowers and seedheads. The waxy, yellow flowers of 'Bill MacKenzie' are still hanging on, and are now joined by its fluffy seedheads. We also grow *C. rehderiana* for its nodding, scented flowers as well as its seedheads, which are strong right up to Christmas. On acid clay, we can't grow the wild old man's beard (*Clematis vitalba*), as it thrives on chalk, but it's a good one to forage.

Finally, one of the best winter harvests are branches. They often form the basis of an arrangement and they are luckily always there, whatever the weather. If you don't have anything growing in the garden you can use, there may be some branches you can forage.

I'm a big fan of alder (*Alnus glutinosa*), which is often found on wet ground by rivers and streams. Its gnarled, contorted branches hold catkins (male) and cones (female) at the same moment. Added to a vase, you need nothing with them, bar a few small Christmas decorations, to make a beautiful arrangement. The same is true of silver birch (*Betula pendula*): its leaves will be turning in November, and as they drop, the catkins start to form. We use silver birch for almost all of our November and Christmas wreaths, and I love picking an odd branch or two for statuesque, simple vases. All they need are some warm fairy lights, and the odd decoration or bauble, and you've made yourself a mini Christmas tree.

We also use boughs or sprigs of olive. Olive is evergreen, but unlike pine, it isn't commonly used in winter. It is light and airy in its feel and I find decorations shine out beautifully against its silvery-grey leaves. With stem ends seared, boughs last three to four weeks in a vase. I place it all around the house in December: I tie stems together to create a simple dining table runner, fill jugs with it, and use it as a base for wreaths.

There's also no better time to look for lichen-covered branches. You can often find small branches that have been blown down by autumn gales and I usually pick some up to bring home from a walk. They are beautiful, just as they are, and can be magical lit by the finest, most delicate string of lights. This is as simple and sustainable as it comes; you can't go wrong.

Picking and Arranging

Opposite Harvesting physalis, which gives a brilliant late-season burst of orange colour for vases and wreaths.

Quite a bit of what we use for arranging comes from harvests we gathered in the more abundant months (see advice on everlastings on p323), but there are still magnificent things out in the garden – and in the wider environment – that are good to hunt for.

The process of picking gives me as much pleasure as the arranging at this time of year. When the bounty is so lean, you find you really value the stems you cut and bring in, and the pleasure of harvesting feels heightened. I regularly remind myself of that, to encourage myself to slow down and not stress about how much I have to do.

Christmas (and Thanksgiving) are now approaching and are the main focus for many of us at this time in the year. A lot of work goes into making the house look good, so I often get started early to maximise the time we have to enjoy the decorations. I have a mother who doesn't see the point of transferring supper from a pan to a serving bowl to make the food look great on the table (it's just more washing-up), so maybe my love of decorating and making things look as good as they can is in revolt. In our house, we go for it at Christmas and I hope we always will.

There is, however, a dilemma for those of us who care about sustainability. We need to become increasingly aware of the impact of classic Christmas decor – tinsel, glitter and plastic used by the skip-load by millions of us. We don't want to wipe out the life-enhancing glamour, glitz, sparkle and joy we need in our lightless winter, but simply to find ways to decorate that aren't rubbish for the environment. The following pages include some ideas for exactly that.

Conditioning

Cobaea, salvias, late-flowering violas and the odd, early polyanthus all last better with stem ends seared (just instantly in and out of boiling water), so even this late in the year, I'll have my kettle on. And particularly with the more fleshy stems, such as amaryllis and hyacinths, I add a slosh of vinegar to vases to keep bacteria at bay.

Keeping cut flowers cool is key all year, but through the winter they need to be placed away from radiators, and ideally, placed in a cool larder or outside on the doorstep (as long as it's not freezing) overnight. This sounds a palaver, and with larger arrangements it is a hassle, but for smaller vases and single stems in jugs, it's easy to do and makes an enormous difference to their longevity, making sure they last twice as long.

Hellebores, hydrangeas and ivy

Hellebores always need careful treatment (see instructions on p106) to make them last as long as possible, including the all-important searing. If time is short, you can pick them as single flower heads and float them in a bowl of water (see p138) – in this case, you can just pick and plonk.

There are a few plants that benefit from submersion in a bath or a deep sink full of water, hydrangeas and long vines of ivy included. These have complex structures with large surface areas, so they have evolved to absorb water over their whole leaf or petal. Submerging them under water gives them much more of a chance to hydrate than purely sucking up fluid through their narrow stems. See p88 for submersion instructions.

Amaryllis

We grow a few amaryllis (*Hippeastrum*) stems for picking (see p358 and p406), though they are readily available to buy at this time of year. The petals of amaryllis bruise easily if you lay them flat once fully open, so if you are buying them, ensure they are in tight bud, so they can be packed in a box safely at least five days before you need them (put them in water and leave them to open standing upright).

Hollow-stemmed plants like this last longer if you insert a cane in the stem. Without it, the weight of the flower tends to break the stem as it ages and you lose their glorious height. Poke a slender cane up the middle of the stem to just beneath the flower head. If you need to, keep the cane in place with a wad of cotton wool poked in behind it. This prevents it dropping out as you lift your amaryllis into a vase.

The cut end also tends to split and then curl up like a pig's tail. Twist a rubber band around the very bottom of the stem to prevent this.

Finally, remove the stamens, ideally before the pollen is dusty and ripe. If the pollen starts to drop, it ages the flower and will probably fertilise the stigma. The flower has then done its job and ages quickly.

And when you're arranging amaryllis, hang the flowers carefully over the edge of the work surface or table, or they'll bruise at that stage.

Opposite top left A cane inserted in the hollow stems of amaryllis makes them last twice as long. *Opposite top right* An elastic band secured tightly on the stem to stop stem ends splitting.

Opposite bottom left Keeping the cane in place with a wad of cotton wool. Opposite bottom right Removing anthers before the pollen starts to drop; this prolongs the vase life of each flower.

Bird Feeder Wreath

One of the things we become obsessed with as winter starts is feeding the birds. This wreath looks jolly on the door in November before we start to decorate for Christmas, and it has a second life as a bird feeder.

The seeds, nuts and peanut butter you add will be stripped by birds in a few days, but the berries and seedheads will last longer. Keep topping up with bird food as and when you want. To make it as sustainable as it can be, aim to pick as much as possible from the garden and hedgerow and use materials that can be chucked on the compost heap.

- Ribbon for hanging
- Twine and wide-eyed needle
- *Hydrangea petiolaris*, 3–5 stems with seedheads, to achieve a wreath ring roughly 35cm (14in)
- Silver birch (*Betula pendula*), 12 stems, each 60cm (24in)
- Hawthorn (*Crataegus*), 6 branches, ideally with berries still on, each 60cm (24in)
- *Viburnum opulus*, 6 berry sprigs, each 20–30cm (8–12in)
- Teasel (*Dipsacus*), 12 seedheads
- Fir cones, 15–20
- Peanut or hazelnut butter
- Bird seed, such as sunflower
- Monkey nuts (obviously these are not locally sourced, but birds adore them)
- Dried apple rounds

Step 1

Start by bending the hydrangea into a circle to create a ring. If the stems don't bend easily, there's a trick to make them more flexible. Find a bucket or pot with a diameter that's roughly that of the wreath ring to use as a mould. Bend the stems around this, binding them together with twine. Allow it to take the ring shape for a few hours before removing. If they are really unyielding, you can also leave the stems in a bath of water overnight, which should make them more pliable by morning. Add a loop of bright coloured ribbon or twine to the wreath ring, so you can hang it up.

Step 2

Attach the end of a ball of strong twine to the hydrangea frame. Lie three stems of silver birch onto the frame. Wrap the stems around the hydrangea ring and bind them in with twine. Aim to keep this fluid, adding more silver birch stems in threes, wrapping them around the ring, and tying them in with the twine. Keep a good tension as you work your way around, so that the stems are held in place firmly, but not too tightly. You are creating a silver birch structural framework into which you can push the rest of your wreath ingredients.

Step 3

Repeat step 2 with the hawthorn branches, so you have a generous covering of berries. Birds love these. I like to hang the wreath up at this stage to carry on working on it, so I can see more clearly what it's going to look like in place, but you can continue working on a flat surface if you prefer.

Step 4

Push the viburnum berries into the silver birch/hawthorn structure, ensuring the berries are arranged evenly across the wreath and securely anchored into the silver birch. Then add the teasels. Add these to the edges as well as the front, and try not to add too much to the centre – keep the middle of the ring open to avoid it turning into a nest.

Step 5

Now attach the fir cones. If the cones are tightly shut, put them in the oven on a low temperature for half an hour to open out the scales. Wind twine around the cone, near to the base. Then add another to the same length of twine, leaving a good gap between each one. You want to create a long garland with all the cones attached. Some of these cones can act as bird feeders; smear those with peanut butter and roll them in birdseed (you can see one at the top of the wreath). Attach the garland of cones to the wreath.

Step 6

You can thread monkey nuts to create a garland using a wide-eyed needle and twine. Tie a knot at each end to secure them and then add them like beads. Wrap the garland around the wreath. Next, use a needle and thread to string together several apple rounds, one on top of the other to create rosettes, which you can then tie to the wreath. The picture here was taken when I was still using wire – the wire would go through the centre of a stack of apple rounds, and the ends brought together at the top, making it easy to attach it to the wreath like a kirby grip. Now I do the same with biodegradable twine.

Fruit and Veg Christmas Wreath

I love a wreath on the door – a cheery sign that festivities are underway. If you don't have a suitable door, you can hang a wreath inside or lay it flat, like a nest, as a table centrepiece.

Colourful flowers that dry well are hard to come by in the middle of December, which is when I'm thinking of making my door wreath to last until the new year. We might have some small, bright crab apples, but I usually make use of the groceries – chillies or mini peppers, cranberries and limes. Clubbing together with friends to share resources – a box of citrus fruits or abundant garden prunings – means you can reduce the cost, plus it's fun doing this as a group activity.

Often I distribute my ingredients evenly across the wreath, but on occasion I use a system that involves two zones. Zone 1 is strong and dramatic, with two bright ingredients, repeated five times. If you think of the wreath like a clock face, you can roughly add these bold elements at 12 o'clock, 3, 5, 7 and 10 o'clock. Zone 2 is for lighter, filler ingredients, which help to create a sense of generosity and abundance in the wreath. Again, these are placed at five points around the wreath to fill in the gaps.

- Twine and wide-eyed needle
- *Cornus* (or any plant with straight branches) 2–3 branches, 1m (3ft)
- Silver birch (*Betula pendula*), 3–5 twiggy branches, about 60cm (24in) long, to achieve a wreath base roughly 35cm (14in)
- Foraged moss, 6–7 handfuls
- Limes, 15
- Red finger chillies, 35
- *Hydrangea*, 7 stems with seedheads
- *Agapanthus*, 5 seedheads
- *Eucalyptus* (or rosemary, bracken, silver birch), 7 springs

Step 1

Make a circular frame from any long, pliable branches you have in the garden or can find in the hedgerow. Tie the branches together using twine to form a strong circular base. Bend the silver birch branches around your wooden/branch circular base and tie the branches in at regular intervals to make sure the base is strong and secure. See step 1 on p417 for more detailed advice.

Step 2

I have padded out the frame with moss. Kept moist, the moss helps to keep the hydrangea, chillies and limes fresh. Tie the end of a ball of twine to the birch base. Then lay an even and generous layer of moss over the frame. Attach this padding to the frame with the twine, binding it tightly as you move it in and out of the centre of the wreath. Aim for the padding to be about 7–8cm (3in) wide at all points around the wreath. Add a loop of bright coloured ribbon to hang the finished wreath.

Step 3

See the introduction to this wreath for an explanation on zones. For zone 1, I've used limes and chillies. Tie these into five, evenly spaced spots in the moss and twig base. Prep them as follows.

Poke a twine-threaded needle about a third of the way up and through a lime. To attach it individually, leave a length of twine long enough so you can easily tie it to the wreath base. You can also thread a few limes onto twine to create a cluster. We used to do this with wire (pictured on p420), but now use twine because it biodegrades. It's a bit more of a fiddle, but works fine.

Wear gloves when handling chillies and do not wipe your eyes after touching them. To string the chillies, thread a length of twine through the middle of about six or so chillies, leaving lots of twine at either end to tie to the wreath base. If you are using smaller fruit, like crab apples or cranberries, thread them like beads on a chain. Always leave plenty of twine at either end so that you can secure them to the frame.

Step 4
Fill in zone 2 with the lighter mix of hydrangea and agapanthus seedheads and leaves: poke them into the moss regularly at five points.

Step 5
Hang the wreath and finish off with smaller silver birch twigs and some sprigs of eucalyptus to loosen the whole thing up and fill in any remaining gaps. Push in the stem ends hard so that they jam into the moss.

Step 6
Rehydrate the moss if it dries out by floating the wreath in a sink of water for a minute or two every week or so. It will last a month, kept cool, hanging outside. If you've used apples, the birds will start to eat them after a bit, but that's only a good thing!

Below left As an alternative to chillies, I love using beans such as borlotti, which give great shapes, bound in the middle with twine and attached as a bundle to the wreath.

Below right Binding chillies into a chain with sections of wire (this can be done with twine), leaving some at each end to tie or poke into the wreath to secure them.

Cranberry and Crab Apple Wreath

I have used a few sprigs of eucalyptus, *Garrya elliptica* catkins and hydrangea heads for the calmer zone 2, with limes, chillies, cranberry and crab apples as a colourful group for zone 1.

Forager's Wreath

I've used fresh dahlias here, as well as pelargonium leaves and physalis, spindle and agapanthus seedheads. The flowers are added to the wreath base in water vials. This wreath is smaller than the others (about 30cm/12in), so I've scaled down the zone system: the dramatic zone 1 (physalis) feature at three points, while the calmer elements of zone 2 fill in the remaining gaps.

Mantelpiece Swag

To give our sitting room a celebratory Christmas feel, I decorate our fireplace with silver birch and dried flowers every year. Here, I've draped the branches with dried straw flowers (*Xerochrysum* syn. *Helichrysum*) and allium heads, together with festive decorations and warm, white fairy lights.

You can also run a silver birch swag all around a room, just as you might hang up a ribbon for Christmas cards.

The ingredients list should give you some inspiration – you can gather as many of them as you can – and you can improvise and supplement with whatever you can find in the garden and beyond.

- Nails or tacks
- Wire or ribbon
- Needle and silk thread
- Christmas decorations
- Clear-flex, warm, white fairy lights
- Silver birch (*Betula pendula*), 5 branches, roughly 1m (3ft) each
- Honesty (*Lunaria*), 3 stems broken down into shorter length
- *Nicandra physalodes* seedheads, 3 stems broken down into shorter lengths
- *Sanguisorba*, 3 stems broken down into shorter lengths
- *Chasmanthium latifolium*, 20 stems
- *Panicum capillare* 'Sparkling Fountain', 20 stems
- Straw flowers (*Xerochrysum* syn. *Helichrysum*), 5–6 stems, plus 40 individual flower heads
- Alliums and/or hydrangea heads, 10–12 (I've used a mix of *Allium hollandicum* 'Purple Sensation', *A. cristophii* and *A. schubertii* for small to large heads)

Step 1

Gather the branches of silver birch to make the base structure. If you have a beam across a fireplace, knock in nails or tacks along the length. Attach taut lines of wire or ribbon between each nail, then attach the branches of silver birch to these, tying them securely to the wire or ribbon. If the birch branches are no thicker than your finger, they won't weigh much, so even thin wire will safely support the structure.

Step 2

Harvest any robust-stemmed seedheads you have in your garden (or you've stored from earlier in the year). I've used honesty (*Lunaria*), nicandra and sanguisorba as they all have good, strong stems, but others such as agapanthus, Japanese anemones and crocosmia do just as well.

Start by adding these larger ingredients. If you can, thread them into the silver birch structure so they build up to create a halo effect around the birch base. If they don't stay where you want them, tie them to the branches with twine.

Step 3

Add the grasses (chasmanthium and panicum), again just wrap and tuck them into the birch and seedhead layer you've already created, tying them in with twine if you need to. Dot them across the swag widely to increase the density of material and to create a multidimensional arrangement.

Step 4

Using a needle and thread, create garlands with the straw flower heads and hang them over the swag. Individually add the alliums and festive decorations (I've used glass birds and baubles). Finally, bring the whole thing to life by adding a string of lights.

PRACTICAL

November & December

Opposite Chucking handfuls of *Narcissus* 'Actaea' on to grass before planting them, wherever they have landed for a natural look.

We have three main jobs to attend to in the last couple of months of the year, and depending on the weather, we usually do them in this order. First, we prune most of our roses, and keep the prunings to lay on top of pots and borders planted with tulips, to protect them from squirrels. Then we move on to our most time-consuming job – planting tons of tulips. The third job is cutting down and mulching the dahlia beds and lifting any tubers in pots.

As we go into the coldest, wettest months with little growing, seeding or fruiting for the birds to eat, we also consciously plan for sources of bird food, making sure we have plenty available until next March and April. At that point, invertebrates reappear in large numbers and garden birds are over the hungry gap and more likely to survive.

If we see that our seed and fruit plants are looking a bit thin on the ground, we top up with bird feeders (using mainly calorific fat balls and protein-rich sunflower seeds). Current advice seems to be that sporadic use of feeders is okay (feast and famine is more natural). The key is proper, regular (weekly) washing of the feeders and to move the feeders around. But, ideally, we need to be growing ever more plants to naturally feed the birds.

We make sure to have sources of water, refilling bird baths with clean water every day. We also supplement our many hedges with nesting boxes placed on the cool, north or east side of our buildings, in hidden places.

Garden birds are key to slug, snail and general pest control in an organic garden (see p201). They are valuable gardener's friends.

PRACTICAL

Previous page Bunches of amaranth and homemade bird feeders hanging in the mist.

Pruning Roses

We aim to prune our roses this side of Christmas, but you can do this anytime until early March. You should complete the job before the roses come into leaf to avoid damaging the leaf buds and shoots.

The bonus of pruning late in the year, rather than early the following year, is we can then use the prunings to form thorny grids over our bulb plantings to help keep squirrels at bay. This is very effective in the garden here.

I was taught a method of rose pruning by the gardeners at Sissinghurst, who follow a training technique that has been passed down from one gardener to the next since head gardener Jack Vass started at Sissinghurst in 1939.

Rather than cutting the whole bush back, leaving stumps about a third of their previous height, we train many of them into domes, attaching the rose stems to a hazel frame, one branch on top of another. By pruning and training in this way, we get roses covered in flowers, from soil level to the apex of their dome. It gives us the very best rose performance and more flowers to harvest.

The basic principle is, treat them mean to keep them keen. If you put every stem of your rose under pressure, bending it and stressing it, it flowers better. Horizontal training overcomes apical dominance (where the main stem is dominant over the side stems) and encourages the side shoots to believe they have an equal chance of flowering – so they do.

Most of our picking roses are shrub types, but we also have a few climbers and some ramblers (such as 'Francis E. Lester'), which we grow for its elegant rosehips.

Shrub Roses
Depending on their habit, our picking shrub roses are treated in one of three ways, which I've outlined here, starting with the simplest.

Contained, well-behaved varieties For the small to medium-sized bush types, we prune back to an outward-facing bud, but don't train them. Examples for cut flowers include 'De Resht', 'Queen of Sweden', 'Julia's Rose', 'Duchess of Cornwall', 'Sweet Juliet', 'Cinco de Mayo', 'Aphrodite', 'Champagne Moment', 'Timeless Purple' and 'Mokarosa'.

- Remember the three Ds of pruning: remove all dead, diseased and damaged wood. Keep the centre as open as possible. Also remove all crossing branches.
- Prune the rest back hard to an outward-facing bud, removing at least one third of the existing stem length.

Larger shrub roses For these, we need to be prepared before pruning, ready to make frames with hazel branches of various thicknesses. These can be bought (good garden centres have them, or you'll find them online) or harvested from hazel trees. They should be cut anytime from November to January, but ideally before the catkins emerge, so the branches are pliable but still bare.

Below top Pruned *Rosa* 'De Resht'.

Below bottom *Rosa* 'Tuscany Superb', pruned and trained into a dome to ensure more prolific flowering.

Some of the large shrub roses are leggy, putting out great, pliable, lax, triffid arms, which are easy to tie down and train, and make neat domes. One example is 'Tuscany Superb'. This is also the pruning treatment of slightly more rangy shrubs such as 'Ispahan' and 'The Generous Gardener'.

Without any sign of a flower, these look magnificent as soon as you've pruned them, and in a few months, each stem – under stress – will flower abundantly and will do so on stems curved almost to ground level.

- Remove all the dead, diseased and damaged wood.
- Using lengths of hazel with a diameter of about 2.5cm (1in), bend three branches to form semi-circles. Ensure the hazel ends are securely pushed into the soil. Form a triangular shape to encircle a single rose or clump of roses.
- Stem by stem, bend last year's wood down and tie it to the hazel frame. Start at the outside and tie that in first, then move towards the middle, using the plant's own stems to build up a web shape, tying one stem to the stem below. In the case of large varieties, such as 'Ispahan', you can create fantastic height, one layer of stems domed and attached to the one below.

PRACTICAL

Below *Rosa* 'Francis E. Lester' covered in hips.

Tall, rangy shrubs with stiffer branches

There are certain roses (such as 'Warm Welcome' and 'Scent from Heaven') that are too stiff to train over hazel hoops. They can be trained along a fence or wall, or pruned to cover a cylindrical frame as outlined here.

- Remove all the dead, diseased and damaged wood.
- Use four lengths of thick hazel (about the diameter of a thumb), to encircle the rose. Hammer the hazel into the soil.
- This structure surrounds the base of the rose and all remaining stems can be twirled up the frame.
- Bend each pruned stem down to form a fan shape and attach to the stem below.

Rambling Roses

We grow *Rosa banksiae*, which flowers in May. We also love 'Francis E. Lester' for its huge flower clouds with fantastic scent in June – one head fills a bowl and its elegant wands of rosehips are fantastic for much of summer and autumn. They're beautiful in a vase and last ages.

As a general rule, these roses are much bigger and best left to their own devices, but old wood needs to be taken out to encourage new growth. We prune out a couple of the oldest stems annually. For *Rosa banksiae* this is best done in summer, soon after flowering; for 'Francis E. Lester' do this in winter.

Below top *Rosa* 'Ispahan', pruned and trained onto an arched hazel frame.

Below bottom The same plant in summer, covered in flowers from soil level to the apex of the dome.

PRACTICAL

Below **Planting tulip bulbs with a trowel.**

Planting Tulips

Depending on how many bulbs we have to plant each season, this is our most time-consuming job. We put in 16,000 tulips in 2025, many of which were on trial.

When I started gardening, I planted tulips into trenches, but we've since learnt that this causes too much damage to the soil structure, and the microorganisms and mycorrhiza on which we depend for good, sustainable gardening. So we now minimise soil disturbance by planting either with a trowel or bulb planter. Which tool we choose depends on whether the ground is clear. If it's clear, we can quickly and easily dig lots of holes with a decent trowel. If it's an already crowded border, we turn to a bulb planter on a spade-style handle.

Either way, we wait until November and December to plant our tulips. That's partly down to tradition, and partly the science. It's true that when we had properly cold Novembers (which I remember from my childhood, frozen to the bone on bonfire night), the hard frosts would do a good job of wiping out fungal spores remaining from any tulip blight infection the previous spring. Now, with our milder, wetter autumns, this is unlikely to be the case. On top of that, tulips don't actually start to root for a good four to eight weeks after most other bulbs we grow in the cutting garden, so they are safe to go in last.

Flower farmers often treat their tulips as annuals, and as result, don't worry about perenniality. When they're picking their flowers, they pull the stem out of the bulb to give long stems. This damages the bulb and means it won't grow again, which feels too extravagant and wasteful to me. We have done lots of trialling and experimentation to ensure we are growing perennial tulips and not putting in the effort and investment for just one harvest.

How perennial they become is partly down to variety, with the green-flashed tulips in the Viridiflora group, the whopper, early tulips in the Darwin Hybrid group and those in the Lily-flowered group the most reliable. There are also some anomalies such as 'Mistress Mystic', which come back year on year.

To plant, use a trowel or a bulb planter (see p390). Here are some extra tips.

Next page Snowy Perch Hill, seen from the west looking over the buildings and garden.

- Plant tulips at 12–15cm (5–6in) apart to allow for good air circulation.
- Aim to get them as deep as the bulb planter will allow, which is about 10cm (4in), and do the same with a trowel. At this depth, the bulb will be cooler and won't produce bulblets (which will drain energy from the mother bulb), and will hopefully keep flowering for several years.
- Plant in unpromising, poor soil if you can. We've found that around the base of fruit trees (with thin, poor topsoil) and beneath a hedge (in a food and water desert), tulips reappear much more reliably than in beds enriched with organic matter, as you might get below roses.
- Protect against rodent (grey squirrel, rat and mouse) attack. You can use chicken wire, but it's hard to secure. We've had much better results from rose prunings laid in a grid over the soil. Chilli flakes scattered densely over the soil surface help deter them, but are not enough at Perch Hill.
- Overplant with early-flowering biennials, such as wallflowers and honesty. You can also add aquilegia seedlings or May-flowering alliums such as 'Purple Sensation'. For wallflowers, choose the taller, highly scented varieties such as *Erysimum* 'Fire King' or 'Blood Red', or any in the Sunset series. If you need to move them from a stock bed, keep as much root intact by digging them up with a spade (not a trowel), and carrying as much soil with the roots as you can.

Cutting Back and Mulching Dahlias

When I started gardening, our average winter was too severe to leave dahlias in the ground, but not these days. We find it's just as reliable – and hugely less labour intensive – to treat them like our hardy perennials and leave them in the ground.

Cut the plants back when flowering starts to tail off, you don't need to wait for a hard frost first. Cut to within 7–8cm (3in) off the ground. Mulch deeply by tipping a bucket of compost or green waste (see p200 for a note of warning) over the head of each one. Dome it over the crown and this will insulate the tender tubers through the winter and direct the rain away a little, so there's less danger of rot. Make sure to label each dahlia clearly so you remember what's what.

Lifting dahlias
If you live in a frost pocket or in an area that experiences high rainfall, or you have dahlias growing in pots, the tubers need to be lifted and brought in for the winter. Dig them up or knock them out of the pot. Dry off the tubers by standing them upside down to drain the stems for a week or two. Remove any loose soil and pack them into boxes of dry compost and store frost-free in a shed or under the bench (in the dark) in the greenhouse. Check in on them occasionally through the winter and if there are any signs of rot, cut that bit straight out then repack. They'll be ready for potting up in spring.

Sowing and Planting Chart

Latin name	Common name	Plant group	Recommended technique
Ageratum houstonianum	Mexican paintbrush	Half-hardy annual	Seed tray
Allium	Allium	Hardy	Plant outside in autumn
Amaranthus	Love-lies-bleeding	Half-hardy annual	Seed tray
Ammi	Bishop's flower	Hardy annual	Guttering, seed tray, module, root trainer or direct
Anemone coronaria	Garden anemone	Semi-hardy. Needs good drainage and sheltered site	Plant inside or out Sept/Oct
Anethum graveolens	Dill	Hardy annual	Guttering, module, small pot or direct
Antirrhinum	Snapdragon	Half-hardy annual	Seed tray then module
Atriplex	Red orache	Hardy annual	Module
Borago officinalis	Borage	Hardy annual	Seed tray, module or direct
Brassica oleracea Acephala G.	Kale	Hardy annual	Guttering or direct
Briza maxima	Greater quaking grass	Hardy annual	Module or direct
Calendula officinalis	English or Pot marigold	Hardy annual	Module, guttering or direct
Callistephus chinensis	China aster	Half-hardy annual	Seed tray
Cardiospermum halicacabum	Love-in-a-puff	Half-hardy annual	Seed tray or module
Centaurea cyanus	Cornflower	Hardy annual	Module, guttering or direct (larger if autumn-sown)
Cerinthe major	Honeywort	Hardy annual	Seed tray then module
Chasmanthium latifolium	North America wild oats	Perennial	Seed tray or direct
Cleome	Spider flower	Half-hardy annual	Seed tray then module
Cobaea scandens	Cup and saucer vine	Half-hardy annual climber	Individual pot
Consolida	Larkspur	Hardy annual	Seed tray then module, or direct (pre-chill)
Cosmos	Mexican aster	Half-hardy annual	Module or direct
Crocus	Crocus	Hardy bulb	Plant outside Sep/Oct
Cynara cardunculus Scolymus G.	Globe artichoke	Perennial	Module
Cynoglossum amabile	Chinese forget-me-not	Hardy annual	Seed tray then module
Dahlia	Dahlia	Semi-hardy tuberous perennial. Needs mulching for protection in winter	Module
Daucus carota	Wild carrot	Biennial	Seed tray, module, root trainer or direct
Delphinium	Delphinium	Perennial	Seed tray then module
Dianthus barbatus	Sweet William	Biennial	Seed tray, module or direct
Digitalis	Foxglove	Biennial	Seed tray or direct
Echinacea purpurea	Coneflower	Perennial	Seed tray, module or direct
Echium vulgare	Viper's bugloss	Hardy annual	Direct
Eryngium alpinum	Sea holly	Perennial	Seed tray then module
Erysimum	Wallflower	Biennial	Seed tray, module or direct
Eschscholzia californica	California poppy	Hardy annual	Direct
Euphorbia oblongata	Spurge	Perennial	Seed tray then module or direct
Galanthus	Snowdrop	Hardy bulb	Plant outside Sep/Oct
Gladiolus	Gladioli	Semi-hardy corm	Plant outside Apr–Jun
Gypsophila elegans	Baby's breath	Hardy annual	Seed tray, module or direct
Helianthus	Sunflower	Hardy annual	Direct or individual pot
Ipomoea lobata	Spanish flag	Half-hardy annual climber	Module
Lagurus ovatus	Bunny's tail grass	Hardy annual	Seed tray, module or direct
Lathyrus odoratus	Sweet pea	Hardy annual climber	Root trainer or direct
Lavandula	Lavender	Perennial	Seed tray
Lavatera trimestris	Annual mallow	Hardy annual	Module
Limonium sinuatum	Annual statice	Half-hardy annual	Seed tray
Linaria maroccana	Toadflax	Hardy annual	Module or direct
Lupinus mutabilis	Lupin	Hardy annual	Seed tray, module or direct

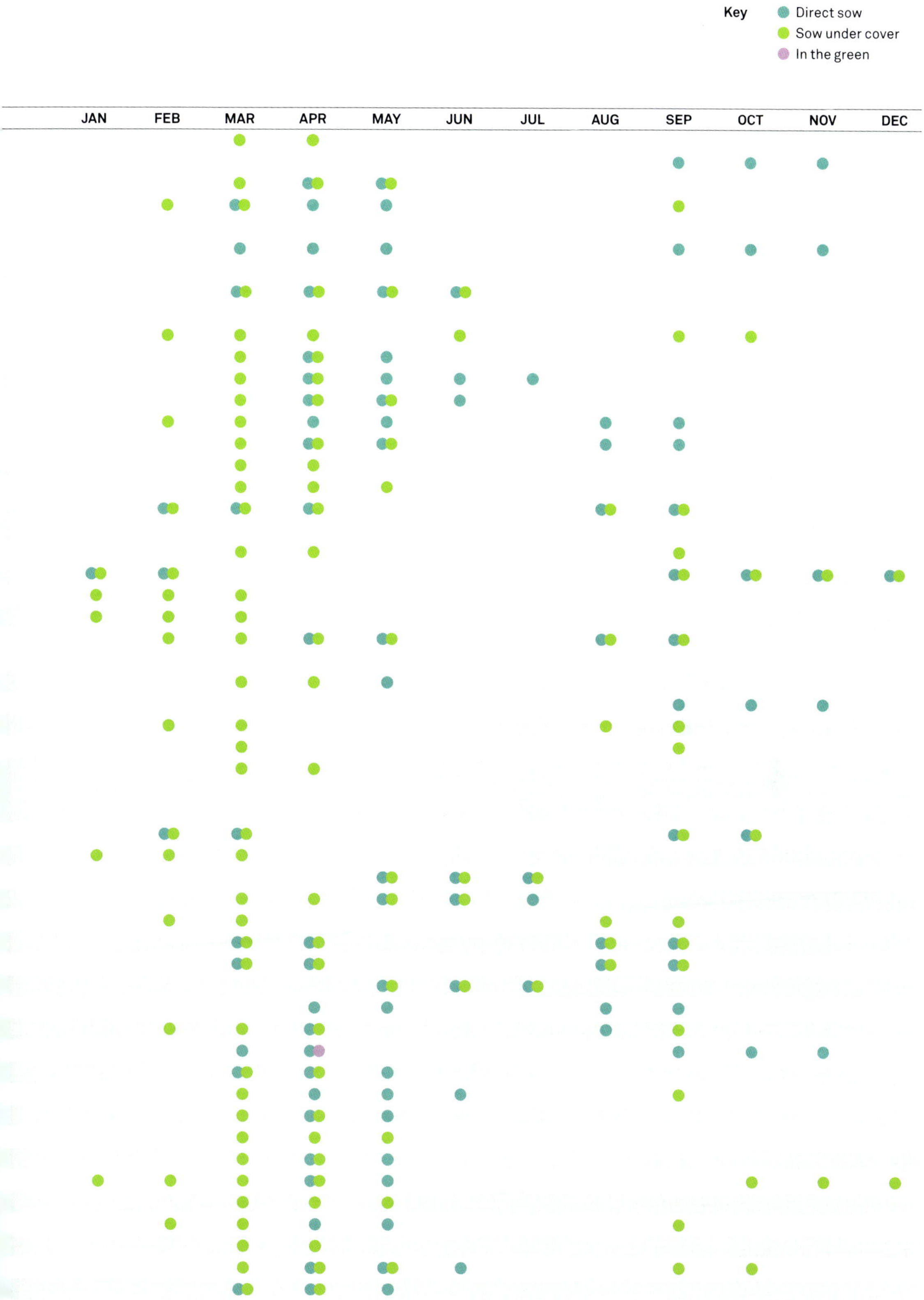

	JAN	FEB	MAR	APR	MAY	JUN	JUL	AUG	SEP	OCT	NOV	DEC

Key
● Direct sow
● Sow under cover
● In the green

Sowing and Planting Chart

Latin name	Common name	Plant group	Recommended technique
Lychnis coronaria	Rose campion	Perennial	Seed tray, module or direct
Malope trifida	Malope	Hardy annual	Module or direct
Matthiola incana	Stocks	Biennial	Module or direct
Moluccella laevis	Bells of Ireland	Half-hardy annual	Seed tray then module, week in freezer first
Myrrhis odorata	Sweet cicely	Perennial	Seed tray or direct
Narcissus	Daffodil	Hardy bulb	Plant inside or out Sep/Oct
Nicandra physalodes	Shoo-fly plant	Hardy annual	Seed tray then module or direct
Nicotiana	Tobacco plant	Half-hardy annual	Seed tray or module
Nigella	Love-in-a-mist	Hardy annual	Direct or guttering
Ocimum basilicum	Basil	Half-hardy annual	Guttering or direct
Oenothera lindheimeri	Guara	Perennial	Module
Orlaya grandiflora	White lace flower	Hardy annual	Seed tray then module or direct
Panicum capillare	Witch grass	Hardy annual	Seed tray, module or direct
Panicum miliaceum 'Violaceum'	Red millet	Hardy annual	Module or seed tray
Papaver commutatum, rhoeas and somniferum	Common poppy, Corn poppy and Opium poppy	Hardy annual	Direct
Papaver nudicaule	Icelandic poppy	Biennial	Seed tray then module or direct
Persicaria	Prince's feather	Hardy annual	Seed tray or module
Petroselinum crispum	Parsley	Biennial grown as annual	Guttering or direct
Petunia	Petunia	Half-hardy annual	Seed tray
Phacelia tanacetifolia	Fiddleneck	Hardy annual	Direct
Phaseolus vulgaris 'Borlotto'	Borlotti bean	Half-hardy annual	Root trainer or pot
Phlox drummondii	Annual phlox	Half-hardy annual	Seed tray, module or direct
Pisum sativum	Pea	Hardy annual	Guttering, root trainer or direct
Primula	Primula, Polyanthus	Perennial	Seed tray
Ranunculus	Ranunculus	Semi-hardy bulb	Plant inside or out Sep/Oct
Rhodochiton	Purple bell vine	Half-hardy annual	Seed tray
Rudbeckia	Coneflower	Half-hardy annual	Module
Salvia patens	Gentian sage	Half-hardy annual	Seed tray then module
Salvia viridis	Clary sage	Hardy annual	Direct, module or guttering
Scabiosa atropurpurea	Sweet scabious	Hardy annual	Seed tray or module
Scabiosa caucasica	Garden scabious	Perennial	Seed tray then module
Scabiosa stellata	Drumstick scabious	Hardy annual	Seed tray or direct
Schizanthus	Butterfly flower	Half-hardy annual	Seed tray or module
Selinum wallichianum	Milk parsley	Perennial	Seed tray
Solanum lycopersicum	Tomato	Half-hardy annual	Module
Tagetes	Marigold	Half-hardy annual	Seed tray, module or direct
Tanacetum parthenium	Feverfew	Perennial	Seed tray, module or direct
Tellima	Fringe cups	Perennial	Seed tray or module
Thalictrum	Chinese meadow rue	Perennial	Seed tray or module
Thunbergia	Black-eyed Susan	Half-hardy annual	Seed tray or module
Tithonia	Mexican sunflower	Half-hardy annual	Module
Tropaeolum majus and minus	Nasturtium	Half-hardy annual	Seed tray, guttering or direct
Tulipa	Tulip	Hardy bulb	Plant outside Oct/Nov
Verbena bonariensis and V. rigida	Purple top, Slender vervain	Perennial	Seed tray then module or direct
Vicia faba	Broad bean	Hardy annual	Root trainer or direct
Viola cornuta / V. wittrockiana	Pansy, Viola	Hardy annual / Perennial	Seed tray
Xeranthemum	Annual everlasting	Half-hardy annual	Direct
Xerochrysum	Straw flower	Half-hardy annual	Seed tray, module or direct
Zinnia	Zinnia	Half-hardy annual	Module, guttering or direct

Key
Direct sow
Sow under cover
In the green
JAN
FEB
MAR
APR
MAY
JUN
JUL
AUG
SEP
OCT
NOV
DEC

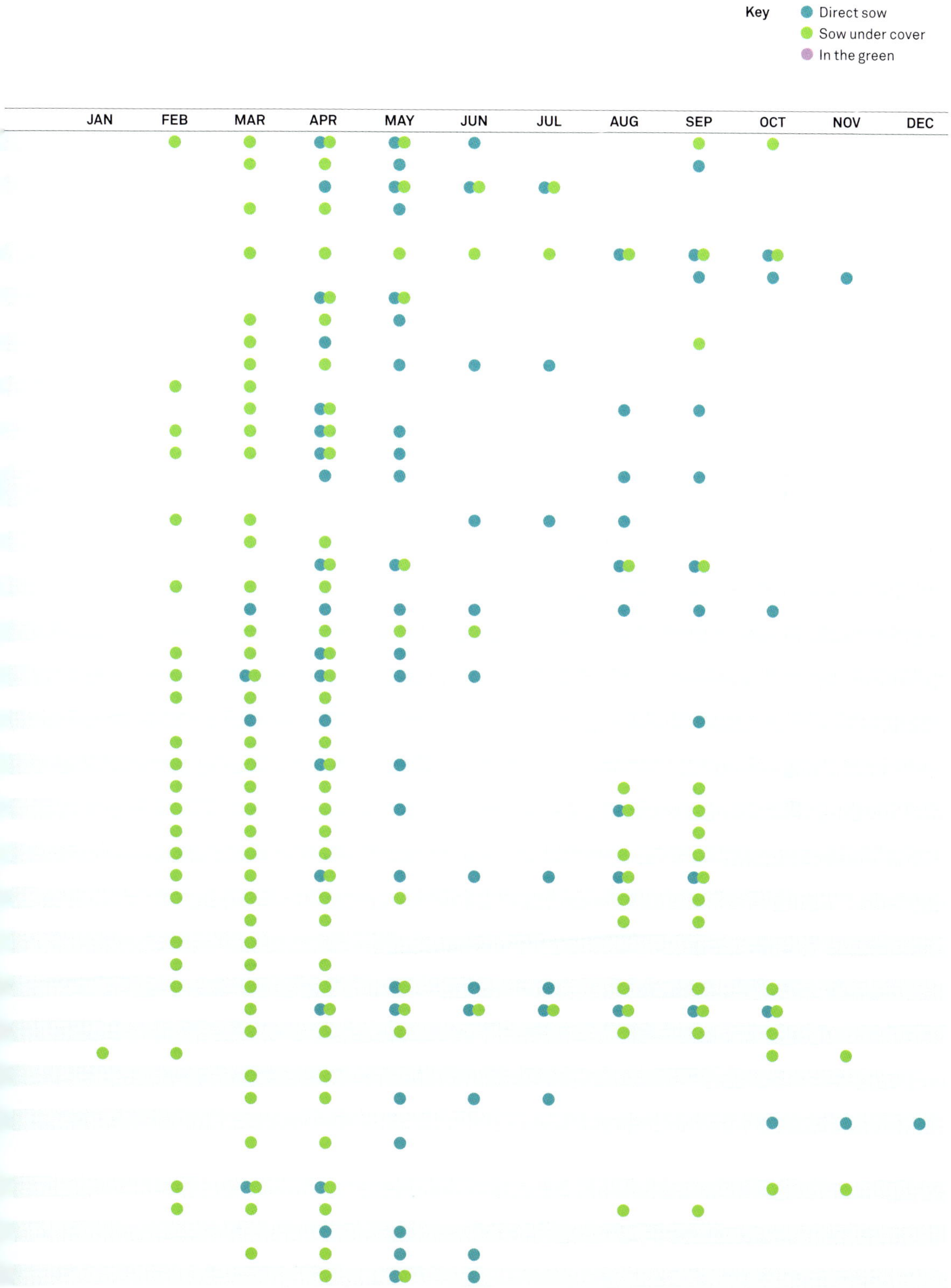

Index

Page numbers in *italic*
refer to the illustrations

A

Acanthus mollis 'Rue Medan'
(bear's breeches) 324
Acer (maple) 363, *365*
Achillea (yarrow) 324
Acidanthera see *Gladiolus murielae*
aconite, winter see *Eranthis hyemalis*
Acrolinium 324
Agapanthus 61, 363, 421, *421*
Agastache (hyssop) *pallidiflora* var. *neomexicana* 'Rose Mint' 283, *285*
Ageratum 45, 65
Alchemilla mollis 35, 213, *256*
alder 411
Allium 35, 82, *83*, 203, 219–21, *220*, 223, *250*, 251, 327, 387, 390–1, *390*, 409, 422–3, *422–3*
 A. *cristophii* 203, 219, 251, *251*, 327, 422–3, *422–3*
 A. *hollandicum* 64, 203, 219, 358
 A. 'Lucy Ball' *83*, 221
 A. 'Purple Rain' *83*, 203, *205*
 A. 'Purple Sensation' 265, 422–3, *422–3*, 431
 A. *schubertii* 203, 219, 251, *252*, 327, 422–3, *422–3*
almond tree blossom 97
Aloysia citrodora (lemon verbena) 314, 408–9
Alstroemeria 28, 38
Amaranthus 28, *39*, 40, 144, 191, 231, 301, 324, 336
 A. *caudatus* 52
 A. *c.* 'Hot Biscuits' *50*, 143, *318*, 319, 324, *342*, 343
 A. 'Red Army' 143, *302*, *318*, 319, *321*, *321*, 324, *334*, *342*, 343
× *Amarine* 374
amaryllis see *Hippeastrum*
Amelanchier lamarckii 168
Aminopyralid 200
Ammi majus 15, 17, *18*, 28, *50*,

51–2, *62*, *63*, *77*, *85*, 118, 142, 195, 197, *197*, *274*, *280*, *282*, 283, *287*, 289–91, *289–91*, 299, 317, *317*, *320*, *320*, 360, 388
A. *visnaga* 21, 41, 52, *65*, *75*, 142, 240, *280*, 283, 360
Anemone 390
 A. *blanda* 136
 A. *coronaria* 30, 34, *42*, *43*, 95, *103*, 123, 126, 154–9, *158*
 A. × *hybrida* (Japanese anemone) 41, 363, 378
 A. *nemorosa* 'Blue Shades' 158
Anethum graveolens (dill) *50*, 52, 61, 340
angelica 87, 327, *409*
annuals: composting 387, 389
 deadheading 357
 planting out 194, *194*, 388
 sowing 142–3, 191, 271, 358–61, 361
Anthriscus sylvestris 'Ravenswing' 163, 217
Antirrhinum (snapdragon) 21, 28, 40, 41, *63*, 87, 118, 120–1, *121*, 143, 144, 231, *256*, 271, 281, 301, 310, 378, 387, *388*
 A. *majus* 'Appleblossom' 281, *282*, *287*
 A. *m.* 'Chantilly Bronze' *36–7*, *63*, *256*
 A. *m.* 'Costa Apricot' *29*, *316*, 317, *338–9*
 A. *m.* 'Costa Silver' *282*, *316*, 317
 A. *m.* 'White Giant' *199*, 281, *287*
aphids 295, 343
apple blossom 107, *207*
Aquilegia 213, 358, 431
Arbutus unedo (strawberry tree) 408
Artemisia dracunculus (French tarragon) *285*
artichoke see *Cynara cardunculus*
asters *39*

Astrantia 213, *401*
Atriplex 51, 52, *71*, 87
axillary buds 12–15

B

baby's breath see *Gypsophila*
basil see *Ocimum*
bay leaves 409
bear's breeches see *Acanthus mollis*
bedside table roses 254, *254–5*
bells of Ireland see *Molucella laevis*
benches, heated 146–7, *147*
Betula pendula (silver birch) 182, 184, *402*, *405*, 409–10, 411, 416–17, *416*, 422–3, *422–3*
Bidens ferulifolia 'Hot and Spicy' *311*
biennials 217, 269–71, 329, 357
birch, silver see *Betula pendula*
bird feeder wreath 416–17, *416*
birds 201, 295, 304, 343, 387, 396, 406, 425
black-eyed Susan see *Thunbergia alata*
blight 170, 177, 200, 390, 430
bluebells 84, 87
Boiled Sweet palette *57*, 60, *60–1*, 67, 68, *68–71*, 70
borage 197, *197*
 Indian see *Plectranthus ciliatus*
borlotti beans *420*
botrytis 304, 331, 357
bottles, mini 384–5, *384–5*
branches 411
Brassica rapa subsp. *nipposinica* var. *laciniata* 182
The Bride 46, *47*–8
The Bridesmaids 46, 48
Briza maxima (great quaking grass) 55, 214, *215*, 306, 326, *326*
broad beans 292–3, *292*
Brunnera 174

bulbs 357
  bulb lasagne 391, *391*
  planting 387, 390–1, *390*
  see also individual plants
bunches: hand-tied 288, 289–91, *289–91*
  summer hand-tied 318–19, *318*
burnet *see Sanguisorba*
buttercups 87

C
Calceolaria 'Kentish Hero' *58*, 72
Calendula (English marigold) *14*, 35, 142, *145*, 146, 195, 198, *198*, 299
  C. officinalis 'Indian Prince' 17, *18*, 44, *71*, 142, 278, *279*
  C. o. 'Neon' *279*
  C. o. 'Sunset Buff' 44, *66*, 74, *74–5*, 142, 278, *279*, *305*, *318*, 319
Camassia 390
camellias 107
Cardiospermum 55
cardoon *see Cynara cardunculus*
carrot, wild *see Daucus carota*
Caryopteris 364
Cashmere Jersey palette *20*, 57, 62, *62–3*, 72, *72–5*, 74
castor oil plant *see Ricinus communis*
caterpillars 343
catkins 411
Centaurea cyanus 60, 278, *279*–80, 324, 360, *361*
Cercidiphyllum japonicum (katsura tree) 365
Cerinthe 34, 43, 87, 195, 214, 296, 299, 359, 388
  C. major 17
  C. m. 'Purpurascens' *18*, *21*, 44, 52, *53*, *66*, *86*, 142, 146, *156*–8, 159, 197–8, *197*–*8*, *215*, *218*, *245*, *271*, *298*, *358–9*, 360, *388*

Chamelaucium uncinatum (wax flower) 98, *99*
Champs-Élysées palette *57*, 64, *64–6*, 76
Chasmanthium latifolium (North American wild oats) 55, *303*, 326, *326*, *401*, 422–3, *422–3*
cherry *see Prunus*
chestnuts 383
chillies *418*, 419–21, *420–1*
Chinese lantern *see Physalis*
Christmas 413
  mantelpiece swag 422–3, *422–3*
  wreaths 110–13, *110*–*13*, *418*, 419–20, *420*
Christmas rose *see Helleborus niger*
Chrysanthemum 28, 40, 41, 43, *80*, 109, 191, 357, 368–73
  cuttings 193, *193*
  C. 'Avignon Pink' *40*, *62*, *75*, 368, *369*, *372*, *374*
  C. 'Pandion Bronze' 368, *369*, *372*
  C. 'Pip Sunny' 368, *370–1*
  C. 'Rosanno Elizabeth' *370–1*
  C. 'Spider Bronze' 368, *370–1*
  C. 'Tarantula Red' *372*
  C. Tula series *40*, 368, *370–1*, *373*
Cirsium rivulare 'Atropurpureum' *250*
Clarkia pulchella 'Snowflake' *280*
Clematis 35, 38, 55, 351
  C. 'Bill Mackenzie' *397*, 411
  C. 'Elizabeth' 207–9, *207*
  C. montana 207–9
  C. 'Nubia' Boulevard Series *257*
  C. rehderiana 411
  C. vitalba (old man's beard) 411
Cleome spinosa 'Colour Mix' *65*
climbing plants: frames 150–1, *151*
  planting out 232, *232*
  see also individual plants
clove knots 267, *267*
Cobaea pringlei 393, *397* *384–5*, *384–5*, 393, *397*

C. scandens (cup and saucer vine) *14*, 38, 41, *42*, *43*, 55, 87, 109, 118, 120, *121*, 146, 148, 191, 231–2, *232*, *335*, 336–40, *337–9*, *369*, *384–5*, *384–5*, 393, *397*, *414*
cold frames 146
colour palettes 57–77
comfrey feed 236, *237*, 297
compost, sowing seeds 143–4
composting annuals 389
conditioning 79, 84–93, 414
  dahlias 352–4
  tulips 178
conkers 383
Connolly, Shane 292
Consolida (larkspur) 324
Convallaria majalis (lily of the valley) 203
Corbett, Graeme 323
Coreopsis 'Redshift' *311*
corn 383
cornflowers 295, 299, 388
Cornus 88
Corsican hellebore *see Helleborus argutifolius*
Corylus (hazel) 43, 110
Cosmos 23, 28, 38, 41, *61*, 143, *145*, 191, 231, 265, 281, 310, *311*, 351, 387, *389*
  C. bipinnatus 'Apricot Lemonade' *282*, 310, *311*
  C. b. 'Apricotta' 55, 143, 281, *311*
  C. b. 'Candy Stripe' *77*, *311*
  C. b. 'Dazzler' 17, *18*, *282–3*, *335*
  C. b. 'Double Click Cranberries' *266*, *280*, 281
  C. b. 'Fizzy Rose Picotee' *23*, *76*, *280*, *311*
  C. b. 'Purity' 17, *18*, *22*, *23*, *64*, *76–7*, 143, *231*, 281, *311*
  C. b. 'Rubenza' *36–7*, *58*, *68*, *72*, 143, *240*, *274*, 281, *282–3*
Cotinus (smoke bush) 88, 365, *366*, 383

crab apple *see Malus*
cranberry and crab apple wreath 421, *421*
Crataegus (hawthorn) 205, *206*, 208–9, 416–17, *416*
Crocosmia (montbretia) 327, 363
Crocus 62, *74*, 98, *100*, 123, 131–2, 136
crown imperial *see Fritillaria imperialis*
cup and saucer vine *see Cobaea scandens*
cutting patches 115–16, *116*
cuttings: chrysanthemums 193, *193*
  dahlias 192, *192*
  tender perennials 331, 357
Cyclamen 98, 123, 131–2
Cynara 324
  C. cardunculus (cardoon/artichoke) 64, 76, *134*, 182, 184, 205, *325*, *401*
Cyperus eragrostis 69

D

daffodils *see Narcissus*
Dahlia 14, 28, 38, *39*, 40, 41, *61*, 63–5, *69*, 71, *73*, 75, 87, 109, 148–9, 191, 231, 265, *274*, 275, 303, *311–12*, 314, 324, 333–47, *334*, *338–9*, *341*, 344, *345–6*, 347, 351, *355*, 365, 367–8, *369*, 374, *379*, 396
  bulb lasagne 391
  cutting and conditioning 352–4
  cutting back and mulching 431
  cuttings 192, *192*
  dahlia groups 344–7
  deadheading 356, 357, 387
  division 192
  floating flowers 352, *353*
  lifting 431
  planting out 233–4, *234*
  staking *268*, 269
  table decorations 354, *354*
D. 'Adam's Choice' *59*, *338–9*, 347
D. 'Autumn Orange' *369*, *379*
D. 'Bishop of Auckland' *336*, *340*, *350*
D. 'Bishop of Llandaff' *18*, 19–20, 348
D. 'Bishop's Children' *342*, 348
D. 'Blue Bayou' *21*, *338–9*, 340, 346, 348, *379*
D. 'Café au Lait' *63*, *75*, 324, *345*, 347
D. 'Chat Noir' 344, *369*
D. 'Copperboy' *59*, *334*, 335, 344, *345*
D. 'Dalaya Aruna' *21*, *338–9*
D. 'Downham Royal' *61*, *369*
D. 'Honka Fragile' 348, *348*, *355*
D. 'Jowey Winnie' *62*, *75*
D. 'Karma Naomi' 321, *321*
D. 'Labyrinth' *21*, *63*, 234, *338–9*, 347, 368
D. 'Linda's Baby' *63*, 344
D. 'Lou Farman' 348, *349*–50
D. 'Manoa' *58*, *68*, *70*, *75*, 334
D. 'Molly Raven' 22, 335, *346*, 347, *350*
D. 'Nicholas' 321, *321*, 347
D. 'Night Silence' 335, *338–9*
D. 'Nuit d'Été' *334*, 344
D. 'Perch Hill' 22, 303, 335, *340*, *346*, 347
D. 'Polka' 314, *350*
D. 'Purple Flame' *61*, *71*
D. 'Rancho' 344, *345*
D. 'Rhubarb and Custard' *75*, *350*, 365
D. 'Rip City' *18*, 19–20, 22, 301, 344
D. 'Rosie Raven' *346*, 347
D. 'Sarah Raven' *69*, *346*
D. 'Schipper's Bronze' *58–9*, *68*, *72*
D. 'Sissinghurst' 22, *72*, *73*, 335–6, *336*, *353*
D. 'Totally Tangerine' *68*–9, 275
D. 'Tsuki-yori-no-shisha' 344, *345*
D. 'Verrone's Obsidian' *348*, *355*
D. 'Waltzing Mathilda' *71*, *336*, *348*, *350*
D. 'Zundert Mystery Fox' *321*, *321*, *379*
Daphne bholua 'Jacqueline Postill' 97
D. odora 'Aureomarginata' 97
Daucus carota (wild carrot) 298
deadheading 356, 357, 387
Delphinium 93
Dianthus (pinks) 79
  D. barbatus (sweet William) 26, 35, *71*, *216*, 217, 269
  D. b. 'Green Trick' *52*, *53*, *71*
  D. b. (Nigrescens Group) 'Sooty' 52, *71*, 269
Didiscus caeruleus 65
Digitalis (foxglove) 26, 28, 35, *63*, 144, 217, 221–3, *221–2*, 249–51, *250*
  D. p. 'Sutton's Apricot' 222, *246–7*, 269–70
dill *see Anethum graveolens*
Dipsacus (teasel) 327, 416–17, *416*
drying flowers 295, *322*, 323–6
Dysphania botrys 377

E

Echinacea 64, 274, 301
Echium 14, 35
  E. vulgare 'Blue Bedder' *36–7*, *287*, *310*
edible arrangements 292–3, *292–3*
Eranthis hyemalis (winter aconite) 98, *100*, 107, 123, 131–2, *139*
Eryngium 19, *256*, *308–9*, *402*
Erysimum 11, 31, 34, *42*, 65, *71*, 87, 159, 163, *171*, 217, 270, 431
  E. cheiri 'Blood Red' 270, 431
  E. c. 'Blood Red Covent Garden' *216*
  E. c. 'Fire King' *71*, 270, 431
  E. c. 'Purple' *162*, *204*
  E. c. 'Sunset Apricot' *162*, *204*, 270
  E. c. 'Sunset Orange' *164–5*, *216*
  E. c. 'Vulcan' *71*, 182, 186, *216*
ethylene gas 93
Eucalyptus 40, 421, *421*
Euonymus (spindle) 366, 383, 421, *421*
  E. europaeus 365–7, *366*, *370–1*, 375
Euphorbia 22, 65, 81, 87, 107, 110, *134*, 153, 191, 198, *198*, 284, 359
  E. amygdaloides var. *robbiae* 46, 217
  E. ceratocarpa 28, 56
  E. characias subsp. *wulfenii* *61*, *208–9*, 250
  E. oblongata *18*, 19, 28, 34, 35, 38, 41, 44, *45*, 50, *51*, *53*, *68*, 240, 265, 266, 274, 283, 378
  E. palustris 19, 28, *59*, *70*, 217
  E. sikkimensis 19, 28
everlasting flowers *322*, 323–6

F

feeding 235, 236, 297
fennel see *Foeniculum*
ferns 87
fertiliser 236
fishbone grass see *Wangenheimia lima*
floating flowers 138, *138–9*, 352, *353*
flower food 93
flower grids 107–9, *107–9*
Foeniculum vulgare 'Purpureum' (fennel) *205*
foliage 48–55
  primary *46, 48*, 51–2
  secondary (filler) *46, 48*, 52
  spiller 55
  upper storey *46, 48*, 54–5
forager's wreath *421*, 421
forcing bulbs 358, 406
forget-me-nots see *Myosotis sylvatica*
foxgloves see *Digitalis*
foxtail see *Setaria viridis*
foxtail barley see *Hordeum jubatum*
frames 148, *148*, 150–1, *151*
French beans 293
Fritillaria 82, 132, *135, 173*, 182
  F. imperialis (crown imperial) *134*, 160
  F. meleagris (snake's head fritillary) *134*, 160, *162, 170*
  F. persica (Persian lily) 102, 160, *162*, 163
  F. raddeana 64, 101–2, 160–3, *182*, 186
frost 357, 390, 393, 430
fruit 406
fruit and veg Christmas wreath *418*, 419–20, *420*
fungal diseases 160, 170, 200, 241–4, 357, 390, 430

G

Gaillardia 308–9
Galanthus (snowdrop) 98, *100–1*, 101, 105, *105*, 107, 109, 110, 123, 131–2, 138
  G. 'Atkinsii' *97*, 101
  G. nivalis 97, 100, 101, *108–9, 139*
Galega officinalis 316, 317
Garrya elliptica 421, 421
Gatecrashers *46*, 48

gates, staking 265–6, *266*
germination 146–7
Geum 213, *213*
Gladiolus 39, 41, *60, 63*, 234, *234*, 301–3, *335*, 336, 351, *351, 376*, 377
grasses 54–5, 306, 326
Grayson, Kitty 323
green waste 199, 200
greenhouses 146, 191, 373
guelder rose see *Viburnum opulus*
gutter pipes 145–6, *145*, 194, 359, *388*
Gypsophila (baby's breath) 324

H

hardy annuals see annuals
hare's tail grass see *Lagurus ovatus*
harvesting seeds *298*, 299
hawthorn see *Crataegus*
hazel see *Corylus*
heated benches 146–7, *147*
Helenium 19, 28, 301, *308–9*, 364
Helianthus (sunflower) 28, 38, *58*, 87, 142, 146, 195, *196*, 267, *267*, 301, 304–6, *312*, 343, 387
  H. annuus 'Claret' *307, 342*
  H. a. 'ProCut Plum' *20*, 62, 74, *74*, 304, *307*, 320, *320*
  H. a. 'Ruby Eclipse' 304, *307, 335*
Helichrysum 323, 324
Heliotropium (heliotrope) 331
  H. arborescens 'Reva' *330*, 357, *376*, 377
Helleborus 29, 43, 79, 87, 88, *96*, 98, 102, 106, *106*, 107, 110, *124, 134*, 138, 404–6, 414
  H. argutifolius (Corsican hellebore) 102, 404
  H. × *ballardiae* 'Maestro' 43, *75*, 102, 406
  H. foetidus 86, 102, 404
  H. niger (Christmas rose) 43, *77*, 102, 404, *404*
  H. × *sahinii* 'Winterbells' 404, *407*
herbicides 200
herbs 87, 283–4
Hesperantha coccinea 377, *378*
Hesperis matronalis (sweet rocket) 205, *205–6*, 207, 217, *218*, 270
Hippeastrum (amaryllis) 358, 374, 406, *407*, 414, *415*

honesty see *Lunaria annua*
honeysuckle see *Lonicera*
honeywort see *Cerinthe major*
Hordeum jubatum (foxtail barley) 326
Hosta 88
Hyacinthus 81, 82, 95, 123–5, *124–5*, 154, 387, 390, 391, 414
Hydrangea 30, 88, *312*, 324, 383, 399–404, 411, 414
  H. arborescens 399–400, *400–1*, 403
  H. macrophylla 374, *398*, 402, 403, 404, *405*
  H. paniculata 'Limelight' 314, *379*, *398*, 400–4, *400*, *403*
  H. petiolaris 402, 403, 416–17, *416*
hyssop see *Agastache*

I

Icelandic poppy see *Oreomecon nudicaulis*
Ilex verticillata 407
Ipheion uniflorum 137
Ipomoea lobata 150, 336
Iris 30, 101, *103*, 123, 131–2, *135*, 209–13, 212, *212*, 223, 374, 391
  I. 'Red Ember' *58, 68, 72, 74*
ivy 88, 383, 414

J

Japanese anemones see *Anemone* × *hybrida*
Jasminum officinale 314
Jiffy 7s 145

K

kale 292, 383, 384–5, *384–5*
katsura tree see *Cercidiphyllum japonicum*

L

Lagurus 306
  L. ovatus (hare's tail grass) 326
large urn 224–6, *224–7*
larkspur see *Consolida*
Lathyrus (sweet peas) 15, *26*, 28, 35, 55, *71*, 87, *92*, 93, *114*, 118–20, 145, 149–51, *149, 151*, 214, 239, 241, *242*, *260–1*, 329
  feeding 297
  maintenance 235–6, 239–40
  picking and arranging 259–62

L. chloranthus 241, *261*
L. × hammettii 'Erewhon' 214, *214*, 241, *286*
L. odoratus 'Albutt Blue' 289–91, *289–91*
L. o. 'Almost Black' *260–1, 274*
L. o. 'Anniversary' 240, 241, *260*
L. o. 'Blue Velvet' 240, 241, *260*
L. o. 'Emilia Fox' *240*, 260–1
L. o. 'Judith Wilkinson' *242*, 261, *274*
L. o. 'King Edward VII' 239, *274*
L. o. 'King's Ransom' 241, *286*
L. o. 'Lord Nelson' 239, *260*, *293*
L. o. 'Matucana' *214*, 239, 240–1, *274*
L. o. 'Mollie Rilstone' *258*, 260
L. o. 'Painted Lady' 214, *214*
L. o. 'Prince Edward of York' 241, *262–3*
L. o. 'Prince of Orange' *242*, 261
L. o. 'Winston Churchill' 240, *240*, 260–1, *274*
Lavandula angustifolia 'Hidcote' (lavender) 329
Lavatera trimestris 'Dwarf Pink Blush' *64*, 317, *317*
lavender *see Lavandula*
leaves, autumn colour 363–5
leek 'St Victor' *172*
lemon verbena *see Aloysia citrodora*
Leucojum aestivum 77, *96*, 131
lichen 411
lilac 84, *87*
Lilium (lily) 82, 303–4, *305*
lily of the valley *see Convallaria majalis*
Limonium (statice) 323, *324*
Linaria maroccana 'Licilia Azure' *66*
Linaria purpurea 'Canon Went' 317, *317*
Lonicera (honeysuckle) 55, 110, 254
love-in-a-mist *see Nigella*
Lunaria (honesty) 31, *32–3*, 34, *162*, 203, 217, 270, 327, *409*, *409*, 422–3, *422–3*, 431
L. annua 71, *163*, 205, 270, 284
Lupinus (lupins) *86*, 145, 203, 209, 210–11, *215*, 218, 219, 223, 295, 301, *308–9*

M
Magnolia 107, 377
Malope 299
M. trifida 14, 15, *21*, 198, *198*, *286*
M. t. 'Alba' *64, 65, 76–7, 280, 281*
M. t. 'Vulcan' *70, 71, 240, 274, 281*
Malus 408
M. hupehensis (crab apple) 205, 224, *224–7*, 367, 408, *408*
M. × robusta 'Red Sentinel' 205–7, *208–9*, 224, *224–7*, 343, 367, *368*, *398*, 408
Malva moschata f. *alba* 65
mantelpiece swag 422–3, *422–3*
maples *see Acer*
marigolds *see Calendula*; *Tagetes*
Matthiola (stocks) 65, *155, 161*, 217
Mentha (mint) 284, *284*
Mexican sunflower *see Tithonia rotundifolia*
mice 119, 431
mildew 160, 297, 357
millet *see Panicum miliaceum*
mimosa 98
mini bottles 384–5, *384–5*
miniature vases 136, *136–7*
mint *see Mentha*
Mizuna 'Red Knight' *182*, 184
Molucella laevis (bells of Ireland) 54, *54*, 323, *324*
montbretia *see Crocosmia*
mulching 199–200, *199*, 296, 431
Muscari 30, 132, *134–7*, 154, 390
Myosotis sylvatica (forget-me-not) *11, 162, 163*, 217
myrtle 408

N
Narcissus (daffodil) 30, *30*, 34, 77–8, 82, 123, *124*, 125–31, *127–8*, *130–1*, 162, 182, 203, 387, 390, 391, 406, *407*
N. 'Actaea' *76–7*, 78, 127–8, *127*, *129, 131, 134*, 189
N. 'Avalanche' *43*, 78, 126, *130*, 182, 186, 189, 406
N. 'Cragford' *43*, 126, 159, 406
N. 'Erlicheer' *43*, 159
N. *fernandesii* var. *cordubensis* 126, 131
N. 'Geranium' *78, 130*, 189
N. 'Jack Snipe' *182*, 186
N. 'Polar Hunter' 126, *127*, 128, 131
N. 'Precocious' *30, 134*
N. 'Prinses Amalia' *124, 128*, 182, 186
N. 'Rip van Winkle' 182, *186*
N. 'Starlight Sensation' 126, *127, 128, 134*
N. *tazetta* 126, 154
nasturtiums 301
nematodes 201
Nerine bowdenii 373–4, *374–5*, 398
Nero vases 314, *315*
netting, as support 266–7, *266*
nettle fertiliser 236
Nicandra (shoo fly plant) 326, *327*, 340, 369, 387, 422–3, *422–3*
Nicotiana 143, *144*, 231
N. *knightiana* 334, *340*
N. *langsdorffii* 'Bronze Queen' *55*
N. 'Lime Green' *45*, 61, *71*, 320, *320*
N. 'Whisper Mixed' *85*, *287*, 289–91, *289–91*
Nigella (love-in-a-mist) 26, 35, *65, 76–7*, 284, 299, 327, 360, *401*
nitrogen 236

O
Ocimum 'African Blue' 384–5, *384–5*
Oenothera lindheimeri 'The Bride' *65, 77*
old man's beard *see Clematis vitalba*
olive branches 98, *99*, 411
Onopordum acanthium (giant thistle) 76
opium poppy *see Papaver somniferum*
Oreomecon nudicaulis (Icelandic poppy) *4*, 26, 31, 34, 35, *63*, 107, 214, *216–17*, 217, 271, 351
oriental poppy *see Papaver orientale*
Origanum laevigatum 'Herrenhausen' *283*
Orlaya grandiflora 65, *74, 75, 77*, *85*, 86, 214, *215*, 289–91, *289–91*, 360

P
Paeonia (peony) 22, 30, 88, 191, 248–9, *257*, 333, 363
P. 'Coral Sunset' *245, 257*
P. *lactiflora* 'Duchesse de Nemours' *19, 88, 223, 248, 249*

P. l. 'Monsieur Jules Elie' *223*, *248*
P. l. 'Sarah Bernhardt' *223*, *248*, 249
Panicum capillare (witch grass) 144, 306
P. c. 'Frosted Explosion' 55, *55*, *65*, *69*, 232, 326, *335*, 343
P. c. 'Sparkling Fountain' *5*, *55*, 143, *303*, 326, *398*, 422–3, *422–3*
P. miliaceum 'Violaceum' (millet) 326, 343
P. 'Sprinkles' 55, *55*
Papaver (poppy) 87, 145, 281, 299, 360–1, *378*
P. orientale (oriental poppy) 30, 358
P. rhoeas 'Amazing Grey' *85*, 142, 278, 289–91, *289–91*
P. somniferum (opium poppy) 36–7, *246–7*, 284, 298, 299, 327, 340
paperwhite narcissus 43, 95, 126, 131, 406, *407*
pasqueflower *see Pulsatilla vulgaris*
paths 116
pear *see Pyrus*
peas *see Pisum sativum*
Pelargonium 43, *69*, 191, 231, 331, 352, *355*, 357, 408–9
peony *see Paeonia*
Persian lily *see Fritillaria persica*
Persicaria orientalis 340, *341*
pests 201, *201*, 295, 343
Petunia × atkinsiana 'Tidal Wave Red Velour' *378*
P. 'Sophistica Lime Green' *64*
P. 'Tidal Wave Silver' *280*, 384–5, *384–5*
Phaseolus coccineus 'Black Knight' 293
P. vulgaris 'Monte Gusto' 293, *307*
Philadelphus 87
Phlox 28, 38, 191
P. drummondii *53*, 143, *240*, 306
P. d. '21st Century Blue Star' 289–91, *289–91*
P. d. 'Cherry Caramel' *5*, *62*, *74*, *75*, *305*, 306
P. d. 'Crème Brûlée' *55*, 289–91, *289–91*, 306, *318*, 319
P. paniculata 19
Phuopsis stylosa 213

Physalis (Chinese lantern) 327, *401*, *412*, *421*, *421*
picking flowers 81–2
pinching out 196, *196*
Pisum sativum (peas) 245, 292–3, 293
Pittosporum tenuifolium Bannow Bay 'Breebay' 182, 186
planting: bulbs 390–1, *390*
planting chart 434–7
planting plans 117, *117*
seedlings 194–5, *194*, 231, *231*, 296, 359, 388, *388*
Plectranthus ciliatus (Indian borage) 384–5, *384–5*
P. argentatus 'Silver Shield' *280*
pollen beetles 259
pollinators 135, 197, 232, 304, 335, 393, 396
polyanthus 28, *29*, 43, 102, *103*, 105, 123, 131–2, *134*, 414
Polygonatum × hybridum (Solomon's seal) 203–5, *204*, 224, *224–7*
polytunnels 146, 191, 373
poppies *see Papaver*
pot frames 148, *148*
potash 236, 297
pots, sowing seeds in 146
pricking out seedlings 148, 388
Primula 132, *133*, 138
P. 'Gold-laced Group' *136*, 138, *138*
P. 'Gold Nugget Apricot' 138, *138*
P. 'Stella Champagne' *30*, 43, *133*, 138, *138*, *156–7*
P. 'Stella Neon Violet' *135*, *156–7*
P. 'Stella Victoriana Lilac Lace' 138, *138*
pruning: Mediterranean shrubs 329, 331
roses 426–8, *427*, 429
Prunus (cherry) 87, 97–8, 107
Pulmonaria 29, 102, *103*
Pulsatilla vulgaris (pasqueflower) 160, *162*
pumpkins 383
pussy willow *see Salix*
Pyrus salicifolia 'Pendula' 317, *317*

Q

quaking grass *see Briza maxima*

R

Ranunculus 71, 159–60, *161*
Raven, Charles 10
Raven, John 7–10, *9*, 132
resting flowers 89
Rhinanthus minor (yellow rattle) 298
Ricinus communis (castor oil plant) 336
root trainers 119, *119*, 145
Rosa (roses) 28, *73*, 87, 241–8, *243*, *249*, 253–6, *254–7*, 367, *380*, 381, 426–8
centrepiece roses 256, *256–7*
pruning 426–8, *427*, 429
R. 'Aphrodite' *257*, *380*, 381, 426
R. banksiae 207, 428
R. 'Calendar Girl' *255*, 381
R. 'Champagne Moment' 28, *243*, 244–8, *244*, 381, 426
R. 'Cinco de Mayo' *243*, *254*, *380*, 381, 426
R. 'De Resht' 426, *427*
R. 'Duchess of Cornwall' 28, *218*, 219, *243*, 244, 245, 381, 426
R. 'For Your Eyes Only' *257*, *380*
R. 'Francis E. Lester' *366*, 367, 426, 428, *428*
R. 'Gertrude Jekyll' *218*, *254*, 381
R. 'Hot Chocolate' *243*, *254*, 256, *380*, 381
R. 'Ispahan' 427, *429*
R. 'Julia's Rose' *243*, *255*, *380*, 426
R. 'Madame Grégoire Staechelin' 107, 241
R. × odorata 'Bengal Crimson' 244, 248
R. × o. 'Mutabilis' 244, *244*, 248, *255*
R. 'Pumpkin Patch' *380*, 381
R. 'Queen of Sweden' *243*, 426
R. 'Rhapsody in Blue' 244, *246–7*
R. 'Sweet Juliet' *257*, 426
R. 'Timeless Purple' *243*, 381, 426
R. 'Tuscany Superb' *243*, *254*, 427, *427*
rosehips 314, *366*, 367, 426, *428*
rosemary *134–5*, 189, 329, 331, 409
rosemary *see Salvia rosmarinus*
Rudbeckia 28, 301, *364*, *378*

R. hirta 20, *69*, *71*, *75*, *318*, 319, 320, *320*, 377
runner beans 293

S

Salix (pussy willow) 43
  S. gracilistyla 'Mount Aso' *96*, 98
  S. purpurea 110, 182, 184
Salvia 35, 45, 242–4, *246–7*, 331, 357, 396, *398*, 414
  S. 'Amistad' 242, *398*, 399
  S. involucrata 'Hadspen' 396, *398*, 399
  S. × *jamensis* 242, *398*
  S. microphylla 364, *398*
  S. rosmarinus 98, 110
  S. viridis 14, 17, *18*, 28, *36–7*, 38, 44, 45, 52, *53*, 56, *89*, 142, 194, 197, *197*, 271, 296, 299, 360
Sanguisorba (burnet) *39*, 324, 422–3, *422–3*
Sarcococca (sweet box) 95–7, 110
Scabiosa (scabious) 15, 28, 299, 327, 351, 378, 388
  S. atropurpurea 266, 271, 360
  S. a. 'Black Cat' *55*, *71*, *75*, 197–8, *197–8*, *280*, 281
Schizanthus 34, *388*
Schizostylis coccinea see *Hesperantha coccinea*
Scilla 105, 123, 131–2, *131*, 135–6
searing 84–7, *85–6*
seasonal succession 31–43
seed packets, storing 146
seed trays 144–5, *144*
seedheads 295, 313, 323, 327, 363, 383, 409
seedlings 120
  pinching out 196, *196*
  planting out 194–5, *194*, 231, *231*, 296, 359, 388, *388*
  pricking out 148, 295–6, 388
  thinning out 296
  watering 147, 235
seeds: germination 146–7
  harvesting *298*, 299
  organising 118
  sowing 118–21, *118–19*, *121*, 141–6, 191, 269, *270*, 357, 358–61, *361*, *388*
  sowing chart 434–7
Selinum wallichianum 39, 327
Setaria 39, 306

S. viridis (foxtail) 54, *55*, 308–9
shoo fly plant see *Nicandra*
Silene dioica 224
silver birch see *Betula pendula*
slugs 201, *201*, 343, 425
smoke bush see *Cotinus*
Smyrnium perfoliatum 68, 69, 107, 203, 327
  S. rotundifolium 327
snails 343, 425
snake's head fritillary see *Fritillaria meleagris*
snapdragon see *Antirrhinum*
snapdragon love heart *316*, 317
snowball tree see *Viburnum opulus*
snowdrops see *Galanthus*
soil: cutting patches 116, *116*
  mulching 199–200, *199*, 296
  sowing direct 360–1, *361*
Solanum lycopersicum 'Micro Cherry' 292
Solomon's seal see *Polygonatum* × *hybridum*
sowing seeds see seeds
spindle see *Euonymus*
spring harvest table 188–9, 189
spring party flowers 182–7, *183–7*
Spry, Constance 292
squash *382*, 383
squirrels 426, 431
staking and supports 265–79, *266–8*
statice see *Limonium sinuatum*
stems, conditioning 79, 84–93
Stipa 306, 326
stocks see *Matthiola*
straw flowers see *Xerochrysum bracteatum*
strawberry tree see *Arbutus unedo*
submersion 88, *88*, 383, 414
succession of plants 27–45
summer hand-tied bunch 318–19, *318*
sunflowers see *Helianthus*
sunrise vase *180*, 181
swag, mantelpiece 422–3, *422–3*
sweet box see *Sarcococca*
sweet peas see *Lathyrus*
sweet rocket see *Hesperis matronalis*
sweet Williams see *Dianthus barbatus*
sweetcorn *382*

Swiss chard *342*
Symphyotrichum 'Vasterival' 378, *379*
Symphytum officinale (comfrey) 236, *237*

T

table decorations, dahlias 354, *354–5*
Tagetes (marigold) *21*, 56, *70*, *72*, 231, *308–9*
tarragon, French see *Artemisia dracunculus*
teasel see *Dipsacus*
thistle, giant see *Onopordum acanthium*
Thlaspi arvense 52, *316*, 317
Thunbergia alata (black-eyed Susan) 20, 150, 232, 336, *337*, 397
Tithonia rotundifolia (Mexican sunflower) 107–9, 267
toad lily see *Tricyrtis formosana*
tomatoes 292
Trachymene coerulea 289–91, *289–91*
Tricyrtis formosana (toad lily) 377, *378*
Tulbaghia violacea 374
Tulipa (tulips) 11, 30, *32–3*, 34, 46, 60–1, *63*, 65, 69, 73, 79, 82, 123, 154, *154–5*, 162, *164–7*, 168, *169–71*, 170, 172, *173–4*, 175, *176*, 177, *177*, 203, *205*, 217, 324, 387, 390
  categories 167–75
  conditioning 178
  planting 430–1, *430*
  tulip blight 126, 177, 200, 390, 430
  T. 'Apricot Beauty' *63*, 177, *180*, 181
  T. 'Apricot Delight' 123, *127*, *134*, *180*, 181
  T. 'Apricot Foxx' *62*, *74*, 177, 204
  T. 'Arjuna' *59*, 61
  T. 'Ballerina' 168, *168*, 213
  T. 'Bastia' *59*, *171*
  T. 'La Belle Epoque' *62*, *72*, *155*, 166, 167, 204
  T. 'Black Parrot' 46, *59*, *171*
  T. 'Blue Heaven' 168, *168–9*
  T. 'Blushing Lady' *62*, 74
  T. 'Campbell' 168, *168*
  T. 'Charming Lady' *62*, 74
  T. 'Chato' *32–3*, 172

T. clusiana 170, 175
T. 'Copex Cairo' 155, *176*
T. 'Exotic Emperor' 123, *134*, *167*, 172
T. 'Flaming Club' 168, *169*
T. 'Green Wave' 172, *173*, 175, 224, *224–7*
T. 'Groenland' *63*, 175
T. 'Ice Stick' 123, *128*, 172, 189
T. 'Istanbul' *32–3*, *156–7*
T. 'Jinan' *166*, 167
T. 'Light and Dreamy' 172, *172*
T. 'Little Beauty' 170, *170*
T. 'Mariette' *60*, 70
T. 'Mistress Mystic' *63*, 175, *175*, 430
T. 'Mystic van Eijk' *177*, *180*, 181
T. 'Orca' 123, *134*, 159, *168*, 172
T. 'Prinses Irene' *60*, 70
T. 'Purissima' 123, *174*, 175
T. 'Request' *59*, *164–5*, 168
T. 'Royal Acres' *60*, 70
T. 'Sanne' *180*, 181
T. 'Sarah Raven' *32–3*, *46*, *58*, *59*, *68–70*, *72*, 154
T. 'Silver Cloud' *180*, 181
T. 'Slawa' *154*, *164–5*, *177*
T. 'Spring Green' *63*, 175, *175*
T. 'Spryng Tide' *32–3*, *156–7*
T. sylvestris 168, *168*, 189
T. 'Victoria's Secret' *171*, 204
T. 'Vovos' *72–3*, 204
T. 'World's Favourite' *32–3*, *156–7*

U
urns 224–6, *224–7*
Urtica dioica (nettles) 236

V
vase life 79–93
vegetables 292–3, *292–3*
Venetian Velvet palette *57*, 58, *58–9*, 67, 68–75, *68–75*
Verbena 87, 348, 387
Veronica gentianoides 213–14
Viburnum 97
  V. opulus (guelder rose) *61*, 87, 153, 205, 224, *224–7*, *366*, 367, 416–17, *416*
Vicia faba 'Crimson Flowered' 292–3
vines 55
Viola 43, *135*, 182, *359*, 360, 414

W
wallflowers *see Erysimum*
Wangenheimia lima (fishbone grass) 55, 306, 326
watering 147, 235, 296
wax flower *see Chamelaucium uncinatum*
weeds 229–31, *230*
white 76, *76–7*
willow *see Salix*
willow wreaths 110–13, *110–13*
winter aconite *see Eranthis hyemalis*
wisteria 207
witch grass *see Panicum capillare*
wood anemone 107
wreaths 399, *401*, *402*, *405*, *408*
  bird feeder wreath 416–17, *416*
  cranberry and crab apple wreath 421, *421*
  forager's wreath 421, *421*
  fruit and veg Christmas wreath *418*, 419–20, *420*
  party wreath 110–13, *110–13*

X
Xerochrysum bracteatum (straw flower) 323, 324, *327*, *401*, 422–3, *422–3*

Y
yarrow *see Achillea*
yellow rattle *see Rhinanthus minor*

Z
Zinnia 28, *29*, 40, *61*, *71*, *82*, 118, 145, 191, 229, 231, *240*, 301, 304, *312*, 324, 387
  Z. elegans 5, *71*, 144, 304, *305–6*, *320*, 320

Acknowledgements

For their incredible hard work and cheerful help in making the cutting gardens – and all of Perch Hill – look so good every month of the year, thank you to Josie Lewis, Rebecca Cocker, Colin Pilbeam, Joe Dallywater, Richard Lambden, Katie Schanche and Adam Punter. And thanks to Tom Stimpson, Bea Andrews, Arthur Parkinson, Tessa Bishop and Jemima Bowker for one or two of the arrangements featured in the book.

For their general kindness and encouragement, thanks to my agent Caroline Michel and her colleagues at PFD. I think this may be our ninth book together! At Bloomsbury, thanks go to Rowan Yapp, Lena Hall and Britt Davies. Thanks to Esther Palmer for her beautiful illustrations. And thanks to our designer Glenn Howard for this, his fourth book in the series. This is a tome – thanks so much for sticking with it.

For being encouraging supporters, thank you Ros Peckham and Nick Sampson, and for being excellent readers and fact-checkers, thank you Josie Lewis and Kate Hubbard. And to Zena Alkayat who has edited and project managed this very complicated book and has always looked to the best of what we can do together.

Finally, thanks to my husband Adam Nicolson who is the greatest fan of the garden, the plants and plant combinations within it. Watching it change from week to week, he always gives invaluable feedback – occasionally critical, but usually admiring – as we walk round the garden, early in the morning or when it's quiet in the evening.

And most of all to Jonathan Buckley, to whom this book is dedicated, for his years of care and skill and affection.

Most of the plants in this book are available from sarahraven.com

Opposite Adam and I, standing in the Perennial Cutting Garden on a late-summer morning. We're checking out the dahlias in our trial; we trial 150 to 200 new varieties every year.
Next page I love picking the edible, ornamental pea, *Pisum sativum* 'Blauwschokker'.